Core Connections, Course 3
Second Edition*, Version 5.0, Volume 2

Managing Editors / Authors

Leslie Dietiker, Ph.D., Director of Curriculum (Both Editions)
Boston University
Boston, MA

Evra Baldinger (First Edition)
University of California, Berkeley
Berkeley, CA

Michael Kassarjian (2nd Edition)
CPM Educational Program
Kensington, CA

Barbara Shreve (First Edition)
San Lorenzo High School
San Lorenzo, CA

Misty Nikula (2nd Edition)
CPM Educational Program
Bellingham, WA

Contributing Authors

Elizabeth Baker
Zane Middle School

Tara Bianchi
American Canyon Middle School

Bev Brockhoff
Glen Edwards Middle School

Clanci Chiu
Santa Barbara Junior High School

Mark Coté
Beaver Lake Middle School

Suzanne Cisco Cox
Turner Middle School

Kathleen Davies
Rincon Valley Middle School

Josea Eggink
Bloomington Public Schools

William Funkhouser
Zane Middle School

Lori Hamada
CPM Educational Program

Brian Hoey
CPM Educational Program

Janet Hollister
La Cumbre Jr. High School

Carol Jancsi
CPM Mentor Teacher

Rakesh Khanna
Hotmath, Inc.

Judy Kysh, Ph.D.
San Francisco State University

Sarah Maile
CPM Educational Program

Bruce Melhorn
International School Bangkok (ISB)

Chris Mikles
Post Falls Middle School

Bob Petersen
CPM Educational Program

Tom Sallee, Ph.D.
University of California, Davis

Lorna Thomas Vázquez
Neillsville, WI Math Consultant

Stephanie Whitney, Ph.D.
DePaul University

Program Directors

Elizabeth Coyner
Christian Brothers High School
Sacramento, CA

Leslie Dietiker, Ph.D.
Boston University
Boston, MA

Lori Hamada
CPM Educational Program
Fresno, CA

Brian Hoey
CPM Educational Program
Sacramento, CA

Michael Kassarjian
CPM Educational Program
Kensington, CA

Judy Kysh, Ph.D.
Departments of Education and
Mathematics San Francisco
State University, CA

Tom Sallee, Ph.D.
Department of Mathematics
University of California, Davis

Karen Wootton
CPM Educational Program
Odenton, MD

*Based on *Making Connections*: *Foundations for Algebra, Courses 1 and 2*.

e-book Manager
Carol Cho
Director of Technology
Martinez, CA

e-book Programmers
Rakesh Khanna
Daniel Kleinsinger
Kevin Stein

e-book Assistants
Debbie Dodd
Shirley Paulsen
Wendy Papciak
Anna Poehlmann
Jordan Wight

Assessment Manager
Karen Wootton
Director of Assessment
Odenton, MD

Assessment Assistants
Elizabeth Baker
Zane Middle School
Eureka, CA

William Funkhouser
Zane Middle School
Eureka, CA

Assessment Website
Elizabeth Fong
Michael Huang
Daniel Kleinsinger

Illustration
Kevin Coffey
San Francisco, CA

Jonathan Weast
Sacramento, CA

Homework Help Manager
Bob Petersen
CPM Educational Program

Homework Help Website
Carol Cho
Director of Technology

Parent Guide with Extra Practice
Elizabeth Coyner
Christian Brothers High School

Brian Hoey
CPM Educational Program

Bob Petersen
CPM Educational Program

Based on the Skill Builder materials created for Foundations for Algebra (2003), created by:

Heidi Ackley	Steve Ackley	Elizabeth Baker
Bev Brockhoff	Ellen Cafferata	Elizabeth Coyner
Scott Coyner	Sara Effenbeck	William Funkhouser
Brian Hoey	Judy Kysh	Kris Petersen
Robert Petersen	Edwin Reed	Stacy Rocklein
Kristie Sallee	Tom Sallee	Howard Webb

Technical Managers
Sarah Maile
Sacramento, CA

Aubrie Maze
Sebastopol, CA

Technical Assistants

Stephanie Achondo	Robert Ainsworth	Bethany Armstrong
Rebecca Bobell	Delenn Breedlove	Jason Cho
Hannah Coyner	Mary Coyner	Carmen de la Cruz
Matthew Donahue	Bethany Firch	Dana Kimball
Leslie Lai	Michael Li	Jerry Luo
Eli Marable	James McCardle	Nyssa Muheim
Alexandra Murphy	Wendy Papciak	Atlanta Parrott
Juanita Patian	Ryan Peabody	Iris Perez
Steven Pham	Anna Poehlmann	Eduardo Ramirez
John Ramos	Ali Rivera	Andrea Smith
Rachel Smith	Claire Taylor	Christy Van Beek
Megan Walters	Sarah Wong	Alex Yu

3 4 5 6 7 8 9 10   18 17 16 15 14   Version 5.0

Printed in the United States of America   ISBN: 978-1-60328-090-7

A Note to Students:

Welcome to a new year of math! In this course, you will learn to use new models and methods to think about problems as well as solve them. You will be developing powerful mathematical tools and learning new ways of thinking about and investigating situations. You will be making connections, discovering relationships, figuring out what strategies can be used to solve problems, and explaining your thinking. Learning to think in these ways and communicate about your thinking is useful in mathematical contexts, other subjects in school, and situations outside the classroom. The mathematics you have learned in the past will be valuable for learning in this course. That work, and what you learn in this course, will prepare you for future courses.

In meeting the challenges of this course, you will not be learning alone. You will cooperate with other students as a member of a study team. Being a part of a team means speaking up and interacting with other people. You will explain your ideas, listen to what others have to say, and ask questions if there is something you do not understand. In this course, a single problem can often be solved several ways. You will see problems in different ways than your teammates do. Each of you has something to contribute while you work on the lessons in this course.

Together, your team will complete problems and activities that will help you discover mathematical ideas and develop solution methods. Your teacher will support you as you work, but will not take away your opportunity to think and investigate for yourself. Each topic will be revisited many times and will connect to other topics. If something is not clear to you the first time you work on it, you will have more chances to build your understanding as the course continues.

Learning math this way has an advantage: as long as you actively participate, make sure everyone in your study team is involved, and ask good questions, you will find yourself understanding mathematics at a deeper level than ever before. By the end of this course, you will have a powerful set of mathematical tools to use to solve new problems. With your teammates you will meet mathematical challenges you would not have known how to approach before.

In addition to the support provided by your teacher and your study team, CPM has also created online resources to help you, including help with homework, and a parent guide with extra practice. You will find these resources and more at www.cpm.org.

We wish you well and are confident that you will enjoy this next year of learning!

Sincerely,

The CPM Team

Core Connections, Course 3
Student Edition

Volume 1

Transformations and Similarity

6

CHAPTER 6   Transformations and Similarity

You may not often take the time to think about how you move objects around as you go about daily life. Many of the movements you make in a given day involve changing directions. In Section 6.1, you will investigate different kinds of motion on a coordinate graph. You will learn how to give directions to slide, flip, turn, and stretch flat shapes. You will also learn how to show where the shapes will be after a series of moves.

In Section 6.2, you will use mathematics you already know to investigate how shapes change size. You will also determine the unknown length of a side in a figure with given information about the lengths of other sides in the figure and in related figures.

Guiding Questions

Think about these questions throughout this chapter:

How can I visualize it?

How can I describe the motion?

How can I transform it?

How do they compare?

What is the relationship?

In this chapter, you will learn how to:

➢ Transform shapes by flipping, turning, and sliding them on a coordinate graph.

➢ Describe movement on a graph using coordinates and expressions.

➢ Compare shapes and use similarity to find missing side lengths of polygons, especially triangles.

Chapter Outline

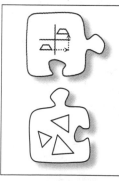

Section 6.1 You will use a technology tool to move a shape on a coordinate graph using slides, flips, and turns, and will use integers to describe those moves.

Section 6.2 This section will introduce similarity and congruence for polygons.

6.1.1 How can I move a shape on a grid?

Rigid Transformations

How can you describe the movement of a figure on a flat surface when it is not moving in a straight line? For example, when you need to move a loose puzzle piece into the puzzle (as shown at right), how can you describe the way its position changes?

Today you will explore mathematical ways of sliding, turning, and flipping an object without changing its size or shape. These types of movements are called **rigid transformations**. You will solve challenge problems as you explore the transformations.

6-1.   KEY-IN-THE-LOCK PUZZLES

Are you ready for a puzzle challenge? You will use the technology tool "Rigid Transformations" (also available at www.cpm.org/students/technology). Your job will be to move the key to the keyhole to unlock the door, using the transformation buttons shown at right.

You will need to tell the computer about how you want the key to move. For example, how far to the left or right and how far up or down do you want the key to slide? In which direction do you want your key to flip?

Your Task: For each puzzle, move the key to the keyhole. Remember that to unlock the door, the key must fit exactly into the keyhole and not be upside down. Also note that your key will not be able to move through walls.

Be sure to record your moves on the Lesson 6.1.1 Resource Page.

Discussion Points

In what direction does the key need to move?

How can we get the key to fit the keyhole?

What information do we need to give the computer so that it moves the key into the lock?

6-2. Describe what moves you could use to create the transformation of the original image shown at right.

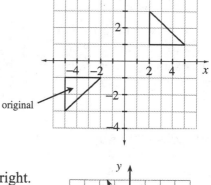

original

6-3. Review what you know about graphs as you complete parts (a) through (d) below.

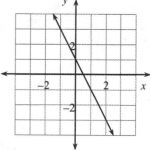

a. Find the equation of the line graphed at right.

b. What are its x- and y-intercepts?

c. On your own graph paper, graph the line.

d. On the same set of axes, graph a line that is *parallel* to the line graphed at right and that goes through the *origin* $(0, 0)$. Find the equation of this new line.

6-4. Which equation below has *no* solution? Explain how you know.

a. $4(x+1) = 2x+4$

b. $9-5x+2 = 4-5x$

6-5. Rena says that if $x = -5$, the equation below is true. Her friend, Dean, says the answer is $x = 3$. Who is correct? Justify your conclusion.

$$9(x+4) = 1+2x$$

6-6. Find the rule for the pattern represented at right.

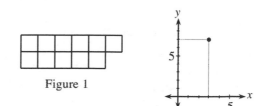

Figure 1

224

6-7.   Homer the Hungry Hippo is munching on the
        lily pads in his pond. When he got to the
        pond, there were 30 lily pads, but he is eating
        5 lily pads an hour. Henrietta the Hungrier
        Hippo found a better pond with 38 lily pads!
        She eats 7 lily pads every hour.

   a.   If Homer and Henrietta start eating at the same time, when will their ponds
        have the same number of lily pads remaining?

   b.   How many lily pads will be left in each pond at that time?

6.1.2   How can I move a shape on a grid?

. . . .

Rigid Transformations on a Coordinate Graph

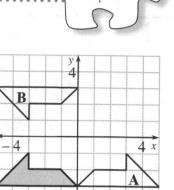

Have you ever had trouble giving directions? Sometimes
describing where something is or how it has moved is
difficult. For this reason, people often use coordinate
graphs like the one shown at right. Coordinate graphs help
you describe directions with words like "left" and "down."
They can also help you measure distances.

Today you will work with your team to describe movement
on a coordinate graph. You will also look at ways to
describe where an object is on the grid before and after a
transformation. As you work, use the questions below to
help start math discussions with your team members.

Is there a different way to get the same result?

Did we give enough information?

How can we describe the position?

6-8.   While solving the key challenge in
Lesson 6.1.1, Rowan made more than
one move to change his key from point
A to point B and from point C to point
D, as shown on the graph at right. Both
of these keys are shown as triangles on
the Lesson 6.1.2 Resource Page.

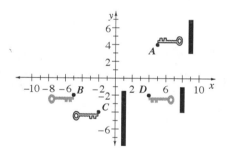

Your Task: With your team, describe how Rowan could have moved each key
from the starting position to the ending position using slides (also called
translations), turns (also called **rotations**), and/or flips (also called
reflections).

- Make sure you provide enough detail to describe the moves completely.

- Try to find more than one way he could have moved each key.

- Be ready to justify your ideas with the class.

Core Connections, Course 3

6-9.   **WHERE DOES IT LAND?**

Felicia found a copy of a puzzle like the one in problem 6-1, but the lock is missing. All she has are the starting points and the moves to unlock the lock. This time her key is shaped like a triangle.

The points are at A(−5, 0), B(−5, 3), and C(−1, 0).

Step 1:   Translate 4 units to the right and 2 units up.

Step 2:   Reflect across the x-axis.

Step 3:   Rotate counter-clockwise 90° about point (3, −2).

Help Felicia find out where the lock is by following her steps. The following questions are designed to help you.

a.   With your team, set up your own coordinate graph on graph paper. The questions below will help.

   • How many quadrants (regions) should the graph have? Should it be a graph with only the first quadrant? Or a graph with four quadrants?

   • How should the axes be scaled? How many units should you use for each side length of a grid square?

b.   Plot triangle *ABC* to represent the key.

c.   Follow Step 1 to translate the triangle. Name the new location of each vertex, or corner, of the triangle in the form (x, y).

d.   Complete Step 2. Sketch the triangle in its new position and label the coordinates of each vertex.

e.   Where does Felicia's triangle end up? Complete Step 3 on the graph and label the coordinates of each vertex.

6-10.   Now compare the triangle in problem 6-9 that you have after Step 3 with the original triangle. How do the lengths of the sides compare? How do the sizes of the angles compare?

6-11.   Could Felicia's team have used different steps to "unlock" her puzzle in problem 6-9? In other words, could she have used different moves and still have the key end up in the same final position?

- If it is possible, list a new set of steps that would move her key from the same starting location to the same final position.

- If it is not possible, explain why not.

6-12.   On graph paper, draw a coordinate graph with x- and y-axes. Graph shapes A, B, and C as described below.

a. Shape A is a triangle with vertices $(1,1)$, $(3,3)$, and $(2,4)$.

b. Shape B is a square with vertices $(2,-1)$, $(4,-1)$, $(2,-3)$, and $(4,-3)$.

c. Shape C is a rectangle with vertices $(-3,1)$, $(-3,4)$, $(-1,4)$, and $(-1,1)$.

6-13.   On the same grid you used in problem 6-12, translate triangle A four units right and three units up to create triangle D. Write the coordinates of the new vertices.

6-14.   Graph each equation below on the same set of axes and label the point of intersection with its coordinates.

$$y = 2x + 3 \qquad\qquad y = x + 1$$

6-15.   Shooter Marilyn is the Spartans' best free-throw shooter. She normally makes three out of every four shots. In an upcoming charity event, Shooter will shoot 600 free-throws. If she makes over 400 baskets, the school wins $1000. Should the Spartans expect to win the cash for the school? Show and organize your work.

6-16.   Examine the tile pattern shown at right.

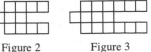

Figure 1   Figure 2   Figure 3

a.   On graph paper, draw Figure 0 and Figure 4.

b.   How many tiles will Figure 10 have? Justify your answer.

6-17.   GETTING IN SHAPE

Frank weighs 160 pounds and is on a diet to gain two pounds a week so that he can make the football team. John weighs 208 pounds and is on a diet to lose three pounds a week so that he can be on the wrestling team in a lower weight class.

a.   If Frank and John can meet these goals with their diets, when will they weigh the same, and how much will they weigh at that time?

b.   Clearly explain your method.

6.1.3   How can I describe it?

· ·

Describing Transformations

In Lesson 6.1.2, you used words and coordinate points to describe how a triangle moved on a graph. These expressions described the starting place, the motion, and the point where the triangle ended up. Today, you will write similar expressions to describe transformations on a grid.

6-18.   Rosa changed the position of quadrilateral *ABCD* to that of quadrilateral *WXYZ*. "*How did the coordinates of the points change?*" she wondered.

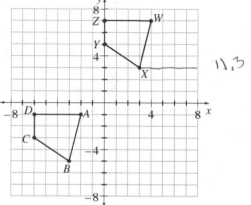

11,3

a.   Describe how Rosa transformed *ABCD*. Was the shape translated (slid), rotated (turned), or reflected (flipped)? Explain how you know.

b.   How far did *ABCD* move? In which direction?

c.   Point *B* became point *X*. What are the coordinates of points *B* and *X*? Name them using (x, y) notation.

d.   How did the *x*-coordinate of point *B* change? How did its *y*-coordinate change? For each coordinate, write an equation using addition to show the change.

e.   Visualize translating *WXYZ* 10 units to the right and 12 units up. Where will point *X* end up? *Without counting on the graph*, work with your team to find the new coordinates of point *Y*. Write equations using addition to show the change.

6-19.   Rosa translated a different shape on a grid. Use the clues below to figure out how her shape was moved.

a.   The point $(4, 7)$ was translated to $(32, -2)$. Without graphing, describe how the shape moved on the grid. 28, -9

b.   Another point on her original shape was $(-16, 9)$. After the translation, where did this point end up? For each coordinate, write an equation using addition to show the change.

Core Connections, Course 3

6-20. Rowan transformed quadrilateral *CDEF* below to get the quadrilateral *PQRS*.

a. Describe how Rowan transformed the quadrilateral. Was the shape translated, rotated, or reflected? Explain how you know.

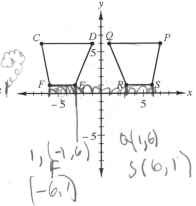

b. Rowan noticed that the *y*-coordinates of the points did not change. What happened to the *x*-coordinates? Compare the *x*-coordinate of point *D* with the *x*-coordinate of point *Q*. Do the same with points *E* and *R* and with points *F* and *S* and with points *C* and *P*. What do you notice?

c. Can you describe the change to all of the *x*-coordinates with addition like you did in problems 6-18 and 6-19? If not, what other operation could you use? Explain.

d. What parts of quadrilateral *CDEF* are the same as quadrilateral *PQRS*? How can you show that the corresponding angles are the same measure and the parallel sides remain parallel?

6-21. Imagine that Rowan reflected quadrilateral *CDEF* from problem 6-20 across the *x*-axis instead. What do you think would happen to the coordinates in that case?

a. First visualize how the quadrilateral will reflect across the *x*-axis.

b. Set up a four-quadrant coordinate graph on graph paper and plot quadrilateral *CDEF* from problem 6-20.

c. Reflect quadrilateral *CDEF* across the *x*-axis to get quadrilateral *JKLM*.

d. Compare the coordinates of point *C* with point *J*, point *D* with point *K*, point *E* with point *L*, and point *F* with point *M*. What do you notice? How can you use multiplication to describe this change?

6-22. In problem 6-20, Rowan noticed that multiplying the *x*-coordinates by −1 reflects the shape across the *y*-axis.

a. Test this strategy on a triangle formed by the points *A* (−3,5), *B*(1,2), and *C*(0,8). Before you graph, multiply each *x*-coordinate by −1. What are the new points?

b. Graph your original and new triangle on a new set of axes. Did your triangle get reflected across the *y*-axis?

6-23.   In the last three lessons, you have investigated rigid transformations: reflections, rotations, and translations. What happens to a shape when you perform a rigid transformation? Do the side lengths or angles in the figure change? Do the relationships between the lines (parallel or perpendicular) change? Why do you think reflections, rotations, and translations are called rigid transformations?

6-24.   Stella used three steps to move the key on the graph at right from *A* to *B*. On your graph paper, draw the key at *A*. (A triangle can be used to represent the key.) Then follow the steps Stella wrote below. What was her last move?

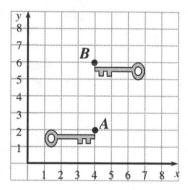

1. Slide the key to the right 3 units and up 6 units.

2. Reflect the key across the line x = 4.

3. ???

6-25.   **Additional Challenge:** Do you think there is a way to use translations to create a reflection or a rotation? Or can reflections be used to move a shape in the same way as a rotation? To investigate these questions, begin by making a graph like the one below. Then complete parts (a) through (c).

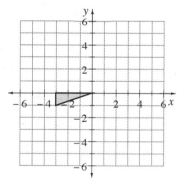

a.   Reflect (flip) the triangle across the *x*-axis. Then reflect the new triangle over the *y*-axis.

b.   Rotate the original triangle 180° around the point $(0,0)$. What do you notice?

c.   Is there a way to use more than one reflection step so that at the end, the triangle looks like it was translated (slid)? If so, describe the combination of moves you would use.

6-26.   LEARNING LOG

In your Learning Log, describe what the terms *translate*, *rotate*, and *reflect* mean in your own words. For each term, demonstrate the movement with a diagram. Title this entry "Rigid Transformations" and include today's date.

Core Connections, Course 3

METHODS AND MEANINGS

Rigid Transformations

MATH NOTES

Rigid transformations are ways to move an object while not changing its shape or size. Specifically, they are translations (slides), reflections (flips), and rotations (turns). Each movement is described below.

A **translation** slides an object horizontally (side-to-side), vertically (up or down), or both. To translate an object, you must describe which direction you will move it, and how far it will slide. In the example at right, Triangle A is translated 4 units to the right and 3 units up.

A **reflection** flips an object across a line (called a **line of reflection**). To reflect an object, you must choose a line of reflection. In the example at right, Triangle A is reflected across the *x*-axis.

A **rotation** turns an object about a point. To rotate an object, you must choose a point, direction, and angle of rotation. In the example at right, Triangle A is rotated 90° clockwise (↻) about the origin $(0,0)$.

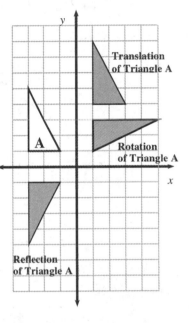

6-27. Erin started with one corner of a figure located at $(-4,5)$ and translated it to end at $(6,8)$. To find out how far the shape moved horizontally, she decided to find the difference between the two x-coordinates. She wrote: $6-(-4)$.

a. When Erin simplified $6-(-4)$, she got 2 as her answer. Is this correct? If not, what is the correct simplification?

b. Write another expression to find out how far the shape moved vertically ($\updownarrow$). Simplify both expressions and describe the translation in words.

c. Describe each of the translations below.

    i. $(3,-2) \rightarrow (5,-9)$ *ii.* $(-1,4) \rightarrow (6,-2)$

    iii. $(0,0) \rightarrow (-4,-7)$ *iv.* $(-2,-9) \rightarrow (2,9)$

6-28. On graph paper, set up x- and y-axes for a four-quadrant graph. Then draw a triangle with vertices at $(1,1)$, $(5,1)$, and $(6,3)$. Label this triangle T.

a. Translate (slide) the triangle left 3 units and down 4 units. Label this triangle A and list the vertices.

b. Reflect triangle T across the y-axis. Label this triangle B and list the vertices.

c. Are triangles T, A, and B **congruent** (that is, do they have the same shape and size)? Explain.

6-29. Change each equation below into $y = mx + b$ form.

    a. $y - 4x = -3$ b. $3y - 3x = 9$

    c. $3x + 2y = 12$ d. $2(x - 3) + 3y = 0$

6-30.   Solve the problem below by defining a variable and then writing and solving an equation.

The perimeter of a triangle is 31 cm. Sides #1 and #2 have equal length, while Side #3 is one centimeter shorter than twice the length of Side #1. How long is each side?

6-31.   Simplify each expression.

a. $\frac{73}{100} \cdot \left(-\frac{2}{7}\right)$

b. $0.4 \cdot 0.3$

c. $5\frac{1}{9} + 8\frac{2}{5}$

d. $-1.2 + \left(-\frac{3}{5}\right)$

6-32.   Each part (a) through (d) below represents a different tile pattern. For each, find the pattern of growth and the number of tiles in Figure 0.

a.   b.

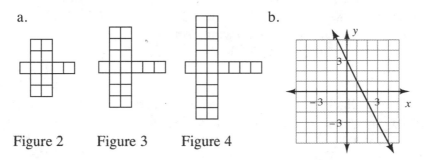

Figure 2   Figure 3   Figure 4

c. $y = 3x - 14$

d.

x	−3	−2	−1	0	1	2	3
y	18	13	8	3	−2	−7	−12

6.1.4 What can I create?

Using Rigid Transformations

In the last several lessons, you have described translations using coordinates. You have also developed strategies for determining where an object started when you know how it was translated and its final position. In this lesson, you will continue to practice transforming objects on a coordinate graph by translating (sliding), rotating (turning), and reflecting (flipping). As you work, visualize what each object will look like after the transformation. Use the graph to check your prediction.

6-33.   BECOMING AN ARTIST

Have you ever seen directions for drawing a cartoon figure such as a face? Usually these directions start by helping you to put some basic shapes together to form an outline. Then they give you ideas for how to finish the drawing. An example showing how you could draw a dinosaur is at right.

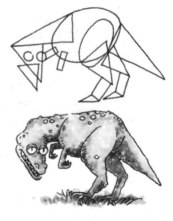

Your Task: Obtain Lesson 6.1.4A Resource Page from your teacher. On it, shapes A, B, and C are provided for you. Follow the directions below to create a design. Whenever one of the shapes is mentioned below, start with the original shape on the left side of the paper. The final result of each step is part of the outline of the design.

Once you have finished following all of the directions, describe the picture that is formed. Then use the outline to create a cartoon drawing, complete with color and other details.

- Draw a rectangle with vertices $(5,0)$, $(9,0)$, $(9,8)$, and $(5,8)$.

- Translate circle A so that its center is at $(7,6)$. Describe how the shape moved.

- Rotate (turn) triangle C 180° clockwise about the point $(-6,3)$. Record the coordinates of the new vertices. Then add 15 to each x-coordinate and graph the final result. What transformation does "adding 15" represent?

Problem continues on next page. →

6-33.   *Problem continued from previous page.*

- Reflect (flip) triangle B across the *y*-axis. Record the new coordinates of the vertices. Describe how the coordinates have changed from the original shape.

- A new shape, triangle D, has vertices at $(-7,13)$, $(-8,11)$ and $(-6,11)$. Translate triangle D so that its top vertex is at $(7,4)$. Describe this translation with words.

- Translate triangle C to the right 11 units. Then reflect the result across the horizontal ($\leftrightarrow$) line that goes through $y = 3$. Record the new coordinates for triangle C.

- Translate circle A so that the *x*-coordinates increase by 13 units and the *y*-coordinates increase by 11 units. Record the coordinates of the center of circle A in its new position.

6-34.   CREATE A DESIGN

Now create your own design using basic shapes A through F on the Lesson 6.1.4C Resource Page. Write complete directions at the bottom of your resource page (such as those in problem 6-33) for creating your design. Make sure you provide all of the necessary information.

6-35.   **Additional Challenge:** Visualize a pattern of squares covering a coordinate graph as show at right. What transformations could you make to move the whole pattern so that the squares and lines in the pattern line up exactly over other squares and lines?

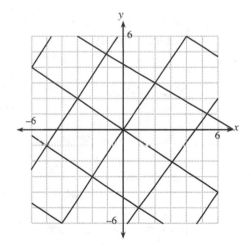

6-36. Sketch the graph at right on your paper.

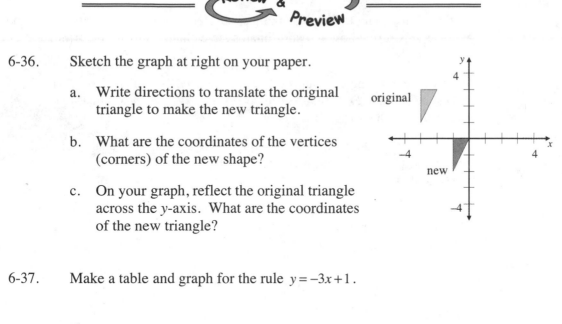

   a. Write directions to translate the original triangle to make the new triangle.

   b. What are the coordinates of the vertices (corners) of the new shape?

   c. On your graph, reflect the original triangle across the y-axis. What are the coordinates of the new triangle?

6-37. Make a table and graph for the rule $y = -3x + 1$.

6-38. Solve the system of equations below using the Equal Values Method.

$$a = 12b + 3$$
$$a = -2b - 4$$

6-39. Ms. Cai's class is studying a tile pattern. The rule for the tile pattern is $y = 10x - 18$. Kalil thinks that Figure 12 of this pattern will have 108 tiles. Is he correct? Justify your answer.

6-40. Angel is picking mountain blueberries for a delicious pie. She can pick $\frac{1}{6}$ cup of blueberries in 2 minutes. If she needs $2\frac{1}{2}$ cups of blueberries for the pie, how long will it take her to pick the berries?

6-41. Juan thinks that the graph of $6y + 12x = 4$ is a line.

   a. Solve Juan's equation for y.

   b. Is this equation linear? That is, is its graph a line? Explain how you know.

   c. What are the pattern of growth and y-intercept of this graph?

6.2.1 What if I multiply?

Multiplication and Dilation

Remember that when an object is translated, rotated, or reflected, it stays the same size and shape even though it moves. For this reason, these types of movements are called rigid transformations. In this lesson, you will explore a new transformation that changes how the object looks. As you work today, ask these questions in your team:

> What parts of the shape are changing? What parts stay the same?

6-42. When all of the x- or y-coordinates of each vertex of a shape are changed by adding or subtracting the same numbers, the shape translates (slides) to a new position on the coordinate graph. You learned in Lesson 6.1.3 that when one of the coordinates of the vertices (either the x- or y-coordinate) is multiplied by -1, the shape is reflected over the y-axis or the x-axis, respectively.

How do you think the shape will change when both the x- and y-coordinates are multiplied by some number? Use the directions below to help you answer this question.

a. Plot the following points on graph paper: $(2,1)$, $(3,1)$, $(5,5)$, $(2,5)$. Connect the points to make a quadrilateral.

b. Without graphing, predict how you think the figure would change if the x- and y-coordinates were multiplied by 2 and then plotted.

c. Test your prediction by doubling the coordinates from part (a) and plotting them on your graph paper. Was your prediction correct?

d. With your team members, look at the figure you just graphed. Transforming a graphed shape by multiplying each coordinate by the same number is called a **dilation**. With your team, discuss how this figure compares to the original. Be specific about changes in side length and area!

6-43.   INVESTIGATING DILATIONS

The students in Ms. Stanley's class were studying what happens to the graph of a shape when both coordinates are multiplied by the same number. They came up with these questions:

- *"What happens when each coordinate is <u>multiplied</u> by one-half?"*
- *"What changes when the coordinates are <u>multiplied</u> by 1?"*
- *"What happens when both of the coordinates are <u>multiplied</u> by –1?"*
- *"What happens when the coordinates are <u>multiplied</u> by –2?"*

a. Use the shape at right to investigate the questions above. Use graph paper to make the dilations.

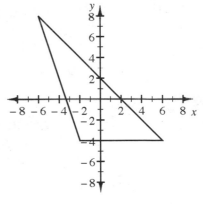

b. How did the figure change in each of the investigations? Compare the side lengths, the angles, and the line relationships. Explain what your team learned about the three questions you investigated.

6-44.   In problem 6-43, you investigated questions about multiplying coordinates that were posed by other students.

a. With your team, write a different question about the effect of multiplying the coordinates of a shape on a grid. This question might start with, *"What happens when you multiply…"*

b. Write a **conjecture** — that is, an educated guess based on the evidence in the last two problems — to answer your question.

c. On graph paper, investigate your question, and see if your conjecture is supported, by multiplying the coordinates of the shape in problem 6-43 as you described in your question. What happened? Was your conjecture correct?

6-45.   LEARNING LOG

In your Learning Log, explain how multiplying the coordinates of a shape affects the shape. How does the size of the shape change (or not change)? How do the angles of the shape change (or not change)? Do these results depend on the multiplier that is chosen? Be as specific as you can and include examples to demonstrate your thinking. Title your entry "Dilations" and include today's date.

Core Connections, Course 3

6-46. Louis is dilating triangle ABC at right. He multiplied each x-coordinate and y-coordinate of triangle ABC by -2.

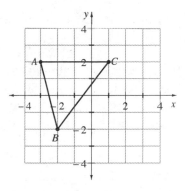

a. What are the new coordinates of the points?

b. Graph Louis' new triangle.

c. Describe how triangle ABC changed.

6-47. On the same set of axes, graph the two rules shown at right. Then find the point(s) of intersection, if one (or more) exists.

$$y = -x + 2$$
$$y = 3x + 6$$

6-48. Evaluate the expression $6x^2 - 3x + 1$ for $x = -2$.

6-49. When Ms. Shreve solved an equation in class, she checked her solution and found that it did not make the equation true! Examine her work below and find her mistake. Then find the correct solution.

$$5(2x - 1) - 3x = 5x + 9$$
$$10x - 5 - 3x = 5x + 9$$
$$7x - 5 = 5x + 9$$
$$12x = 4$$
$$x = \frac{1}{3}$$

6-50. Determine if the statement below is true or false. Justify your conclusion.

$$2(3 + 5x) = 6 + 5x$$

6-51. Complete the missing entries in the table below. Then write the rule.

IN (x)	2	10	6	7	-3		-10	100	x
OUT (y)	4	28	16			10			

6.2.2 How do shapes change?

Dilations and Similar Figures

Have you ever wondered how different mirrors work? Most mirrors show you a reflection that looks just like you. But other mirrors, like the mirrors commonly found at carnivals and amusement parks, reflect back a face that is stretched or squished. You may look taller, shorter, wider, or narrower. These effects can be created on the computer if you put a picture into a photo program. If you do not follow the mathematical principles of proportionality when you enlarge or shrink a photo, you may find that the picture is stretched thin or spread out, and not at all like the original. Today you will look at enlarging and reducing shapes using dilations to explore why a shape changes in certain ways.

6-52. UNDOING DILATION

In Lesson 6.2.1, you looked at dilations and multiplied each of the coordinates of a shape to change its size. Now you will explore how to undo dilations.

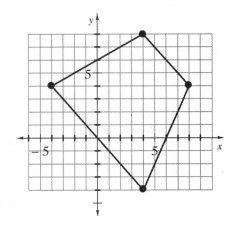

Charlie multiplied each coordinate of the vertices of a shape by 4 to create the dilated shape at right.

a. If Charlie multiplied to find this shape, what operation would undo his dilation? Why?

b. On a Lesson 6.2.2A Resource Page, undo the dilation on the graph above. Label the vertices of Charlie's original shape. How does the shape compare to the dilated shape?

Core Connections, Course 3

6-53.   Alana was also working with dilations. She
         wondered, *"What would happen if I multiplied
         each coordinate of a shape by $\frac{1}{3}$?"* On the
         Lesson 6.2.2A Resource Page, graph and connect
         the points below to form her dilated shape. Be
         sure to connect them in the order given.

$$(-1,-1) \quad (-1,1) \quad (1,2) \quad (2,-1)$$

a.   Alana graphed this shape by multiplying each of her original coordinates by
      $\frac{1}{3}$. What do you think Alana's shape looked like before the dilation? Make
      a prediction.

b.   On the same graph, undo the dilation to show Alana's original shape. List
      the coordinates of the vertices of Alana's original shape.

c.   What did you do to each coordinate to undo the dilation? How did the
      shape change?

d.   Why do you think the shape changed in this way?

6-54.   With your team, look carefully at Alana's dilated and original shapes in
         problem 6-53 and describe how the two shapes are related. Use the questions
         below to help you.

         •   How are the sides of the small and large shape related?

         •   How many of the small sides does it take to measure the
              corresponding (matching) side of the large shape? Is this true for all
              of the sides?

         •   Compare the four angles of the smaller shape to those of the larger
              shape. What can you say for sure about one matching pair of these
              angles? What appears to be true about the other three pairs?

6-55.   CHANGING SHAPE

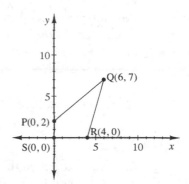

When you multiplied each coordinate of a
shape by the same constant, you saw that
sometimes the shape became smaller and
sometimes it became larger. In this chapter,
you moved shapes on a graph without
changing their size or shape by rotating,
reflecting, and translating them. In what other
ways can you change a shape?

Your Task: Work with your team to make predictions about what you could do
to the coordinates of the shape above to make it look stretched or squished, and
what actions will keep the shape the same. Make predictions for the situations
presented below. You will test these predictions in problem 6-56.

Discussion Points

What do you think will change if both the *x*- and *y*-coordinates of the points
P, Q, R, and *S* are multiplied by the same number, such as 4?

What do you think will happen if only the *x*-coordinates are multiplied by 3?

What do you think will happen if just the *y*-coordinates are multiplied by 2?

What do you think will happen if the *x*- and *y*-coordinates
are multiplied by different numbers, like 2 for *x* and 3 for *y*?

6-56.   Test the predictions your team made in problem 6-55. On the Lesson 6.2.2B
Resource Page, graph each of the shapes described below.

a.   Dilate each coordinate of shape *PQRS* by multiplying each *x*-coordinate
and each *y*-coordinate by 4. Graph the dilated shape on the same graph
using a color other than black.

b.   Go back to the original shape, and this time multiply only the *x*-coordinates
by 3. Leave the *y*-coordinates the same. Find, graph, and connect the new
coordinates.

c.   What happened to the shape in part (b)? Why did this happen?

d.   Look at the predictions your team made in problem 6-55. Do you still
agree with your predictions? Revise your predictions if necessary, based on
your work so far. What do you think will happen if you multiply only the
y-coordinates of the vertices by a number? Be ready to explain your
reasoning.

6-57. **Similar figures** are figures that have the same shape, but not necessarily the same size. One characteristic of similar shapes is that the sides of one shape are each the same number of times bigger than the corresponding sides of the smaller shape.

Which pairs of shapes that you have worked with in this lesson are similar and which are not? Justify your answer using specific examples.

METHODS AND MEANINGS

MATH NOTES

Corresponding Parts of Similar Shapes

Two figures are **similar** if they have the same shape but not necessarily the same size. For example, all semi-circles are similar, as are all squares, no matter how they are oriented. Dilations create similar figures.

To check whether figures are similar, you need to decide which parts of one figure **correspond** (match up) to which parts of the other. For example, in the triangles at right, triangle *DEF* is a dilation of triangle *ABC*. Side *AB* is dilated to get side *DE*, side *AC* is dilated to get side *DF*, and side *BC* is dilated to get side *EF*. Side *AB* **corresponds** to side *DE*, that is, they are **corresponding sides**. Notice that vertex *A* corresponds to vertex *D*, *C* to *F*, and *B* to *E*.

Not all correspondences are so easily seen. Sometimes you have to rotate or reflect the shapes mentally so that you can tell which parts are the corresponding sides, angles, or vertices. For example, the two triangles at right are similar, with *R* corresponding to *X*, *S* to *Y*, and *T* to *Z*. You can get triangle *XYZ* from triangle *RST* by a dilation of $\frac{1}{2}$ followed by a 90° counter-clockwise (↺) turn.

Shapes that are similar and have the same size are called **congruent**. Congruent shapes have corresponding sides of equal length and corresponding angles of equal measure. Rigid transformations (reflections, rotations, and translations), along with dilations with a multiplier of 1 or -1, create congruent shapes.

6-58.   Create a large coordinate graph on graph paper and graph the triangle at right. Multiply the y-coordinate of each point by 4. Then graph the new shape. Make sure you connect your points. List the points for the new shape. Are the two figures similar? Why or why not?

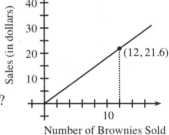

6-59.   Lashayia is famous for her delicious brownies, which she sells at football games. The graph at right shows the relationship between the number of brownies she sells and the amount of money she earns.

a.   How much should she charge for 10 brownies? Be sure to demonstrate your reasoning.

b.   During the last football game, Lashayia made $34.20. How many brownies did she sell? Show your work.

6-60.   Figure 3 of a tile pattern has 11 tiles, while Figure 4 has 13 tiles. The pattern grows at a constant rate.

a.   Write an equation to represent this situation.

b.   Which figure number will contain 1015 tiles?

6-61.   Normally, the longer you work for a company, the higher your salary per hour. Hector surveyed the people at his company and placed his data in the table below.

Number of Years at Company	1	3	6	7
Salary per Hour	$7.00	$8.50	$10.75	$11.50

a.   Use Hector's data to estimate how much he makes, assuming he has worked at the company for 12 years.

b.   Hector is hiring a new employee who will work 20 hours a week. How much should the new employee earn for the first week?

6-62.   Mr. Greer solved the equation as shown below. However, when he checked his solution, it did not make the original equation true. Find his error and then find the correct solution.

$$4x = 8(2x - 3)$$
$$4x = 16x - 3$$
$$-12x = -3$$
$$x = \frac{-3}{-12}$$
$$x = \frac{1}{4}$$

6-63.   The box plot below shows the different grades (in percents) that students in Ms. Sanchez's class earned on a recent test.

a.   What was the median score on the test? What were the highest and lowest scores?

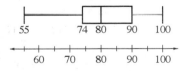

b.   Did most students earn a particular score? How do you know?

c.   If Ms. Sanchez has 32 students in her class, about how many students earned a grade of 80% or higher? About how many earned more than 90%? Explain how you know.

d.   Can you tell if the scores between 80% and 90% were closer to 80% or closer to 90%? Explain.

6.2.3 Are they similar?

Identifying Similar Shapes

Have you ever noticed how many different kinds of cell phones there are? Sometimes you might have a cell phone that is similar to one of your friends' cell phones because it is the same brand, but it might be a different model or color. Occasionally, two people will have the exact same cell phone, including brand, model, and color. Sorting objects into groups based on what is the same about them is also done in math. As you work with your team to sort shapes, ask the following questions:

How do the shapes grow or shrink?

What parts can we compare?

How can we write the comparison?

6-64.   WHICH SHAPES ARE SIMILAR?

If two shapes appear to have the same general relationship between sides, how can you decide for sure if the shapes are similar? Work with your team to:

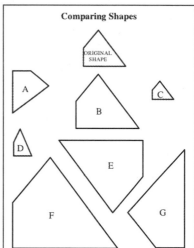

- Carefully cut out the original shape and shapes A through G from one copy of the Lesson 6.2.3 Resource Page.

- Decide how each shape is related to the original shape. (Each person should use an uncut copy of the resource page and the team's cut out shapes to help decide.)

- Compare the angles and the sides of shapes A through G to the original shape.

a.   Which shapes are similar to the original shape? Give specific reasons to justify your conclusions.

b.   Now look only at the shapes that are similar to the original shape. What do these shapes have in common? What is different about them? Be specific.

c.   When two shapes are similar, the **scale factor** is the number you multiply the length of the side of one shape by to get the length of the corresponding side of the new shape. What is the scale factor between the original shape and shape E? Is each side of the shape enlarged the same number of times? Use a ruler to help you decide, if needed.

d.   What is the scale factor between the original shape and shape C? Why is it less than 1?

248   *Core Connections, Course 3*

6-65.   Shapes that are similar but do not grow or shrink are called **congruent** shapes.

   a.   Which shape from problem 6-64 is exactly equal to the original shape in every way?

   b.   Record the pairs of shapes below that appear to be congruent to each other.

   c.   Get a piece of tracing paper from your teacher and use it to check that the shapes you identified as congruent have exactly the same size and shape. Were you correct? If not, why not?

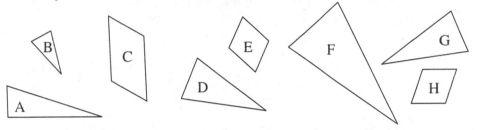

6-66.   Quan enlarged shape Q to make shape P, below. Are his shapes similar? If they are similar, identify the scale factor (multiplier). If they are not, demonstrate that at least one pair of sides does not share the scale factor.

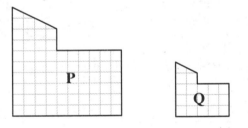

6-67.   Draw each of the shapes in problem 6-66 on graph paper. Color-code the corresponding sides on each shape using the colors suggested by your teacher.

   a.   Compare the green sides of each shape. What do you notice about those sides?

   b.   Compare each of the other five sides of shape P with their corresponding sides on shape Q. What do you notice about those pairs of sides?

   c.   Imagine enlarging shape P to make a new shape R that has a base 25 units long. If shape R is similar to shape P, predict the length of the shorter vertical side of shape R *without drawing the shape*. What is the scale factor in this situation?

6-68.   Using the triangle shown at right as the original figure, *predict* which of the scale factors below would enlarge (make bigger) or reduce (make smaller) the shape. (Do not actually make a new shape.)

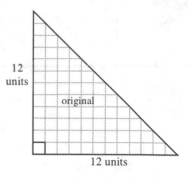

$$\frac{5}{3} \qquad \frac{3}{4} \qquad \frac{7}{6} \qquad \frac{2}{3}$$

After you write down your prediction, decide which scale factor each member of your team will use. Then copy the original figure on graph paper and draw a similar triangle using your scale factor.

a.   Show your new triangle to your teammates and check your predictions. Which scale factors made the triangle larger? Which made the triangle smaller? Is there a pattern?

b.   Which parts of the new triangles remained the same as the original triangle? Which parts changed? How do you know?

c.   Each of the new triangles is similar to the original triangle used to create it. Compare the corresponding (matching) sides and angles to each other. Describe the relationship or explain why you think there is no relationship.

d.   What scale factor could you use to create a triangle that is congruent to the original? Explain.

e.   **Additional Challenge:** Find a scale factor that will make a similar shape that is larger than the original but has a scale factor less than 2.

6-69.   LEARNING LOG

In your Learning Log, explain how to determine when shapes are similar. To decide if two shapes are similar, what do you need to know about the side lengths? The angles? Title your entry "Finding Similar Shapes" and include today's date.

6-70.   Which of the shapes at right appear to be similar? Explain how you know.

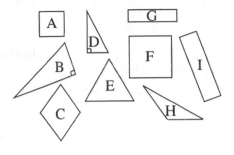

6-71.   A local deli sells 6-inch sub sandwiches for $2.95. Now the deli has decided to sell a "family sub" that is 50 inches long. If they want to make the larger sub price comparable to the price of the smaller sub, how much should it charge? Show all work.

6-72.   Represent the tile pattern below with a table, a rule, and a graph.

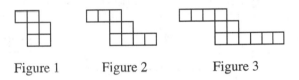

Figure 1   Figure 2   Figure 3

6-73.   How many solutions does each equation below have? How can you tell?

a. $4x - 1 + 5 = 4x + 3$

b. $6t - 3 = 3t + 6$

c. $6(2m - 3) - 3m = 2m - 18 + m$

d. $10 + 3y - 2 = 4y - y + 8$

6-74.   Simplify each expression below.

a. $-2\frac{3}{10} - 1\frac{2}{5}$

b. $3 \div -\frac{5}{4}$

c. $\frac{3}{4} + 5\frac{7}{8}$

d. $5\frac{1}{6} \cdot \left(-\frac{7}{9}\right)$

6-75.   Look carefully at the key at right. Which of the keys below could you create by spinning (rotating) the original key? Which keys could you create by flipping (reflecting) the original key?

original

a.   b.   c.   d.

6.2.4 What sequence makes them the same?

Similar Figures and Transformations

So far in this chapter you have investigated transformations and similar figures. Recall that reflections, rotations, and translations are all special cases of transformations that are called rigid transformations. Today you will investigate how to use transformations to show that two figures are similar.

6-76.   Copy the graph at right.

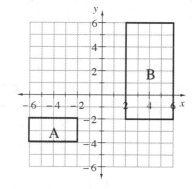

a.   Do you think the figures are similar? Why or why not?

b.   Describe a sequence of transformations (reflections, rotations, translations, and dilations) to change Figure A to Figure B.

c.   How does your sequence of transformations prove that the figures are similar?

6-77.   Figures that are congruent are the same shape and the same size. You can also say they have a scale factor of 1. Which transformation(s) can you use to show that two figures are congruent? Which transformation(s) will cause figures that are not congruent, but similar?

6-78.   Angelina and Vee have each made a challenge for you. Begin with Figure A at right, and then follow the steps of their transformations to find the coordinates of the new figure, Figure B. Record your work on graph paper.

a.   Angelina's steps:

- Reflect the triangle across the x-axis.

- Rotate the triangle about the origin counter-clockwise (↺) 90°.

- Dilate the figure by a scale factor of $\frac{1}{2}$ (multiply the coordinate of each point by $\frac{1}{2}$).

Problem continues on next page. →

6-78.   *Problem continued from previous page.*

    b. Vee's steps:

- Translate the triangle 4 units right and 3 units down.

- Rotate the triangle clockwise (↻) 180° about its top vertex (point).

- Reflect the triangle across the line $x = 3$.

    c. Were your resulting figures congruent, similar, or neither? Explain.

6-79.   With your team, find a sequence of transformations that will transform Figure C to become Figure D.

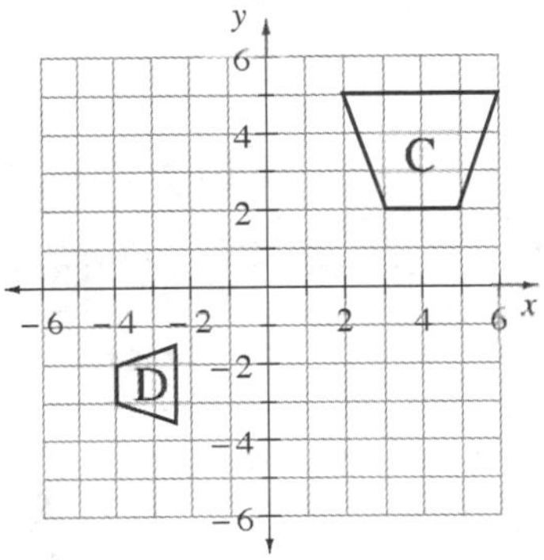

6-80.   On your paper, sketch the graph at right.

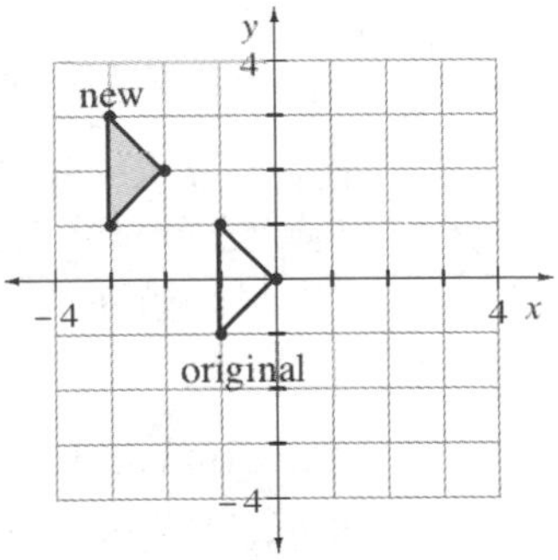

    a. Write directions for translating the original triangle to make the new triangle.

    b. What are the coordinates of the vertices (corners) of the new shape?

    c. On your graph, reflect the original triangle over the y-axis. What are the coordinates of the new triangle?

6-81.   Hannah thinks the solution to the system below is $(-4, -6)$. Wirt thinks the solution is $(20, 10)$.

$$2x - 3y = 10$$
$$6y = 4x - 20$$

    a. Is Hannah correct?   b. Is Wirt correct?

    c. What do the answers to (a) and (b) tell you about the lines in the problem?

6-82. Figure 2 of a tile pattern is shown at right. If the pattern grows linearly and if Figure 6 has 18 tiles, then find a rule for the pattern.

Figure 2

6-83. Solve the following equations for x, if possible. Check your solutions.

a. $-(2-3x)+x=9-x$

b. $\frac{6}{x+2}=\frac{3}{4}$

c. $5-2(x+6)=14$

d. $\frac{1}{2}x-4=-3-\frac{1}{3}x$

6-84. Kevin found the box plot below in the school newspaper.

Number of hours spent watching TV each week

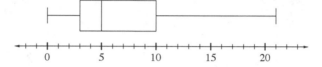

a. Based on the plot, what percent of students watch more than 10 hours of television each week?

b. Based on the plot, what percent of students watch less than 5 hours of television each week?

c. Can Kevin use the box plot to find the mean (average) number of hours of television students watch each week? If so, what is it? Explain your reasoning.

6-85. Solve each equation. Show all work.

a. $0.85x=200$

b. $\frac{7}{6}x=140$

6.2.5 What do similar shapes tell us?

Working With Corresponding Sides

Graphic artists often need to make a shape larger to use for a sign. Sometimes they need to make a shape smaller to use for a bumper sticker. They have to be sure that the shapes look the same no matter what size they are. How do artists know what the side length of a similar shape should be? That is, does it need to be larger or smaller than the original?

6-86.   With your team, find the scale factor between each pair of similar shapes. That is, what are the sides of each original shape multiplied by to get the new shape?

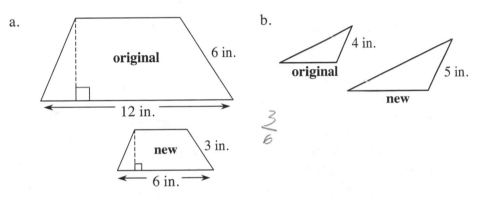

6-87.   It may have been easier to recognize the scale factor between the two shapes in part (a) of problem 6-86 than it was to determine the scale factor between the two shapes in part (b). When sides are not even multiples of each other (like the sides labeled 4 in. and 5 in. in part (b), it is useful to have another strategy for finding the scale factor.

Your Task: Work with your team to describe a strategy for finding the scale factor between any two shapes. Refer to the questions below to begin your discussion.

Discussion Points

How can we use pairs of corresponding sides to write the scale factor?

Will the scale factor between the shapes be more or less than 1?

Does it matter which pair of corresponding sides we use?

6-88.   A study team was working together to find the scale factor for the two similar triangles at right.

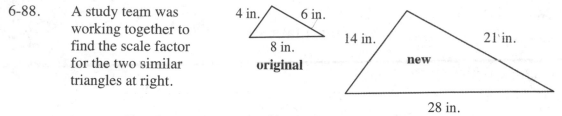

*   Claudia set up the ratio $\frac{14}{4}$ to find the scale factor.

*   Issac set up the ratio $\frac{28}{8}$ to find the scale factor.

*   Paula set up the ratio $\frac{21}{6}$ to find the scale factor.

a. What did the students do differently when they found their scale factors?

b. Do the triangles have more than one scale factor? If not, show how they are the same.

c. Why does it make sense that the ratios are equal?

6-89.   Alex was working with the two triangles from problem 6-86, but he now has a few more pieces of information about the -sides. He has represented the new information and his scale factor in the diagram reprinted at right. Sketch his diagram on your own paper.

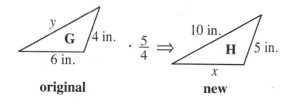

a. Use the scale factor to find the length of the side labeled x. Show your work.

b. Since Alex multiplied the side lengths of triangle G to get triangle H, he needs to undo the enlargement to find the side labeled y. What math operation would he use to undo the enlargement? Write an expression and be prepared to explain your reasoning. If you are able, simplify the expression to find y.

c. If triangle H had been the original triangle and triangle G had been the new triangle, how would the scale factor change? What would the new scale factor be? Explain.

6-90.   For the pairs of similar shapes below, find the lengths of the missing sides. Be
         sure to show your calculation. You can choose which shape is "new" and
         which is "original" in each pair. Assume the shapes are all drawn to scale. The
         shapes in part (b) are parallelograms and the shapes in part (d) are trapezoids.

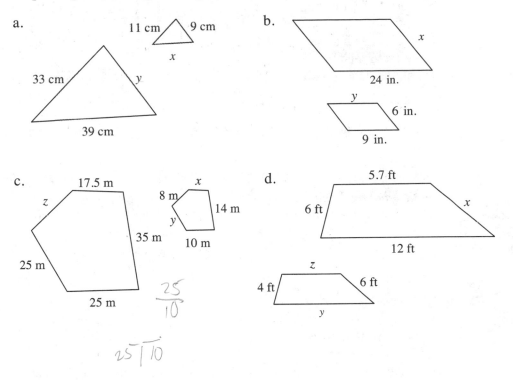

a.

b.

c.

d.

$$\frac{25}{10}$$

$$25 \overline{\smash{\big)}10}$$

6-91.   **Additional Challenge:** On graph paper, copy
         the figure shown at right.

     a. Find the area of the shape.

     b. Enlarge the shape by a scale factor of 2,
         and draw the new shape. Find the area.

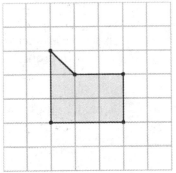

6-92. Sketch the two similar triangles at right on your own paper. Find the scale factor and the missing side lengths.

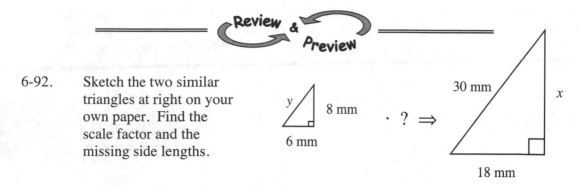

6-93. Alex and Maria were trying to find the side labeled x in problem 6-92. Their work is shown below.

Alex: *"I noticed that when I multiplied by 3, the sides of the triangle got longer."*

Maria: *"I remember that when we were dilating shapes in Lesson 6.2.2, my shape got bigger when I divided by $\frac{1}{3}$."*

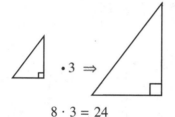

$8 \cdot 3 = 24$

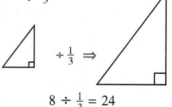

$8 \div \frac{1}{3} = 24$

a. Look at each student's work. Why do both multiplying by 3 and dividing by $\frac{1}{3}$ make the triangles larger?

b. Use Alex and Maria's strategy to write two expressions to find the value of y in problem 6-92.

6-94. Consider these two equations:
$$y = 3x - 2$$
$$y = 4 + 3x$$

a. Graph both equations on the same set of axes.

b. Solve this system using the Equal Values Method.

c. Explain how the answer to part (b) agrees with the graph you made in part (a).

6-95. Hollyhocks are tall, slender, flowering plants that grow in many areas of the U.S. Here are the heights (in inches) of hollyhocks that are growing in a park: 10, 39, 43, 45, 46, 47, 48, 48, 49, 50, and 52.

a. Find the median.

b. Find the quartiles.

c. Make a box plot of the data.

6-96. Use the graph at right to add points to the table below.

a. Write the rule in words.

b. Explain how to use the table to predict the value of y when x is -8.

6-97. Use these following directions to create a mystery letter. On a piece of graph paper, draw a four-quadrant graph. Scale each axis from 6 to -6. Plot these points and connect them in order to create a rectangle: $(2,1)$, $(2,4)$, $(3,4)$, $(3,1)$. Be sure to connect the last point to the first point. Then follow the directions in parts (a) through (c) below.

a. Rotate the rectangle 90° clockwise (↻) about the point $(2,1)$ and draw the rotated rectangle.

b. Reflect the new rectangle over the line $y = 2$ and draw the reflected rectangle.

c. Name the letter of the alphabet that your graph resembles.

6.2.6 How do I find a missing side?

Solving Problems Involving Similar Shapes

Architects create scaled plans for building houses. Artists use sketches to plan murals for the sides of buildings. Companies create smaller sizes of their products to display in stores. Each of these models is created to show all of the information about the real object, without being the actual size of the object. Today you will work with your team to find strategies that you can use when you are missing some of the information about a set of similar shapes. As you work, look for more than one way to solve the problem.

6-98.   MODEL TRAINS

Kenen loves trains, especially those that run on narrow-gauge tracks. (The gauge of a track measures how far apart the rails are.) He has decided to build a model train of the Rio Grande, a popular narrow-gauge train.

Use the following information to help him know how big his model should be:

- The real track has a gauge of 3 feet (36 inches).

- His model railroad track has a gauge of $\frac{3}{4}$ inches.

- The Rio Grande train he wants to model has driving wheels that measure 44 inches high.

Your Task: With your team, discuss what you know about the model train Kenen will build. What scale factor should he use? What will be the height of the driving wheels of his model? Be prepared to share your strategies with the class.

6-99.   Heather and Cindy are playing "Guess My Shape." Heather has to describe a shape to Cindy accurately enough so that Cindy can draw it without ever seeing the shape. Heather gives Cindy these clues:

> Clue #1:   The shape is similar to a rectangle with a base of 7 cm and a height of 4 cm.
>
> Clue #2:   The shape is five times larger than the shape it is similar to.

a.   Has Heather given Cindy enough information to draw the shape? If so, sketch the shape on your paper. If not, write a question to ask Heather to get the additional information you need.

b.   Use what you know about similar shapes to write a set of "Guess My Shape" clues to describe each of the mystery shapes below. Your clues should be complete enough for someone in another class to be able to read them and draw the shape. Be sure to include at least one clue about the relationship between the mystery shape and a similar shape.

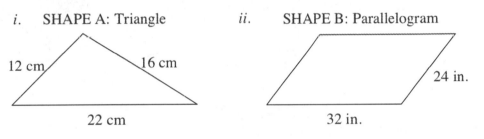

i.   SHAPE A: Triangle

12 cm   16 cm

22 cm

ii.   SHAPE B: Parallelogram

24 in.

32 in.

6-100.   Nick enlarged figure A at right so that it became the similar figure B. His diagrams are shown at right.

4 mm   7 mm
2 mm   A
10 mm
x
5 mm   B

a.   Write all of the ratios that compare the corresponding sides of figure B to figure A.

b.   What is the relationship between these ratios? How do you know?

c.   Use two different ways to find the value of x in this quadrilateral. Does your solution seem reasonable? Be ready to share your strategies with the class.

6-101.   Fatima solved for p in the diagram of similar triangles below and got $p = 30$. Looking at her answer, she knows she made a mistake. What would make Fatima think that her answer is wrong?

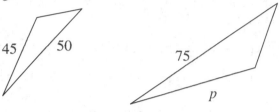

6-102.   LEARNING LOG

In your Learning Log, write a description about how to find the missing side of a similar shape. Be specific about your strategy and include a picture with labels. Put today's date on your entry and title it "Finding Missing Sides of Similar Shapes."

METHODS AND MEANINGS

Scale Factor

A **scale factor** is a ratio that describes how two quantities or lengths are related. A scale factor that describes how two similar shapes are related can be found by writing a ratio between any pair of corresponding sides as $\frac{\text{new}}{\text{original}}$.

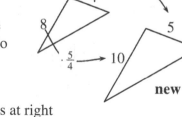

For example, the two similar triangles at right are related by a scale factor of $\frac{5}{4}$ because the side lengths of the new triangle can be found by multiplying the corresponding side lengths of the original triangle by $\frac{5}{4}$.

A scale factor greater than one **enlarges** a shape (makes it larger). A scale factor between zero and one **reduces** a shape (makes it smaller). If a scale factor is equal to one, the two similar shapes are identical and are called **congruent**.

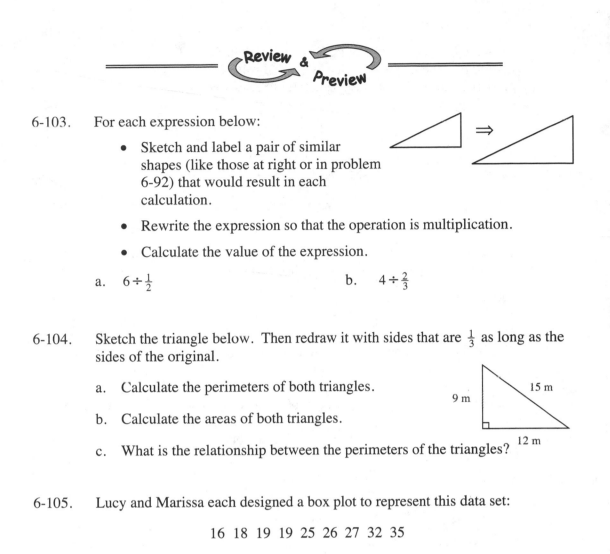

6-103.   For each expression below:

- Sketch and label a pair of similar shapes (like those at right or in problem 6-92) that would result in each calculation.

- Rewrite the expression so that the operation is multiplication.

- Calculate the value of the expression.

a. $6 \div \frac{1}{2}$ b. $4 \div \frac{2}{3}$

6-104.   Sketch the triangle below. Then redraw it with sides that are $\frac{1}{3}$ as long as the sides of the original.

a.   Calculate the perimeters of both triangles.

b.   Calculate the areas of both triangles.

c.   What is the relationship between the perimeters of the triangles?

6-105.   Lucy and Marissa each designed a box plot to represent this data set:

16 18 19 19 25 26 27 32 35

Their plots are shown below. Which plot is scaled correctly and why? Explain the mistakes in the incorrect plot.

a.   b.

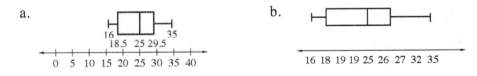

6-106.   Draw a coordinate graph, and then plot and connect the following points:
$A(-3,1)$, $B(-1,3)$, $C(4,2)$, $D(2,0)$.

a.   What is the shape you created?

b.   Reflect the shape across the x-axis. List the coordinates of the new points.

c.   Multiply each coordinate of the original shape by 3. Graph the dilated shape. What are the new coordinates of the points?

6-107. Examine the diagram at right. The smaller triangle is similar to the larger triangle. Write and solve a proportion to find x. It may be helpful to draw the two triangles separately.

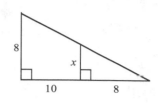

6-108. SEQUENCES OF TRANSFORMATIONS

    a. A figure is rotated and reflected. What can you say about the new figure in relation to the original figure?

    b. A figure is translated, reflected, and then dilated. What can you say about the new figure in relation to the original figure?

6-109. This problem is a checkpoint for multiple representations of linear equations. It will be referred to as Checkpoint 6.

For each situation given below, complete the Representations of Patterns Web by finding the missing $x \rightarrow y$ table, graph, and/or rule. Since there are many possible patterns, it is not necessary to create one.

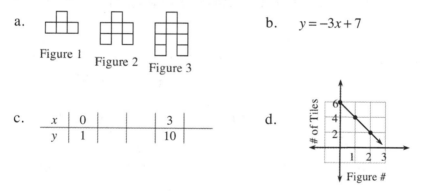

    a. Figure 1 Figure 2 Figure 3

    b. $y = -3x + 7$

    c.

x	0			3	
y	1			10	

    d.

Check your answers by referring to the Checkpoint 6 materials located at the back of your book.

If you needed help solving these problems correctly, then you need more practice. Review the Checkpoint 6 materials and try the practice problems. Also, consider getting help outside of class time. From this point on, you will be expected to do problems like these quickly and easily.

Chapter 6 Closure   What have I learned?

Reflection and Synthesis

The activities below offer you a chance to reflect about
what you have learned during this chapter. As you work,
look for concepts that you feel very comfortable with,
ideas that you would like to learn more about, and topics
you need more help with.

①   SUMMARIZING MY UNDERSTANDING

This section gives you an opportunity to show what you know about certain
math topics or ideas. Your teacher will give you specific directions for exactly
how to do this and will provide you with instructions about how to summarize
your understanding of transformations and undoing transformations. In this
activity, you will use a triangle to review transformations.

Predict and Order: Predict how each
transformation will change or move the shape.
Select an order for the four transformations
and predict what the new coordinates of the
vertices will be after each step.

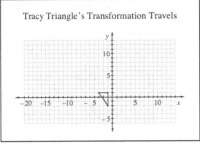

Apply Transformations: Follow the
transformation steps you described
on the graph. Use color and written descriptions to show how each
transformation alters the shape and its position on the coordinate graph. Check
that the coordinates you predicted were correct.

Tracy Triangle's Transformative Travels	Tracy Triangle's Transformative Travels
Add 5 to each *x* coordinate.	Multiply each *y*-coordinate by –1.
Tracy Triangle's Transformative Travels	**Tracy Triangle's Transformative Travels**
Multiply each coordinate by 2.	Add –8 and then 3 to each *x*-coordinate. Add 9 and –4 to each *y*-coordinate.

Undo Transformations: To get the triangle back to the original position, undo
your transformations. You may choose to undo *each* transformation step or to
find a new series of steps to return the shape to its original position. Using
color, symbols, and written descriptions, show how each transformation
changes the shape's size and position on the coordinate graph.

WHAT HAVE I LEARNED?

Doing the problems in this section will help you to evaluate which types of problems you feel comfortable with and which ones you need more help with.

Solve each problem as completely as you can. The table at the end of this closure section provides answers to these problems. It also tells you where you can find additional help and where to find practice problems like them.

CL 6-110. Priscilla and Ursula went fishing. Priscilla brought a full box of 32 worms and used one worm every minute. Ursula brought a box with five worms and decided to dig for more before she began fishing. Ursula dug up two worms per minute. When did Priscilla and Ursula have the same number of worms? Show how you know.

CL 6-111. Copy the graph at right on your paper. You will need a second graph for List II. Complete each list of transformation steps you could use to move triangle B back to where it started at position A, and show each transformation on your graph.

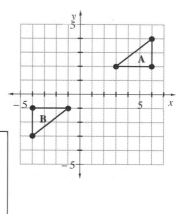

List I	List II
1. Rotate triangle B 180° about point (−1,−1)	1. Reflect triangle B across the y-axis
2. ?	2. ?
	3. ?

CL 6-112. Neatly graph the points (−2,9), (−3,7) and (−5,10) on a four-quadrant graph. Connect them to make a triangle. Then, for each transformation described below:

• Write and simplify an expression to find the new coordinates.

• Check your answer on your graph.

a. Slide the triangle right 4 units and down 6 units.

b. Reflect the triangle across the y-axis.

CL 6-113.   The shapes at right are similar.

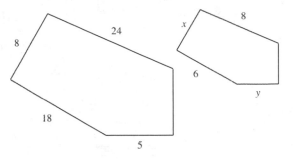

a.   What is the scale factor?

b.   Find the sides labeled x and y.

CL 6-114.   As Khan and Jorman practice for college entrance tests, their scores increase. Khan's current score is 750 and is rising 8 points per week. Jorman's current score is 650 but is growing by 30 points per week. Write an equation or system of equations to determine when Jorman will catch up with Kahn. Be sure to define your variable(s).

CL 6-115.   Solve each equation.

a. $3(2+x) = 4 - (x-2)$ b. $\frac{x}{2} + \frac{x}{3} - 1 = \frac{x}{6} + 3$

CL 6-116.   Samantha is dilating triangle ABC at right. She multiplied each x-coordinate and y-coordinate of triangle ABC by -2.

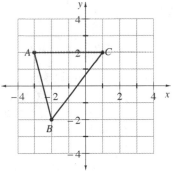

a.   Graph Samantha's new triangle.

b.   Describe how triangle ABC changed.

CL 6-117.   A trapezoid has a perimeter of 117 cm. The two shortest sides have the same length. The third side is 12 cm longer than one short side. The final side is 9 cm less than three times one short side. How long is each side of the trapezoid?

Define a variable and write an equation to represent this problem. Solve your equation and write your answer in a complete sentence.

CL 6-118.   For each of the problems in this section of closure, do the following:

- Draw a bar or number line like the one below that represents 0 to 10.

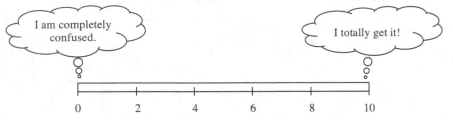

- Color or shade in a portion of the bar that represents your current level of understanding and comfort with completing that problem on your own.

If any of your bars are less than a 5, choose *one* of those problems and do one of the following tasks:

- Write two questions that you would like to ask about that problem.
- Brainstorm two things that you DO know about that type of problem.

If all of your bars are a 5 or above, choose one of those problems and do one of these tasks:

- Write two questions you might ask or hints you might give to a student who was stuck on the problem.
- Make a new problem that is similar and more challenging than that problem and solve it.

③   WHAT TOOLS CAN I USE?

You have several tools and references available to help support your learning – your teacher, your study team, your math book, and your Toolkit, to name only a few. At the end of each chapter you will have an opportunity to review your Toolkit for completeness as well as to revise or update it to better reflect your current understanding of big ideas.

The main elements of your Toolkit should be your Learning Log, Math Notes, and the vocabulary used in this chapter. Math words that are new to this chapter appear in bold in the text. Refer to the lists provided below and follow your teacher's instructions to revise your Toolkit, which will help make it a useful reference for you as you complete this chapter and prepare to begin the next one.

Learning Log Entries
- Lesson 6.1.3 – Rigid Transformations
- Lesson 6.2.1 - Dilations
- Lesson 6.2.3 – Finding Similar Shapes
- Lesson 6.2.6 – Finding Missing Sides of Similar Shapes

Core Connections, Course 3

Math Notes

- Lesson 6.1.3 – Rigid Transformations
- Lesson 6.2.2 – Corresponding Parts of Similar Shapes
- Lesson 6.2.6 – Scale Factor

Mathematical Vocabulary

The following is a list of vocabulary found in this chapter. Some of the words you have been seen in previous chapters. The words in bold are the words new to this chapter. Make sure that you are familiar with the terms below and know what they mean. For the words you do not know, refer to the glossary or index. You might also add these words to your Toolkit so that you can reference them in the future.

congruent	**conjecture**	**corresponding parts**
dilation	**enlarge**	linear equation
point of intersection	**reduce**	**reflection**
rigid transformation	**rotation**	**scale factor**
similar figures	system of equations	**translation**
y-intercept		

Answers and Support for Problems
What Have I Learned?

Note: MN = Math Note, LL = Learning Log

Problem	Solution	Need Help?	More Practice
CL 6-110.	Let w = # worms and t = time in minutes. $w = 32 - t$ and $w = 2t + 5$ 9 minutes	Lessons 5.2.2 and 5.2.3 MN: 5.2.2, 5.2.3, and 5.2.4	Problems 5-32, 5-33, 5-36, 5-41, 5-43, 5-44, 5-52, and 5-59
CL 6-111.	List I: 2. Translate (slide) triangle B right 4 units and up 3 units. List II: 2. Reflect triangle B across the *x*-axis. 3. Translate triangle right 2 units and up 1 unit.	Lesson 6.1.1 MN: 6.1.3 LL: 6.1.3	Problems 6-1, 6-2, 6-8, 6-9, 6-18, 6-22, 6-24, 6-25, 6-27, 6-36, and 6-79

Problem	Solution	Need Help?	More Practice
CL 6-112.	a. x: $-2+4=2$, y: $9-6=3$; $(2,3)$ x: $-3+4=1$, y: $7-6=1$; $(1,1)$ x: $-5+4=-1$, y: $10-6=4$; $(-1,4)$ b. y-coordinates remain the same. x: $-2\cdot(-1)=2$; $(2,9)$ x: $-3\cdot(-1)=3$; $(3,7)$ x: $-5\cdot(-1)=5$; $(5,10)$	Lesson 6.1.1 MN: 6.1.3 LL: 6.1.3	Problems 6-20, 6-25, 6-28, 6-33, 6-78, 6-80, 6-97, and 6-106
CL 6-113.	a. Divide by 3 or multiply by $\frac{1}{3}$ b. $x=\frac{8}{3}$ or $2\frac{2}{3}$ $y=\frac{5}{3}$ or $1\frac{2}{3}$	Lesson 6.2.3 MN: 6.2.2 and 6.2.6	Problems 6-64, 6-66, 6-68, 6-70, 6-77, 6-78, 6-87, 6-88, 6-91, and 6-92
CL 6-114.	$x=$ number of weeks $750+8x=650+30x$ approximately 5 weeks (4.76)	Lessons 5.2.2 and 5.2.3 MN: 5.2.2, 5.2.3, and 5.2.4	Problems 6-7 and 6-17
CL 6-115.	a. $x=0$ b. $x=6$	Lessons 2.1.8 and 2.1.9 MN: 2.1.8 and 2.1.9 LL: 2.1.9	Problems 6-5, 6-49, 6-62, and 6-83
CL 6-116.	a. b. The sides are twice as long and the triangle is reflected over both the x- and y-axes.	Lessons 6.2.1 and 6.2.2 MN: 6.2.2 and 6.2.6	Problems 6-34, 6-43, 6-46, 6-52, 6-53, 6-54, and 6-86
CL 6-117.	$x=$ length of short side $x+x+(x+12)+(3x-9)=117$ The side lengths are 19 cm, 19 cm, 31 cm, 48 cm	MN: 1.1.3	Problem 6-30

Slope and Association

7

CHAPTER 7

Previously you used histograms and box plots to answer statistical questions involving a single piece of data. In this chapter, you will learn how to use scatterplots to find relationships between *two* different measures for a set of objects. For example, you could analyze amounts of fertilizer and plant height to answer a question like, *"If I give a plant more fertilizer, will it grow taller?"*

In Section 7.2, you will examine races called triathlons to discover when rates are the same or different. You will also measure of the steepness of lines, a concept called slope, for situations, tables, and graphs.

Finally, you will look at how to make predictions about future events from existing data using trend lines and equations. You will learn about the concept of association that helps describe the relationship between two pieces of data.

Guiding Questions

Think about these questions throughout this chapter:

What would a graph of this data look like?

Can I make a prediction?

Is there a relationship?

What is slope?

What information is needed to find the equation of a line?

In this chapter, you will learn how to:

> ➤ Create scatterplots that show the relationship between two variables.
> ➤ Identify associations between sets of data and represent the relationship with a trend line.
> ➤ Measure the steepness of a line by using slope.
> ➤ Find the slope of a line given its equation, its graph, or any two points on the line.
> ➤ Find the equation of a trend line to fit linear data.

Chapter Outline

Section 7.1 In this section, you will first create and interpret circle graphs. You will also learn how to make graphs that compare two sets of data. Then, you will use scatterplots and linear graphs to make observations and predictions about the data based on correlations.

Section 7.2 Here, you will compare ratios and rates using different representations, including numbers, tables, and graphs. You will find out how to measure the steepness of a line on a graph.

Section 7.3 In this section, you will find equations of lines that fit data and will use them to make predictions based on trends.

7.1.1 How can I represent the data?

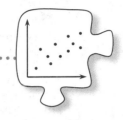

Circle Graphs

Data can be found everywhere in the world. When scientists conduct experiments, they collect data. Advertising agencies collect data to learn which products consumers prefer. In previous courses, you developed histograms and box plots to represent the center and spread of data. How can you represent data that is non-numerical or that cannot be represented on a number line? Today you will look at a data display that is used for data that comes in categories or groups. As you work, keep these questions in mind:

What portion is represented?

Should I use a fraction or a percent?

Am I measuring in percents or degrees?

7-1.   HUMAN CIRCLE GRAPH

Get a shape card from your teacher. Look at your shape and decide if your shape is a parallelogram, another form of a quadrilateral, a triangle, or some other shape. Follow your teacher's directions to create a linear model and **circle graph**. Then answer the questions below.

a.   Your class built a circle graph with your bodies. How can this model be drawn on paper? Work with your team to sketch a picture of your class circle graph showing the portion of your class that held parallelograms, other quadrilaterals, triangles, and other polygons. Be sure to label each section with the category of shape it represents and with an estimated percentage or angle measure.

b.   Approximately what portion of the class held triangles? Write your answer as a percent. Then estimate the measure of the **central angle** on the graph for that portion. A central angle is an angle with its vertex at the center of a circle. Its sides are formed by two radii, and its measure is a portion of 360°.

c.   Was there a section of the circle that had a central angle of approximately 90°? If so, what type of figure is represented in that section?

7-2.   Nate and Rick are interested in buying a car. According to an ad in the paper, they found that there were 12 cars, 9 pickup trucks, 6 SUVs, and 3 minivans for sale in their price range.

   a.   How many vehicles were in Nate and Rick's price range?

   b.   What portion of the total does each type of vehicle represent?

   c.   On the Lesson 7.1.1B Resource Page, create a circle graph of the vehicles in Nate and Rick's price range. Label each section of the graph with the type of vehicle along with the fraction or percent of the circle it represents.

   d.   Calculate the central angle created by each section in the circle graph.

   e.   Is there another way to represent this data? Is a box plot, stem-and-leaf plot, histogram, or bar graph an appropriate way to display this data? Why or why not?

7-3.   Circle graphs can be used to compare data at different points in time. Use the questions that follow to analyze the two circle graphs below.

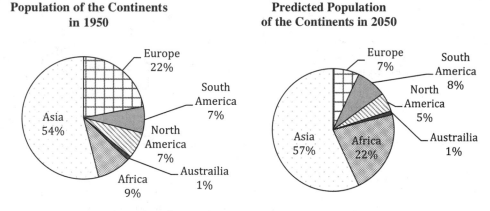

Population of the Continents in 1950

Predicted Population of the Continents in 2050

   a.   According to the circle graphs, which continent had the largest population in 1950? Which has the largest predicted population in 2050? Do they represent the same percent of the world's population in both graphs?

   b.   Which continent is predicted to have its percent of world population increase the most between 1950 and 2050? By what percent is it expected to increase?

   c.   Which continent is expected to have its portion of the total population shrink the most between 1950 and 2050? By how much will its percentage of world population change?

   d.   Is it reasonable to say that continents with a small percentage of the world population in 1950 will have a small percentage of the world populatation in 2050? What evidence from the graphs can you provide to justify your answer?

7-4.   The world's landmasses are divided into seven continents. The largest continent in terms of landmass is Asia, representing almost 30% of the earth's land area. In contrast, the smallest continent is Australia, at about 6% of the earth's land area. Use the circle graph at right to help you make the following comparisons.

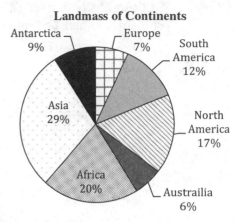

Landmass of Continents

a. Which continents are approximately the same size?

b. Which continent is about one-half the size of Asia?

c. Which continents together make up about half of the world's land mass?

7-5.   The population of the world's people is not evenly divided over the earth's surface. In 2009, only 0.0002% of people in the world lived in Antarctica, while 60% of people lived in Asia.

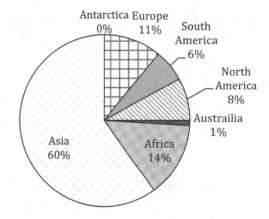

Population of the Continents in 2000

a. Where is the portion representing Antarctica's population? Explain.

b. What similarities and differences do you notice about the landmass and population circle graphs in problem 7-4 and this problem?

c. Is it reasonable to say that larger continents have larger populations? Why or why not?

7-6. **Additional Challenge:** Take another look at the population graphs from problems 7-3 and 7-5, shown below.

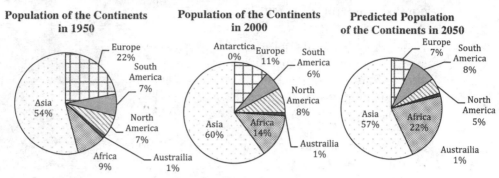

Population of the Continents in 1950

Population of the Continents in 2000

Predicted Population of the Continents in 2050

a. Note that Asia's population percentage goes from 54% to 60% to 57%. However, the population of Asia is not expected to shrink between 2000 and 2050. How could this be true?

b. What kind of graph could be used so that misunderstandings like the one in part (a) would not occur?

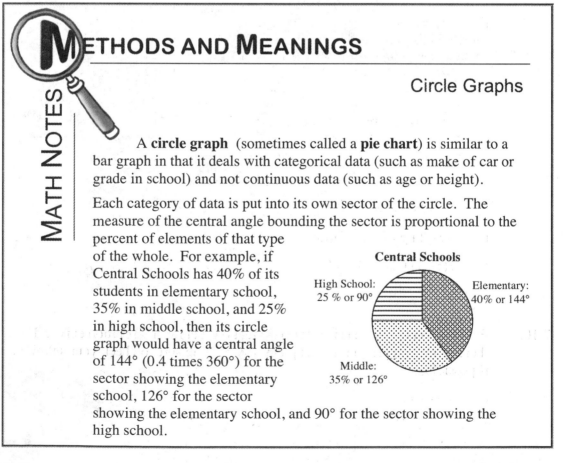

M ETHODS AND MEANINGS

MATH NOTES

Circle Graphs

A **circle graph** (sometimes called a **pie chart**) is similar to a bar graph in that it deals with categorical data (such as make of car or grade in school) and not continuous data (such as age or height).

Each category of data is put into its own sector of the circle. The measure of the central angle bounding the sector is proportional to the percent of elements of that type of the whole. For example, if Central Schools has 40% of its students in elementary school, 35% in middle school, and 25% in high school, then its circle graph would have a central angle of 144° (0.4 times 360°) for the sector showing the elementary school, 126° for the sector showing the elementary school, and 90° for the sector showing the high school.

Central Schools

High School: 25 % or 90°

Elementary: 40% or 144°

Middle: 35% or 126°

7-7.   Answer the following questions about the graph below.

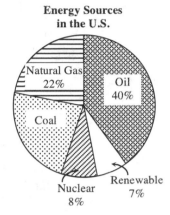

Energy Sources in the U.S.

   a.   According to the graph, what percent of the
        energy in the United States comes from coal?

   b.   Which two sources of energy equal about
        one-third of the total energy for the United
        States?

   c.   What combination of energy sources
        provides about half of the total energy for the
        United States?

7-8.   A group of classmates surveyed how other students
        travel to school. The results of the survey are
        shown in the table at right. Make a circle graph
        showing the results of the survey using percents.

Mode of Transportation	Number of Students
Bus	90
Ride Bike	30
Ride in Car	75
Walk	45

7-9.   Solve each equation below for the indicated variable.

   a. $4x - 2 + y = 6 - 2x$ for y

   b. $4x - 2 + y = 6 - 2x$ for x

   c. $3(6 - x) + 2x = 15$ for x

7-10.   Find the solution for each system of equations below, if a solution exists. If
        there is not a single solution, explain why not. Be sure to check your solution,
        if possible.

   a. $x + 4y = 2$
        $x + 4y = 10$

   b. $2x + 4y = -10$
        $x + 2y = -5$

7-11. Graph the following points on a coordinate grid: $A(-3,-3)$, $B(3,0)$, $C(3,6)$, $D(-3,6)$. Connect the points as you plot them. Then connect point A to point D.

a. Describe the shape you have created.

b. Identify the angles at points C and D.

c. Record the coordinates of the new points if you were to translate the original points three units left and five units up.

7-12. Use proportions to solve each of the problems below.

a. At the zoo, three adult lions together eat 250 pounds of food a day. If two more adult lions joined the group and ate food at the same rate as the original three, how much food would the zoo need to provide all five lions each day?

b. Byron can read 45 pages in an hour. At that rate, how long would it take him to read the new 700-page Terry Cotter book?

c. What is the unit rate of pounds of food per lion in part (a)?

7.1.2 Is there a relationship?

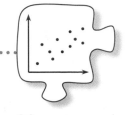

Organizing Data in a Scatterplot

In Lesson 7.1.1, you looked at single data sets, such as world population. Often, you need to compare two measurements to answer a question or to see a connection between two types of data. For example, comparing the odometer reading of a car to the price of a car can help determine if these factors are related. In this lesson, you will study scatterplots, a new tool for visually presenting data, as a way to relate two sets of measurements. You will be asked to analyze the data to see if you can make predictions or come to any conclusion about the relationships that you find.

As you work with your team today, use these focus questions to help direct your discussion:

How can I organize data?

Can I use this data to make a prediction?

What does a point represent?

Is there a connection between the two variables?

7-13.   HOW MUCH IS THAT CAR?

Nate and Rick were discussing cars again. Nate claimed that cars with lower odometer readings were more expensive than cars with higher odometer readings. His evidence was that his car with 23,000 miles was worth more than Rick's car with 31,000 miles. To investigate Nate's claim, the boys collected data from several car advertisements and found the information in the table at right.

Nate's Data from Car Ads

Odometer Reading (thousands of miles)	Price (thousands of $)
35	$38
55	$16
6	$50
28	$30
50	$26
31	$35
15	$28
99	$10
99	$13

Does the information in the table support Nate's claim? That is, do you believe Nate's claim that cars with a lower odometer reading cost more money?

7-14.   Melissa looked at the data from problem 7-13 and said, *"I need to be able to see the data as a picture. I cannot tell if there is a relationship from the lists of numbers."* She decided to use a box plot. Her box plots for odometer reading and price are shown below. Do these pictures help you decide if Nate is correct? Why or why not?

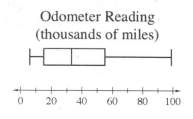

7-15.   Melissa wondered if a coordinate graph could help determine if there was a relationship in Nate's data from problem 7-13.

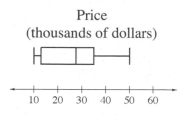

a.   Follow the directions below to create a scatterplot of the data for Melissa.

- Set up a graph showing Odometer Reading on the *x*-axis and Price on the *y*-axis.

- Label equal intervals on each axis so that all of the data will fit on the graph.

- Plot the data points from problem 7-13.

b.   Describe the scatterplot you just created. What do you notice about how the points are placed on the graph? Do you see any patterns?

c.   Place an additional point on your graph for Nate's car that has an odometer reading of 23,000 miles. Explain your strategy for deciding where to put the point.

d.   When a relationship exists, one way to help show a trend in the data is to place a line or curve that, in general, represents where the data falls. This line, sometimes called a **line of best fit**, does not need to touch any of the actual data points. Instead, it shows where the data generally falls. The line is a mathematical model of the data. Models of data help you describe the data more easily and help you make predictions for other cars with different mileages.

With your team, decide where a line of best fit could be placed that would best model the data points. Are there any limits to where your line makes sense?

Problem continues on next page. →

Core Connections, Course 3

7-15.   *Problem continued from previous page.*

   e.   Using the line of best fit, can you predict the price of a car with an
        odometer reading of 80,000 miles? If so, explain how the line of best fit
        helps. If not, explain why it is not helpful.

   f.   Based on the scatterplot, would you agree with Nate's claim that cars with a
        higher odometer reading cost less? Use the scatterplot to justify your
        answer.

7-16.   Sometimes what you know about relationships can help you predict what data
         will look like when it is graphed. For each situation below:

   •   Look at the scatterplots and use your experience to decide which
       statement fits each scatterplot.

   •   Decide if there is a relationship between the data. That is, as one
       quantity changes, does the other change in a predictable way?

   •   If there is a relationship, describe it in a sentence.

   •   If there is no relationship, explain why you think there is not one.

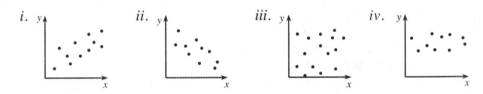

   a.   How fast a dog can run and
        the length of the dog's fur.

   b.   A person's age and his or
        her body temperature.

   c.   A child's age and the size of
        his or her feet.

   d.   Outdoor temperature and the percent of people wearing long-sleeved shirts.

(M)ETHODS AND MEANINGS

Line of Best Fit

A **line of best fit** is a straight line drawn through the center of a group of data points plotted on a scatterplot. It represents a set of data for two variables. It does not need to intersect each data point. Rather, it needs to approximate the data. A line of best fit looks and "behaves" like the data, as shown in the example at right.

Review & Preview

7-17.   HOW MUCH IS THAT CAR?

Nate and Rick were still talking about cars. Nate claimed that cars with more horsepower were more expensive than cars with less horsepower. His reason was that his 300-horsepower sports car was worth more than Rick's 120-horsepower small economy car. To investigate Nate's claim, the boys looked up information about their friends' cars. The table at right shows their results.

Rick and Nate's Data	
Horsepower	Price (Thousands $)
500	$38
160	$16
453	$23
505	$23
228	$30
311	$26
335	$15
197	$40

a.   Does the information in the table support Nate's claim that cars with more horsepower cost more? Is there a relationship between horsepower and the price of a car?

b.   Set up a graph and plot the points from the table. Now do you believe Nate's claim? Explain your reasoning.

7-18.   Look at the scatterplots and use your experience to decide which statement fits each scatterplot. If there is a relationship, describe it in a sentence.

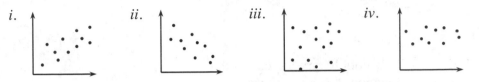

a.   A city's average daytime temperature in January and its latitude. Recall that the equator is at 0° latitude and the poles are at 90° latitude.

b.   Weight of a car and its speed in a traffic jam on the freeway.

c.   Number of pets a student has at home and his or her grades.

d.   Cost of a person's home and the value of his or her car.

7-19.   Match the system of equations in the left column with its solution in the right column.

a. $6x - y = 4$ 1. $(0, -4)$
     $3x + y = 5$

b. $x = y + 4$ 2. $(3, 7)$
     $2x + 3y = -12$

c. $5x - 2y = 1$ 3. $(1, 2)$
     $y = 2x + 1$

7-20.   Use the rectangle at right to answer the following questions.

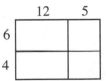

a.   Find the area of the entire rectangle. Explain how you found your solution.

b.   Calculate the perimeter of the figure.

7-21.   Evaluate each expression below for a when $a = \frac{2}{3}$, if possible.

a. $24a$ b. $3a$ c. $\frac{a}{0}$ d. $\frac{0}{a}$

7-22.   The school library has 6500 titles in its collection of books, magazines, and reference materials. The librarian is presenting information about the library to the parent association, and she made the graph at right.

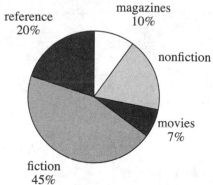

a.   According to the graph, what percent of the collection are nonfiction books?

b.   Could the librarian have presented this information in a histogram? Why or why not?

c.   How many of the books in the library are fiction?

7.1.3 What is the relationship?

Identifying and Describing Association

When is it reasonable to make a prediction? For example, when you know the height of a tree, can you predict the size of its leaves? Or if you know the outdoor temperature for the day, can you predict the number of glasses of water you will drink during the day?

In Lesson 7.1.2, you found that some data sets were related and others were not. In this lesson, you will look at different situations and decide if they show relationships that allow you to make predictions. As you work with your team today, use these focus questions to help direct your discussion:

When one value goes up, what happens to the other one?

Is there a relationship between one measurement changing and the other changing?

Can I make a prediction?

7-23. The students in Mr. Carle's science class have been experimenting with different factors that they think may affect how tall a plant will grow. Each team planted seeds in several pots using different experimental conditions.

With your team, read the questions that the students investigated. Write a team prediction (hypothesis) for the results for each experiment. Assume that all other variables are controlled (meaning that they will not affect the experimental outcome). Write your hypothesis so that it indicates a directional relationship between the independent and dependent variables.

a. Does the amount of fertilizer affect the plant height?

b. Does how deep the seed is planted in each pot affect the plant height?

c. Does the number of seeds in each pot affect the plant height?

d. Does the size of the pot affect the plant height?

e. Does the number of hours of sunlight per day affect the plant height?

7-24.   After three weeks, the teams measured the
         heights of their plants and recorded the data.
         The Team 1 data table and the question Team 1
         investigated are included below. On graph
         paper, make a scatterplot for the data gathered.
         Be sure that you:

- Clearly label your axes.

- Mark the scale at equal intervals.

- Title your graph appropriately (such
  as with the experimental question).

Team 1: Does the amount of fertilizer affect the plant height?

Amount of fertilizer over 3 week period (ml)	5	10	15	20	25	30
Height of plant (cm)	14	17	21	31	33	40

7-25.   Your teacher will assign your team one of the remaining sets of data. Prepare a
         scatterplot poster for your assigned set of data. Be sure your graph has a title
         and that the axes are correctly labeled. Also make sure that the points on your
         graph will be easily seen from across the room.

Team 2: Does the depth of seed in each pot affect the plant height?

Depth of seed in pot (cm)	3	6	9	12	15	18
Height of plant (cm)	24	21	18	12	6	0

Team 3: Does the number of seeds in each pot affect the plant height?

Number of seeds planted in pot	1	2	3	4	5	6
Height of plant (cm)	21	24	27	21	25	20

Team 4: Does the size of the pot affect the plant height?

Diameter of pot (cm)	3	6	9	12	15	18
Height of plant (cm)	21	20	16	20	22	17

Team 5: Does the number of hours of sunlight per day affect the plant height?

Amount of light per day (hours)	1	3	5	7	9	11
Height of plant (cm)	3	10	11	24	30	34

7-26.   Examine your scatterplot for Team 1 from problem 7-24. Also look at the scatterplot posters created by your classmates for Teams 2 through 5. Then answer the following questions.

a.   For each of the graphs of data, does there appear to be a relationship? Describe the relationship by completing the appropriate sentence below.

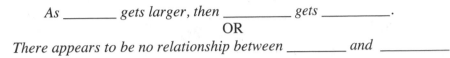

As _____ gets larger, then _____ gets _____.
OR
There appears to be no relationship between _____ and _____.

b.   DIRECTION OF ASSOCIATION

In a scatterplot, if there appears to be no relationship between the variables, then the points in the scatterplot have **no association**. But if one variable generally increases as the other variable increases, there is said to be a **positive association**. If one variable generally decreases as the other variable increases, there is said to be a **negative association**. See some examples below.

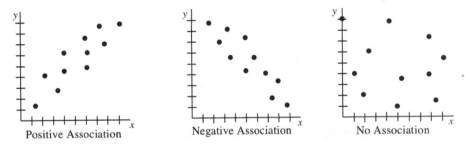

Positive Association   Negative Association   No Association

Review each of the graphs of the plant-experiment data and decide on the direction of the association. That is, decide if there is a positive association, a negative association, or no association.

Problem continues on next page. →

7-26.   *Problem continued from previous page.*

   c.   FORM OF ASSOCIATION

   When there is a positive or negative association, the shape of the pattern is called the **form** of the association. Associations can have a **linear form** or a **non-linear form**, and the form can be made up of **clusters** of data. See some examples below.

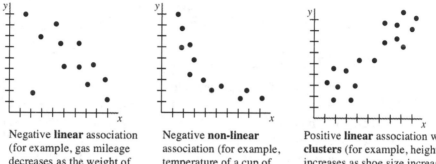

Negative **linear** association (for example, gas mileage decreases as the weight of cargo on a truck increases)

Negative **non-linear** association (for example, temperature of a cup of coffee decreases over time)

Positive **linear** association with **clusters** (for example, height increases as shoe size increases; one cluster is mostly girls and the other cluster is mostly boys)

   Review each of the graphs of the plant-experiment data that has an association, and decide on the form of the association. That is, decide if it is linear or non-linear, and whether it has clusters or no clusters.

   d.   OUTLIERS

   An **outlier** is a piece of data that does not seem to fit into the pattern. Do there appear to be any outliers in any of the example scatterplots above?

   e.   Now go back and look at your team predictions (hypotheses) for each question in problem 7-23. Were your predictions accurate? Explain your reasoning.

288

7-27. When there is an association, predictions can be made. One way to help make predictions is to draw a line (or curve) of best fit for the data.

    a. Find your graph of Team 1's data from problem 7-24. Work with your team to draw a *straight* line that models (represents) the trend of the data on this graph. The line does not need to intersect each of the points, and the line does not need to pass through the origin.

    b. Now use your line of best fit to predict the height of the plant when 12 milliliters of fertilizer are given to the plant over a 3-week period.

    c. What is the *y*-intercept? Interpret the *y*-intercept in this situation.

7-28. LEARNING LOG

In this Learning Log entry, describe how a graph can help you tell if there is an association between two sets of data. That is, what does it look like if there is an association? What does it look like if there is no association? What are the forms an association might have? What does an outlier look like? Title this entry "Associations" and label it with today's date.

MᴇᴛHODS AND Mᴇᴀɴɪɴɢѕ

Describing Association – Part 1

An association (relationship) between two numerical variables can be described by its form, direction, strength, and outliers.

If one variable increases as the other variable increases, there is said to be a **positive association**. If one variable increases as the other variable decreases, there is said to be a **negative association**. If there is no relationship between the variables, then the points in the scatterplot have **no association**. An example of each situation is illustrated below.

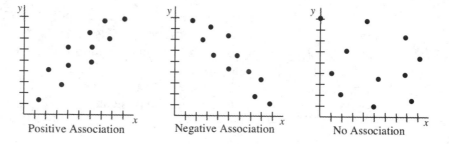

Positive Association   Negative Association   No Association

When there is a positive or negative association, the shape of the pattern is called the **form** of the association. Associations can have a **linear form** or a **non-linear-form**, and the form can be made up of **clusters** of data. See some examples below.

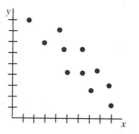 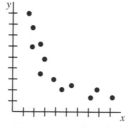 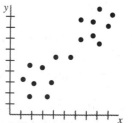

Negative **linear** association (for example, gas mileage decreases as the weight of cargo on a truck increases)

Negative **non-linear** association (for example, temperature of a cup of coffee decreases over time)

Positive **linear** association with **clusters** (for example, height increases as shoe size increases; one cluster is mostly girls and the other cluster is mostly boys)

7-29.   For each scatterplot below, determine if there is an association between the points. Label each graph as showing a positive association, negative association, or no association. If there is an association, write a sentence describing it.

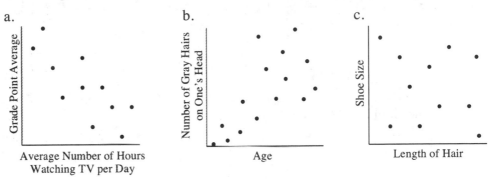

a.

Grade Point Average

Average Number of Hours
Watching TV per Day

b.

Number of Gray Hairs
on One's Head

Age

c.

Shoe Size

Length of Hair

7-30.   Make a graph of Team 2's data from problem 7-25.

   a.   Draw a *straight* line that models the trend of the data on this graph. Remember, the line does not need to intersect each of the points.

   b.   Use your line of best fit to predict the height of the plant when the seed is planted 14 cm deep.

   c.   What is the y-intercept? Interpret the y-intercept in this situation.

7-31.   During a given week, the museum had attendance as shown in the table at right.

   a.   Numerically summarize the center and spread of attendance by finding the median and interquartile range (IQR).

Day	Attendance
1	870
2	940
3	731
4	400
5	861
6	680
7	593

   b.   The museum management needs to tell the staff members their work schedules a week in advance. The museum wants to have approximately one staff member for every 150 visitors. How many staff members should be scheduled to work each week? Explain your reasoning.

   c.   Why is a scatterplot *not* an appropriate display of this data?

7-32.   Simplify each expression.

   a. $\frac{2}{3}(0.8)$ b. $\frac{4}{3} \cdot \frac{3}{7}$ c. $-\frac{5}{6} \cdot \frac{4}{7}$ d. $-\frac{4}{5} \cdot (-1\frac{1}{3})$

7-33.   Solve each equation below for x. Check your solution.

   a. $\frac{3x}{4} - 2(4+2x) = -\frac{1}{2}x + \frac{1}{4}$ b. $\frac{-5}{3}x + \frac{2}{5} - \frac{1}{3}x + 1 = 0$

7-34.   The figures at right are similar. Describe a
         sequence of transformations that will exhibit
         the similarity between them. Transform
         KITE to LOWR.

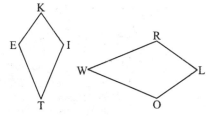

7.2.1 What is the equation of the line?

$y = mx + b$ Revisited

Previously, you developed ways to find the growth of a line using its rule, table, and graph. You also learned how the y-intercept is present in each of the representations. In this lesson, you will enhance your study of lines and will develop ways to find the equation of a line using different pieces of information about the line, such as two points that are on it. Today's lesson will help you review connections you made in previous chapters by challenging you to find equations for lines from multiple representations.

7-35.   THE LINE FACTORY

Congratulations! You have recently been hired to work at the city's premiere Line Factory. People from all over the country order lines from your factory because of their superior quality and excellent price.

Quality Control Lately, however, the Line Factory is having a serious problem: Too many customers have placed orders and then have received lines different from the ones they wanted. The factory has hired your team to correct this problem.

Your Task: Review the recent orders below and decide if there is anything wrong with each customer's order. If the order is correct, then pass it on to your production department with a rule, a table, and a graph (on graph paper). If the order is incorrect, explain to the customer how you know the order is incorrect and suggest corrections.

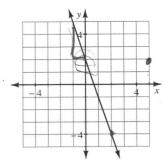

- **Customer A** wants a line with a y-intercept of $(0, -3)$ and that grows by 4. She ordered the line $y = -3x + 4$.

- **Customer B** wants the line graphed at right. He ordered the line $y = 3x + 2$.

- **Customer C** wants a line that passes through the points $(2, -4)$ and $(5, 2)$. She ordered the line $y = 2x - 8$.

Problem continues on next page. →

7-35.   *Problem continued from previous page.*

- **Customer D** wants the line that is represented by the table below.

IN (x)	−3	−2	−1	0	1	2	3
OUT (y)	−4	−1	2	4	7	10	13

- **Customer E** ordered the line $2x - y = 4$ and wants the line to grow by 2 and pass through the point $(5, 6)$.

- **Customer F** wants a line that starts at $(0, 1)$, grows first by 3, and then grows by 5.

7-36.   For the customer order that your team is assigned, prepare a team poster with your analysis from problem 7-35. Every team poster should include:

- The original customer order, complete with any given table, rule, graph, or statements.

- An explanation of any errors your team found in the order. If your team did not find any errors, the poster should justify this fact as well.

- Suggestions for how the customer can fix his or her order. You may want to suggest an equation that you suspect the customer wanted. If no mistake was made, then write a note to the company's production department with a rule, a table, and a graph for the order.

7-37.   Would you expect a scatterplot comparing "speed of a car" and "time it takes to drive 10 miles" to show a positive association, a negative association, or no association? Explain your thinking.

7-38.   Okie is a western lowland gorilla living at the Franklin Park Zoo near Boston, MA. He loves to finger paint! Many of his paintings have been sold because their colors are so interesting. One painting was sold for five times the amount of a second, and a third was sold for $1500. If the total sale was for $13,500, how much did the most expensive painting sell for?

Define a variable and then write and solve an equation to solve the problem. Remember to write your answer as a complete sentence.

Core Connections, Course 3

7-39.   Mt. Rose Middle School collected canned food to donate to a local charity. Each classroom kept track of how many cans it collected. The number of cans in each room were: $107, 55, 39, 79, 86, 62, 65, 70, 80,$ and 77. The principal displayed the data in the box plot below.

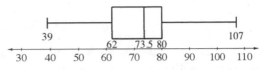

a.   What is the range of the data? Are there any outliers?

b.   The main office staff collected 55 cans, the counseling staff collected 74 cans, and the custodial staff collected 67 cans.

On graph paper, make a new box plot that includes this data. Clearly label the median and the upper and lower quartiles.

7-40.   The trapezoids at right are similar shapes.

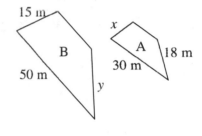

a.   What is the scale factor between shape B and shape A?

b.   Find the lengths of the missing sides.

7-41.   MORE OR LESS

Judy has $20 and is saving at a rate of $6 per week. Ida has $172 and is spending at a rate of $4 per week. After how many weeks will each have the same amount of money?

a.   Write an equation using x and y for Judy and Ida. What does x represent? What does y represent?

b.   Solve this problem using any method you choose.

7-42.   Simplify the following expressions.

a. $-\frac{3}{4}-\frac{2}{5}$

b. $\frac{7}{8}-\frac{2}{3}$

c. $\frac{1}{3}-\frac{5}{6}$

d. $1\frac{2}{3}+(-\frac{2}{5})$

e. $\frac{4}{7}-(-\frac{3}{8})$

f. $-4\frac{1}{2}+3\frac{1}{9}$

7.2.2 How does y change with respect to x?

Slope

Can you imagine swimming 1.5 km (just less than a mile), getting dressed as fast as you can, hopping on a bicycle to race 40 km (almost 25 miles), then getting off your bike to run 10 km (just over 6 miles)? Athletes who compete in Olympic distance triathlons do exactly that! In the 2008 Summer Olympic Games, Jan Frodeno of Germany won the gold medal by finishing the triathlon in 1 hour, 48 minutes and 53.28 seconds. Frodeno did not finish the swimming section in first place, though. In fact, he was not even one of the first ten people to finish that part of the race. While Frodeno may not have been the fastest swimmer, what mattered most was his overall rate.

As you compare rates today, you will learn a new way to describe the growth rate of a line called **slope**. As you investigate rates of change, use the following questions to facilitate mathematical discussions with your team:

> How can I use the graph to figure out which racer is faster?

> How can we find the unit rate for each racer?

> What if the line does not pass through $(0,0)$?

7-43.   BIKING THE TRIATHLON

The second part of the triathlon is a bicycle race. Since participants do not start the bicycle race until they complete the swimming portion, the bicyclists have varying starting times.

The graph at right shows information about four bicyclists during a 20-minute portion of a race.

a.   Based on the graph, list the bicyclists from slowest to fastest. How can you tell?

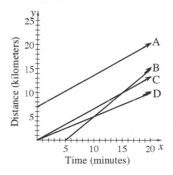

Problem continues on next page. →

Core Connections, Course 3

7-43.   *Problem continued from previous page.*

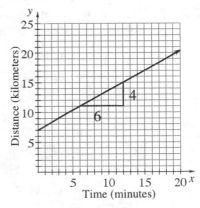

b.   Lydia wants to describe each bicyclist's rate in kilometers per minute for an article in the school paper. To do this, she sketched triangles like the one for line A on the graph at right.

Where do the 4 and 6 come from on Racer A's triangle? What do they represent?

c.   These numbers can be written as a rate in kilometers per hour to describe the distance the bicyclist rides as time passes. The fraction $\frac{4}{6}$ represents how the graph of the line goes up 4 units for every 6 units that it moves to the right. The number $\frac{4}{6}$ is called the **slope** of the line.

On the Lesson 7.2.2 Resource Page, find the slope of each of the other three lines.

d.   Did the slopes in part (c) confirm your ranking from slowest to fastest in part (a)? If not, review your slopes and your comparison of rates based on the graph to find any mistakes.

7-44.   Look at your "Biking The Triathlon" Resource Page from problem 7-43. Slope can also be thought of as a unit rate.

a.   Remember that a unit rate compares the change in one quantity to a one-unit change in another quantity. Find the unit rate for each of the triathlon bicyclists. Make sure you label the units.

b.   Write each of the bicyclists' rates as a decimal rounded to the nearest one-hundredth of a kilometer per minute. When you order the bicyclists' rates, do you get the same results as in problem 7-43?

7-45.   While comparing the rates from problem 7-43, a study team is struggling to decide how to tell which athlete is moving faster.

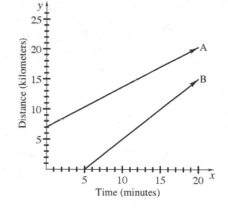

- Leo thinks that because athlete A's line is highest on the graph, he is traveling faster.

- Kara disagrees. *"He starts first, but racer B is moving faster."*

Which person do you agree with? Look at the graph of bicyclists A and B at right and discuss this with your team. Be prepared to explain your reasoning to the class.

7-46.   In Chapter 4 (problems 4-8 through 4-10), you looked at how tile patterns grow. You examined how the growth rate could be seen in the table, graph, and rule for the pattern. One of the patterns that you looked at and its graph are shown below.

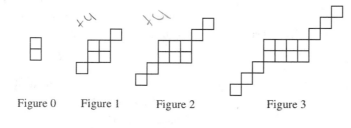

Figure 0   Figure 1   Figure 2   Figure 3

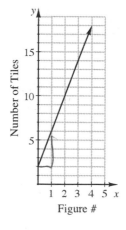

a. What is the growth rate for this pattern? How can you tell?

b. What is the slope of the line on the graph? How does this value compare to the growth rate for the pattern?

7-47. Mr. Regnier's class has been struck with hiccups! Three of the students track their number of hiccups over time. Assume each student hiccups at a constant rate.

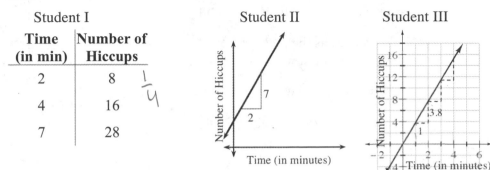

Student I

Time (in min)	Number of Hiccups
2	8
4	16
7	28

$\frac{1}{4}$

Student II

Student III

a. Which student has the most hiccups per minute? Justify your answer.

b. Find the slope that describes the rate of hiccups for each student. What does the slope tell you about each student?

c. If you graphed a line for the student who hiccups 4 times per minute, would the line be steeper, less steep, or the same steepness as the line in the graph for Student II? Explain your reasoning.

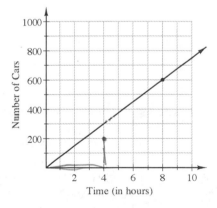

7-48. **Additional Challenge:** CHANGING LINES

Lupe is a manager of an assembly line at a manufacturing company that makes cars. The speed at which the cars are usually built is represented by the graph at right.

Lupe has decided to increase the number of cars built each day and has written directions for her employees. How would each of her directions below change the number of cars built each day? Explain how you know.

a. Build 200 cars every 4 hours.

b. Build 75 cars every hour.

c. Build 500 cars every 5 hours.

d. Decrease the time it takes to make each car.

7-49.   Compare the graphs of lines A, B, and C at right.

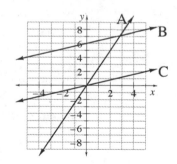

a.   Which line has the greatest slope?
       Justify your answer.

b.   What is the *y*-value of line A when $x = 2$?

c.   Compare the slopes of lines B and C.

7-50.   Lydia drew a graph of four athletes in the final part of the triathlon, the 10 km
         run. She found the slope of each runner's line. Her results are listed below.

   Runner A: slope $= \frac{2}{6}$ Runner B: slope $= \frac{3}{7}$

   Runner C: slope $= \frac{5}{12}$ Runner D: slope $= \frac{4}{10}$

   List the runners from slowest to fastest.

7-51.   If a car is parked on the side of the road and not moving, what is its speed?
         What would it look like on a graph of time and distance?

7-52.   The class advisor was helping students plan an end-of-
         year trip. The students were surveyed about their choices.
         The results are shown in the circle graph at right.

a.   What percent of the students chose the water park?

b.   Which two results are very close?

c.   Write a recommendation to the class advisor regarding what the next step
      would be.

7-53.   Solve this problem by defining a variable, writing an equation, and solving it. Write your solution in a sentence.

The number of students attending the fall play was 150 fewer than three times the number of adults. Together, students and adults purchased 1778 tickets. How many students attended the fall play?

7-54.   The figures below are similar. Use the information given about the lengths of the sides to solve for *x* and *y*.

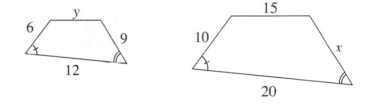

7.2.3   How can I find the slope ratio?

Slope in Different Representations

In Lesson 7.2.2, you learned about how to use a number to describe the steepness of a line. Today, you will work with different representations of lines and look for how the slope can be found in each representation. As you work with your study team today, keep the following questions in mind.

What is being compared to find the slope ratio?

What would it look like in another representation?

7-55.   A planting manual printed the graphs below so that gardeners could predict the height of trees after planting. Jill wants to figure out the rate that each tree will grow.

She remembers that slope is a ratio of the vertical change to the horizontal change between any two points on a line. The units for the vertical change are the same as the *y*-axis, and the units for the horizontal change are the same as the *x*-axis. Finding the slope for each graph will allow her to compare the change in height to the change in time.

a.   On a Lesson 7.2.3 Resource Page, draw and label a slope triangle on the line in graph (*i*). Then write the slope ratio. How fast does the tree in graph (*i*) grow?

b.   Can you find the slope on graph (*ii*) just by looking at the line? Why or why not? When it is difficult to read the slope on a graph, look for points where the line appears to pass through **lattice points** (where the grid lines intersect). Then use those points to create a slope triangle and find the slope for graph (*ii*).

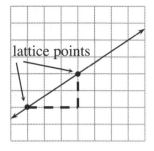

c.   On the resource page, use lattice points to draw a slope triangle for each of the lines in graphs (*iii*) and (*iv*). Then label each slope triangle with its dimensions and calculate the slope ratio.

Slope Triangle

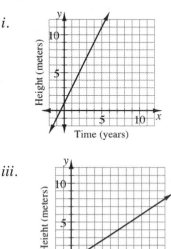

i.

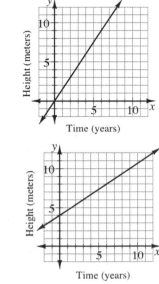

ii.

iii.

iv.

7-56.   Three different students looked at the line graphed at right, and each drew a different slope triangle. Their slope triangles are labeled A, B, and C in the graph at right.

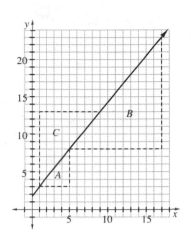

a.   Find the length of the horizontal and vertical sides of each slope triangle A, B and C on the Lesson 7.2.3 Resource Page. What is the relationship between triangles A, B, and C? Explain your answer. Using what you learned in Chapter 6 about the ratios of side lengths of similar figures may be helpful.

b.   Find each slope using the slope triangles.

c.   The numbers in the slope ratios found by the students are all different. Does this mean that the slope of the line changes depending on which points you pick? Discuss this with your team and be ready to share your reasoning with the rest of the class.

d.   Another student said her slope triangle goes up 20 units for every 16 units to the right. Where could her slope triangle be? Draw a possible slope triangle for this student.

e.   Simplify each of the four slope ratios and compare them. Describe what you find.

7-57.   IS SEEING BELIEVING?

Did you know that a bank will pay you money
(called **interest**) when you place your money in a
savings account? The amount you receive is a
portion of the amount you deposit. The interest rate
often varies with each bank.

Thomas and Ryan have each invested the same amount of money in different
bank accounts that earn **simple interest**. Simple interest means the same
amount of interest is added for each time period. In this case, the interest is
added each week. Thomas and Ryan decided to compare their rate of earnings
by graphing how much interest each of them has earned over time. Their
graphs are shown below.

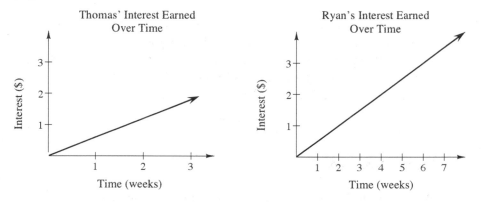

a.   When you look at the graphs, which investment seems to be growing
     fastest? Explain how you decided.

b.   The tables for Thomas'
     and Ryan's accounts are
     shown at right. Which
     table reflects Thomas'
     interest? Which one
     reflects Ryan's interest?
     How do you know?

Time (in weeks)	Interest Earned ($)	Time (in weeks)	Interest Earned ($)
1	0.60	2	1.00
4	2.40	3	1.50
7	4.20	6	3.00
10	6.00	12	6.00

c.   Use the tables to find the rate of *interest earned (in dollars)* to *time (in
     weeks)* for each of them. Whose money is growing faster?

d.   Did your answers from parts (a) and (c) agree? If not, compare the tables
     and graphs with your team to find out why the line that is less steep actually
     represents the bank account that grows faster. Be ready to share your ideas
     about why the graphs look the way they do.

7-58. The students in a study team are now arguing about who has graphed the steepest line. Assume that they set up their axes with the same scale. Here is some information about their lines:

Lucy: slope = $\frac{7}{5}$ Bree: slope = $\frac{5}{7}$

Cliff: slope = $\frac{14}{10}$ Geetha: slope = $\frac{12}{10}$

Can you use the slopes of their lines to visualize how each of the lines would look on a graph? Discuss their lines with your team, and then settle their argument without graphing. Explain completely who has the steepest line and who has the least steep line.

7-59. Which lines on the graph at right and on your resource page appear to have the same slope? Which line or lines are steepest? First, make a prediction. Then check your prediction by finding the slope of each line in the graph on the Lesson 7.2.3 Resource Page.

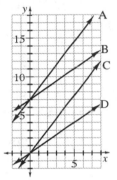

7-60. **LEARNING LOG**

What is slope? How is it calculated? In your Learning Log, sketch a graph of a line and explain how to find its slope. How would the slope be different if the line was steeper? Explain as completely as you can. Title this entry "Slope and Steepness" and include today's date.

7-61. Graph the points in the table at right and draw a line. Then, find three different ratios to describe the slope of this line.

x	y
0	1
2	6
5	13.5
–2	–4
–4	–9

7-62.   Find the slope of each line below.

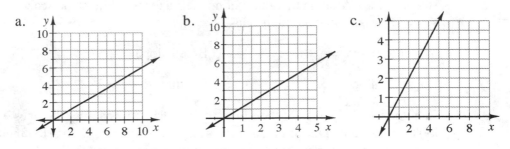

a.

b.

c.

7-63.   For each equation below, solve for x and check your answer.

a. $10(0.02x - 0.01) = 1$

b. $\frac{1}{3}x - 6 = 8$

c. $\frac{x}{3} + 1 = \frac{x}{4} - 1$

d. $0.9x - 2.1 + 0.9 = 0.2(5 - x)$

7-64.   Write and solve an equation for the situation below. Define any variables and write your solution as a sentence.

Jennifer has a total of four-and-a-half hours to spend on the beach swimming and playing volleyball. The time she spends playing volleyball will be twice the amount of time she spends swimming. How long will she do each activity?

7-65.   When Yoshi graphed the lines $y = 2x + 3$ and $y = 2x - 2$, she got the graph shown at right.

a.   One of the lines at right matches the equation $y = 2x + 3$, and the other matches $y = 2x - 2$. Which line matches which equation?

b.   Yoshi wants to add the line $y = 2x + 1$ to her graph. Predict where it would lie and sketch a graph to show its position. Justify your prediction.

c.   Where would the line $y = -2x + 1$ lie? Again, justify your prediction and add the graph of this line to your graph.

7-66.   Solve each of the following equations. Be sure to show your work and check your answers.

a. $2(3x - 4) = 22$

b. $6(2x - 5) = -(x + 4)$

c. $2 - (y + 2) = 3y$

d. $3 + 4(x + 1) = 159$

7.2.4   What else can slope tell you?

More About Slope

In recent lessons, you have learned how to find the slope of a line. You have also learned how slope describes the rate of change and the steepness of a line on a graph. In this lesson, you will learn about other information that the slope of a line can tell you.

7-67.   Which is steeper: a line with a slope of $\frac{2}{5}$ or a line with a slope of $\frac{5}{2}$? How do you know? Explain.

7-68.   Compare the two lines in the graph at right.

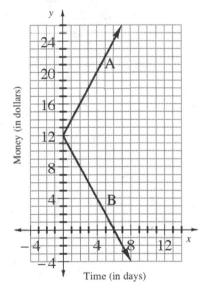

a. How are the two lines the same? How are they different?

b. Each line on this graph describes how much money a person has in his or her wallet over time (in days). Explain what is happening to the amount of money each person has. Be specific.

c. To describe how person A's amount of money is changing, the unit rate (slope) represents the amount that is added each day. Since the value of money is increasing, the slope is positive. But what should you do when the value is decreasing? How should the decrease be reflected in the rate (slope)? Discuss this with your team.

d. Remember that the slope ratio compares how the change on the *y*-axis compares to the change on the *x*-axis. Lines that go up from left to right show positive rates of change, or **positive slopes**, while lines that go down from left to right show negative rates of change, or **negative slopes**.

Find the slope of each line in the graph.

7-69.   WHAT IF IT DOES NOT GROW?

The graph at right shows three different
lines.

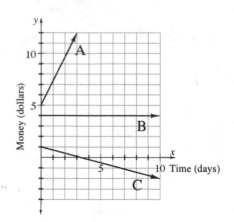

a.   Describe each line in words. Is it
     increasing or decreasing? Quickly or
     slowly?

b.   Line B is different from the other
     two lines. As the x-value increases,
     what happens to y?

c.   Slope is a comparison of $\frac{\text{change in } y}{\text{change in } x}$. Pick two points on line B. How can
     you use a number to represent the change in y between these two points?
     Use this number or the change in y to write a slope ratio for line B.

d.   Recall that the units for the "change in y" are the same as the y-axis, and
     that the units for the "change in x" are the same as for the x-axis. What are
     the rates of growth for lines A and C? Be sure to include units.

e.   Express the rates in part (d) as unit rates.

7-70.   PERSONAL TRAINER

To prepare for biking long distances, Antoine has
been trying to keep a steady pace as he bikes.
However, since his hometown has many hills, he
ends up biking faster and slower during different
parts of his ride.

To track the distance and time when he trains
for the triathlon, Antoine purchased a special watch
that tells him how far he has traveled at specific
time intervals. With the push of a button, he can set
it to record data. Then, at the end of his
workout, the watch gives him a list of the data.

Antoine's Data

Time (minutes)	Distance (miles)
3	0.5
5	1
8	2
12	3
16	4.5
19	6

a.   On his first bike ride around town, he
recorded several times and distances.
These measurements are shown in the table
at right. According to the table, does he
appear to be traveling at a constant rate?
Explain your reasoning.

b.   Draw and label a graph that extends to
40 minutes on the *x*-axis and to at least
15 miles on the *y*-axis. Plot Antoine's time
and distance data on the graph. What type of graph is this?

c.   Draw a trend line that best represents Antoine's data. Then extend it to
predict about how long it will take him to bike 10 miles (his normal long
distance workout).

d.   What is Antoine's general rate during his bike ride? Find the slope (rate of
change) of the trend line you drew in part (c) to determine his general rate.

METHODS AND MEANINGS

MATH NOTES

Slope of a Line

The **slope** of a line is the ratio of the change in y to the change in x between any two points on the line. To find slope, you compute the *ratio* that indicates how y-values are changing with respect to x-values. Essentially, slope is the unit rate of change, because it measures how much y increases or decreases as x changes by one unit. If the slope is positive (+), the y-values are increasing. If it is negative (–), the y-values are decreasing. The graph of a line goes up for positive slopes and down for negatives slopes as the line moves across the graph from left to right.

$$\text{slope} = \frac{\text{vertical change}}{\text{horizontal change}} = \frac{\text{change in } y\text{-values}}{\text{change in } x\text{-values}}$$

Some textbooks write this ratio as $\frac{\text{rise}}{\text{run}}$.

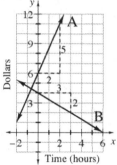

In the graph at right, the slope of line A is $\frac{5 \text{ dollars}}{2 \text{ hours}}$ because for every 2 hours the line increases horizontally, the line increases 5 dollars vertically. Since y increases by $\frac{5}{2}$ dollars when x increases by 1 hour, the unit rate is $\frac{\frac{5}{2}\text{ dollars}}{1 \text{ hour}}$ or 2.5 dollars per hour.

To find the slope of line B, notice that when x increases by 3 hours, y *decreases* by 2 dollars, so the vertical change is –2 dollars and the slope is written as $-\frac{2 \text{ dollars}}{3 \text{ hours}}$ or $-\frac{2}{3}$ dollars per hour.

It is important to notice that horizontal lines do not increase or decrease vertically, so they are described with a slope of 0. The slope of a vertical line is undefined. This is because the horizontal change is 0, resulting in a slope of $\frac{y}{0}$, which is undefined.

slope = 0   slope is undefined

310

Core Connections, Course 3

7-71.   For each pair of slope ratios, decide if they are equivalent (=), or if one slope is greater. If the slopes are not equal, use the greater than (>) or less than (<) symbol to show which is greater.

a. $\frac{6}{7}$, $\frac{5}{6}$ b. $\frac{3}{2}$, $\frac{15}{10}$ c. $\frac{12}{10}$, $\frac{7}{5}$

7-72.   Describe the associations in the two graphs below. Remember to describe the form, direction, and outliers.

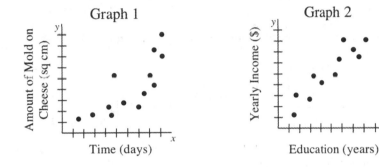

Graph 1

Graph 2

7-73.   Ella and her study team are arguing about the slope of the line in the graph at right. They have come up with four different answers: $\frac{3}{4}$, $-\frac{4}{3}$, $-\frac{3}{4}$, and $\frac{4}{3}$. Which slope is correct? Justify your answer.

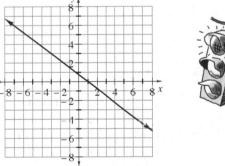

7-74.   Solve each of the following equations.

a. $\frac{1}{6}x + \frac{2}{3} = \frac{1}{4}x - \frac{1}{3}$ b. $0.15(w+2) = 0.3 + 0.2w$

c. $\frac{8x}{6} = \frac{72}{54}$ d. $3(2x-7) = 5x + 17 + x$

7-75.   Salami and More Deli sells a 6-foot sandwich for parties. It weighs 8 pounds. Assume the weight per foot is constant.

    a.   How much does a sandwich 0 feet long weigh?

    b.   Draw a graph showing the weight of the sandwich (vertical axis) compared to the length of the sandwich (horizontal axis). Label the axes with appropriate units.

    c.   Use your graph to estimate the weight of a 1-foot sandwich.

    d.   Write a proportion to find the length of a 12-pound sandwich.

7-76.   Find the area of the entire rectangle in each diagram below. Show all work.

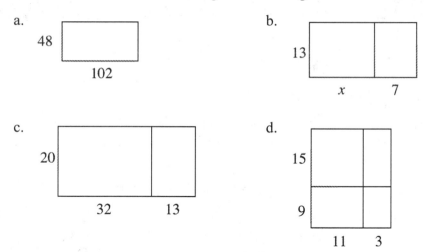

a.
48
102

b.
13
x 7

c.
20
32   13

d.
15
9
11   3

7.2.5 Can I connect rates to slopes?

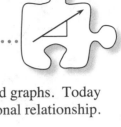

Proportional Equations

In Chapter 1, you identified proportional relationships in both tables and graphs. Today you will look at the connection between slope and graphs of a proportional relationship.

7-77.　　POLITICAL POLL

Mr. Mears was running for mayor of Atlanta. His campaign managers were eager to determine how many citizens of Atlanta would vote for him in the upcoming election. They decided to pay a respected, impartial statistical company to survey potential voters (a process called "polling") to find out how many people would probably vote for Mr. Mears.

One afternoon, pollsters called 100 random potential voters in Atlanta to ask them how they would vote in the election. During that survey, 68 people indicated that they would vote for Mr. Mears.

a.　If the pollsters had instead called 50 randomly selected potential voters, predict how many of them would have said that they would vote for Mr. Mears.

b.　Do you suppose that this relationship is proportional? Why or why not?

c.　Carina's neighborhood has 327 potential voters. If voting in her neighborhood is similar to that of the poll, how many neighbors will probably vote for Mr. Mears? Complete the table at right.

Number of Potential Voters	Number of Votes Expected for Mr. Mears
50	34
100	68
327	x

d.　Make a graph of the data Carina has collected, and draw a line through the points. Should your line go through the origin? How do you know?

e.　What is the equation of the line in $y = mx + b$ form?

$$\frac{25 - 17}{5} - 3.4$$

f.　Use the equation to help Carina figure out how many people will probably vote for Mr. Mears if 350,125 people vote in the election. What do x and y represent in your equation?

g.　What information would the unit rate give Carina? What is the unit rate? How does the unit rate compare to the slope?

7-78.   In two minutes, Stacie can write her name 17 times.

    a.   Use a proportion (write equivalent ratios) to find how long it will take Stacie to write her name 85 times.

    b.   Make a graph of this situation. Which piece of information is on the dependent axis?

    c.   Another name for the slope in a proportional relationship is the **constant of proportionality**. Find the constant of proportionality and write an equation in $y = mx + b$ form for Stacie's situation. What do x and y represent in this situation?

    d.   Use the equation to find how many minutes it will take Stacie to write her name 85 times.

    e.   What is the advantage of the equation in part (d) compared to the proportion (equivalent ratios) in part (a)? What is the advantage of the proportion?

    f.   What is the unit rate at which Stacie writes her name?

7-79.   Beth and her father have a large model railroad in their basement. Beth figured out that the equation $y = \frac{260}{3}x$ relates the length of an item on her model railroad to the length of the real thing, where x is the size on the model and y is the real object's size. Beth's uncle has a different model railroad in his home. It has a different scale. He put together the following table for Beth.

	Height on Model Railroad (inches)	Height of Real Object (inches)
Human	0.94	60
Tree	4.70	300
Apartment Building	7.52	480

    a.   In decimal notation, what is the unit rate for Beth's railroad? For her uncle's railroad? Make sure you show units on your unit rate.

    b.   On which model would a horse be taller? Use the unit rates to justify your answer without making any calculations.

7-80. Eight of 29 students in your class want to attend the Winter Ball.

   a. Find the constant of proportionality, and then write an equation in $y = mx + b$ form. What do x and y represent?

   b. If your class represents the entire school, how many of the 1490 students will probably attend the dance? Solve your equation from part (b).

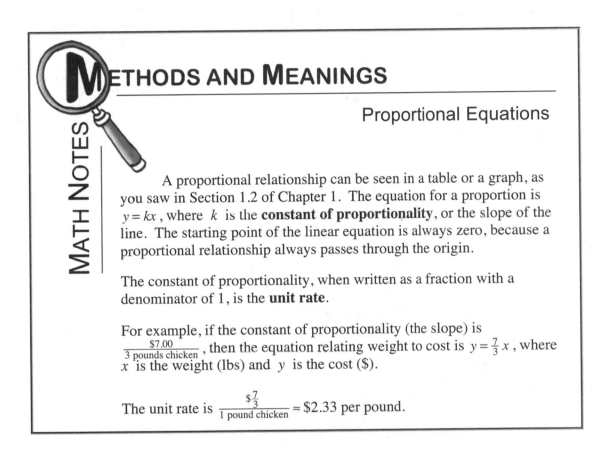

METHODS AND MEANINGS

Proportional Equations

MATH NOTES

   A proportional relationship can be seen in a table or a graph, as you saw in Section 1.2 of Chapter 1. The equation for a proportion is $y = kx$, where k is the **constant of proportionality**, or the slope of the line. The starting point of the linear equation is always zero, because a proportional relationship always passes through the origin.

   The constant of proportionality, when written as a fraction with a denominator of 1, is the **unit rate**.

   For example, if the constant of proportionality (the slope) is $\frac{\$7.00}{3 \text{ pounds chicken}}$, then the equation relating weight to cost is $y = \frac{7}{3}x$, where x is the weight (lbs) and y is the cost ($).

   The unit rate is $\frac{\$\frac{7}{3}}{1 \text{ pound chicken}} \approx \$2.33$ per pound.

Review & Preview

7-81. Aja and Emilie were riding their skateboards. They knew that they could ride 3 miles in 20 minutes.

   a. How far can the girls ride in 45 minutes?

   b. If y represents the distance in miles and x represents the time in minutes, write an equation to represent the distance traveled for any time.

7-82. Joe is downloading songs from the Internet. He can download them at a rate of 8 songs every 10 minutes. Jasmine, who is also downloading songs, can download at a rate of 12 songs every 15 minutes. Who is downloading songs faster?

7-83. Reflect quadrilateral ABCD across the line $y = -2$. Write the new coordinate points.

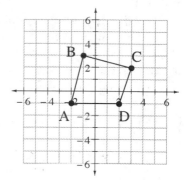

7-84. Copy and complete each of the Diamond Problems below. The pattern used in the Diamond Problems is shown at right.

a.

2.4   1.5

b.

4.2

0.6

c.

3.1

11.1

d.

−49

0

7-85. On graph paper, graph the line that goes through the points $(-6, 3)$ and $(-3, -1)$.

a. What is the slope of the line?

b. What is the y-intercept?

c. Find the equation of the line.

7-86. Mr. Crow, the head groundskeeper at High Tech Middle School, mows the lawn along the side of the gym. The lawn is rectangular, and the length is 5 feet more than twice the width. The perimeter of the lawn is 250 feet.

a. Define a variable and write an equation for this problem.

b. Solve the equation that you wrote in part (a) and find the dimensions of the lawn.

c. Use the dimensions you calculated in part (a) to find the area of the lawn.

7.3.1 How can I use an equation?

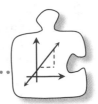

Using Equations to Make Predictions

Previously, you have learned to find and extend patterns in data and to make predictions using rules, equations, and graphs. Today you will apply these mathematical tools to a real situation in which your data does not make a perfect pattern.

7-87. AURÉLIE'S BIKE RIDE

To prepare for a 30-mile ride for charity, Aurélie has been biking every weekend. To predict how long the charity event will take her to complete, Aurélie has been keeping track of her time and distances. She tries to ride at a constant pace, but of course that is not easy to do.

a. Would a box plot, scatterplot, or histogram be most useful in helping Aurélie make a prediction?

b. Considering that Aurélie is trying to predict how long it will take to complete the ride, which is the independent variable and which is the dependent variable? Make a scatterplot.

c. Use a line of best fit to predict how long it will take Aurélie to complete the charity ride. Remember that the line does not need to intersect each of the points and that the line does not need to pass through the origin to model the data.

Aurélie's Data

Weekend	Time (minutes)	Distance (miles)
Feb 6	68	7
Feb 13	88	17
Feb 20	35	3.5
Feb 27	150	25
Mar 6	104	14
Mar 13	80	11

7-88.   USING AN EQUATION TO MAKE PREDICTIONS

Sometimes it is more convenient and more accurate to use an equation to make a prediction rather than making a prediction by reading a graph.

a.   Choose two points that lie on your line of best fit. These points can be given data points or lattice points on the coordinate grid. Use these two points to calculate the slope of your line of best fit. What does the slope mean in terms of Aurélie's bike riding?

b.   What is the y-intercept of your line of best fit? What does the y-intercept mean in terms of Aurélie's training?

c.   Write the equation of the line of best fit in $y = mx + b$ form. Identify your variables.

d.   Use your equation to predict how long the charity ride would take Aurélie to complete. How did your prediction compare to the prediction you made from the graph in part (c) of problem 7-87?

7-89.   Westland Workers Union's Health and Wellness Department started a voluntary lunchtime running club. Members kept track of how much they ran each week for exercise and how much their resting heart rate dropped over several weeks. Their data is in the table at right. Note that a negative heart rate change is actually a *gain* in heart rate.

Average Distance Run per Week (miles)	Resting Heart Rate Change (beats per minute)
5	6
3	4
1	-2
7	-1
4	2
8	8
5	4.5
6	8

a.   Make a scatterplot of the data.

b.   Describe the association.

c.   Draw a line of best fit for the data. Find the equation of the line of best fit.

d.   Use the equation to predict the heart rate change for an employee who ran 10 miles a week.

e.   Interpret the slope and y-intercept in this situation.

7-90.   LEARNING LOG

In your Learning Log, describe how to find the equation of
a line in $y = mx + b$ form from a graph of points. Include an
example of how to calculate the slope from two points.
Title this entry "Line From Data Points" and label it with
today's date.

7-91.   Anthony has added a line of best fit to the
scatterplot at right. Do you agree with where he
put the line? Explain your reasoning.

7-92.   Graph $y = -\frac{1}{2}x + 6$. Find its x- and y-intercepts.

7-93.   Graph a line that goes through the points $(0, 3)$ and $(2, -1)$. What is the slope of
the line?

7-94.   How many yearbooks should your school order? Your student government
surveyed three homeroom classes, and 55 of 90 students said that they would
definitely buy a yearbook. If your school has 2000 students, approximately
how many books should be ordered? Show and organize your work.

7-95.   Find the perimeter and area of each triangle below.

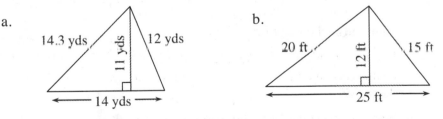

a.
14.3 yds   11 yds   12 yds
14 yds

b.
20 ft   12 ft   15 ft
25 ft

7-96.   Graph the lines $y = -4x - 3$ and $y = -4x + 1$ on graph paper.

a.   Where do they intersect?

b.   Solve this system using the Equal Values Method.

c.   Explain how your graph and algebraic solution relate to each other.

7.3.2 How can I describe the association?

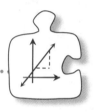

Describing Association Fully

You have already seen that form, direction, and outliers can be used to describe an association. Today you will complete the description of an association by considering strength.

7-97.   Do you remember the "Newton's Revenge" roller-coaster problem from Chapter 1? You will now return to the problem, using your knowledge of $y = mx + b$ to solve it. The problem (problem 1-24) is summarized below.

Newton's Revenge, the new roller coaster, has a tunnel that thrills riders with its very low ceiling. The closest the ceiling of the tunnel ever comes to the seat of the roller-coaster car is 200 cm. Although no accidents have been reported yet, it is said that very tall riders have stopped riding the roller coaster.

a.   To help determine whether the tunnel is safe for any rider, no matter how tall, you collected data in problem 1-24. The height and reach were both measured in centimeters. Use the data from the class at the right. Which is the dependent variable? As you plot the data, consider whether the plot is useful for making predictions. If not, can you change the plot to make it more useful?

Height (cm)	Reach (cm)
166.4	127
169	133
172.8	133
179	139
170	139
183	137
162.5	121
165	126
157.5	128
165	123
169	132
156	119

b.   Work with your team to draw a straight line that models the data on this graph. Use two points from the line that you drew to calculate the slope. Then find the equation of this line. Identify the variables.

7-98.   Once you have an equation that can best represent the data in problem 7-97, you will be able to use the equation to verify that the roller coaster is safe. The amusement park wants Newton's Revenge to be safe for tall riders. For example, remember that one of the tallest NBA players in history was Yao Ming, who is 7 feet 6 inches (about 228.6 cm) tall. Is the roller coaster safe for him? Explain.

7-99.   The slope and y-intercept can sometimes give you more information about the situation you are studying, but sometimes their interpretation makes no sense.

   a.   What is the slope of the line of best fit in Newton's Revenge? Interpret the slope in this problem situation. Does your interpretation make sense?

   b.   Interpret the y-intercept in this situation. Does your interpretation make sense?

   c.   Make a conjecture about why your interpretation for the y-intercept does not make sense in a real-world situation, but can still be part of the equation to model this situation.

7-100.   STRENGTH OF ASSOCIATION

   Although considering the direction of an association (positive or negative) is important in describing it, it is just as important to consider the **strength of the association**. Strength is a description of how much scatter there is in the data away from the line of best fit. Some examples are below.

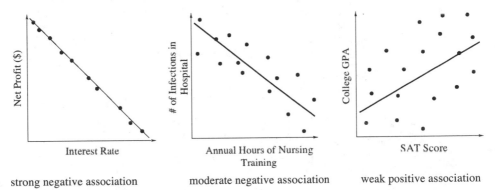

strong negative association   moderate negative association   weak positive association

   a.   Fully describe the association in "Newton's Revenge" (problem 7-97), considering the form, direction, strength, and outliers. See the Math Notes box in Lesson 7.1.3 to review some of these terms.

   b.   Look back at Aurélie's scatterplot from the previous lesson (problem 7-87). Fully describe the association between the distance she bikes and the time it takes her.

7-101.   LEARNING LOG

   Make an entry in your Learning Log. Title it "Describing Association" and label it with today's date. What are the four things you need to consider when describing an association? Give examples of each item. What information does an equation give you? When might an equation be more useful than a graph? What additional information does the slope tell you about the association?

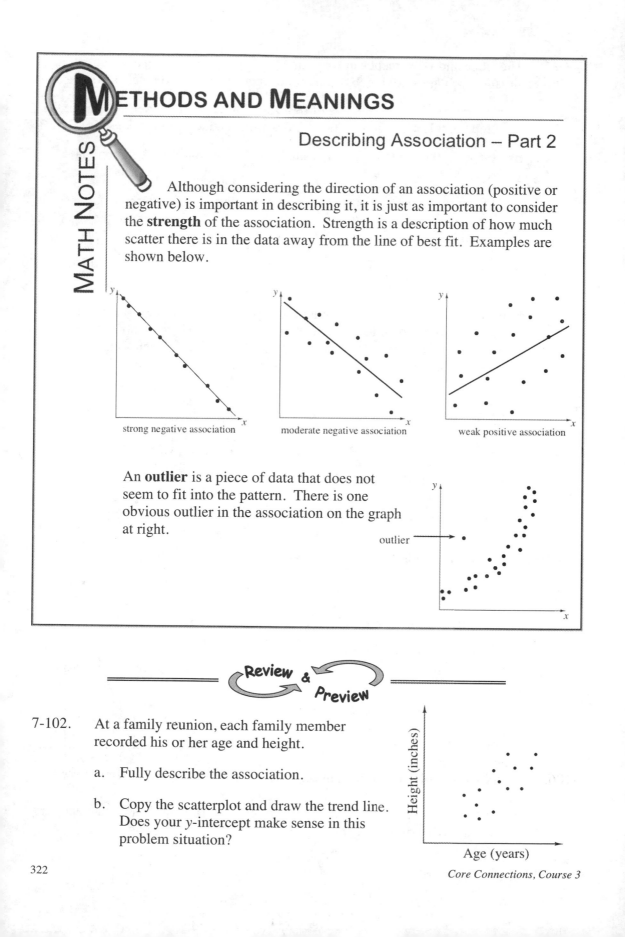

METHODS AND MEANINGS

MATH NOTES

Describing Association – Part 2

Although considering the direction of an association (positive or negative) is important in describing it, it is just as important to consider the **strength** of the association. Strength is a description of how much scatter there is in the data away from the line of best fit. Examples are shown below.

strong negative association

moderate negative association

weak positive association

An **outlier** is a piece of data that does not seem to fit into the pattern. There is one obvious outlier in the association on the graph at right.

outlier ⟶

Review & Preview

7-102. At a family reunion, each family member recorded his or her age and height.

a. Fully describe the association.

b. Copy the scatterplot and draw the trend line. Does your y-intercept make sense in this problem situation?

Height (inches)

Age (years)

7-103.   Marissa's older sister was discussing purchasing a car with her summer job earnings. Marissa collected data from her friends at her job.

Age of Car (years)	Avg. Miles per Gallon
9	34
2	30
5	30
1	35
4	34
10	28
9	27
3	40
8	29

a.   Marissa would like to know the typical age of her friends' cars. What kind of graphical display should she use?

b.   Marissa wants to convince her dad that newer cars are more fuel-efficient. What kind of graph(s) should Marissa make to convince her dad?

c.   Make a scatterplot of the data.

d.   Fully describe the association.

e.   Draw a line of best fit on the data. Find the equation of thc line of best fit.

f.   Use the equation to predict what the correct mileage for a 7-year-old car should be.

g.   Interpret the slope and y-intercept in this situation.

7-104.   When Malcolm hops 10 times down the hallway, he travels 12 feet. How many times would he need to hop to travel to his class, 90 feet away?

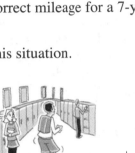

7-105.   Jeff and Liz are each saving money for college. Their savings are shown in the graph at right.

a.   Based on the graph, who is saving money fastest? Justify your answer.

b.   What is the slope of each line? What does the slope tell you about this situation?

7-106.   Simplify and solve the following equations.

a. $\frac{1}{4}x + \frac{1}{10} = -\frac{3}{20}x - \frac{7}{10}$

b. $3x + 4.5 = 4.5x - 18$

c. $\frac{1}{12}x - \frac{1}{12} = \frac{1}{8}x + \frac{1}{6} - \frac{1}{6}x$

d. $6.25x + 7.5 - 2.5x = 3.75x - 8.75$

7.3.3 What if the data is not numerical?

Association Between Categorical Variables

In previous lessons, you described the association between two numerical variables, such as the amount of fertilizer used and the height of the plant. Some variables, however – such as gender, eye color, names of countries, or weather conditions – are not numerical. Since the data are in categories, non-numerical variables are called **categorical variables**. Another type of categorical variable occurs when numerical variables are lumped into categories, such as in age groups. Today you will look for relationships in variables that are not numerical.

7-107.   The experiments students did with plants and different growing conditions in Lesson 7.1.3 caught the attention of a local farmer. He was interested in whether the type of soil made a difference in the height of his corn crop. He planted 2500 stalks of corn and collected the following data. This type of table is called a **frequency table** because it shows counts, or frequencies, in each of the cells of the table.

	Height of Corn (ft)				
	0-3 ft	**3-4 ft**	**4-6 ft**	**7-8 ft**	**Total**
Sandy Soil	150	200	575	750	1675
Clay Soil	225	150	200	250	825
Total	375	350	775	1000	2500

a.   Make a conjecture about the effect of soil type on the height of the corn.

b.   The table of data on corn height used counts because it counted the number of stalks of corn. When analyzing categorical data, percents are much easier to analyze. But first, you need to determine the independent variable so that you can determine, "Percent of what?" What is the independent variable in this situation?

c.   Create a second table that contains the data above but as percentages instead of counts. The percentage should be the count for each height category out of the total number for that soil type. For example, the height of the bar for 0-3 ft will be 9.0%, because $\frac{150}{1675}$ is 0.090. The third row of the table is not needed in this case.

7-108.   The farmer is interested in the height of his corn for each of the two soil types. A straightforward way to compare the effect of the independent variable is to make a different bar graph for each independent variable.

   a.   Make a bar graph for the sandy soil. The horizontal axis should be the height categories. The vertical axis will represent the percent of the corn in sandy soil that grew to that height.

   b.   Make a similar bar graph for the other independent variable.

   c.   Is the height of corn associated with the soil type? That is, does the soil type have an impact on height? Report your conclusions to the farmer.

   d.   Why did you make a bar graph instead of a histogram for the height of the corn?

7-109.   The nutrition staff at CPM Diabetic Institute is interested in the impact of three new energy bars on blood sugar levels. The staff conducted a study on 1000 volunteers and collected the following data.

	Mighty Bar	Force Bar	Strength Bar
Lower Blood Sugar	30	91	66
Higher Blood Sugar	120	409	284

   a.   Complete the table by computing row and column totals. What is the independent variable?

   b.   A **relative frequency table** displays the percents in a table instead of a bar graph. Change the frequency table at the beginning of this problem to a relative frequency table by changing the counts to percents. For example, the 30 Mighty Bars that lowered blood sugar will be displayed as 20%.

   c.   Use your data from the relative frequency table to make a bar graph for each of the independent variables. The horizontal axis should be the dependent variable.

   d.   Is there an association between blood sugar level and the choice of energy bar?

7-110. An unusually severe increase in gasoline prices may have motivated full-sized pickup truck buyers to purchase a highly fuel-efficient vehicle. Purchase behavior was collected in one area for one year and reported below.

	Low Fuel Prices	High Fuel Prices
Number of Highly Fuel Efficient Trucks Purchased	392	442
Number of Ordinary Cars and Regular Trucks Purchased	36,929	42,255

a. Complete the row and column totals. What is the independent variable?

b. Create a relative frequency table. Is there an association between fuel prices and the number of highly fuel-efficient trucks purchased?

7-111. Researchers have determined that teenagers' memories are negatively affected by getting less than 10 hours of sleep. Being good scientists, the math students at North Middle School were skeptical, so they did their own study. They asked 300 students to memorize 10 objects. The next day, each student was asked how much sleep he or she got and then was asked to list the ten items. The results are below.

	Remembered all 10 items?		
	Yes	**No**	**TOTAL**
Less than 7 hours sleep	6	149	155
7-9 hours sleep	11	109	120
At least 10 hours sleep	5	20	25 ·
TOTAL	22	278	300

Make a relative frequency table to determine if there is an association between hours of sleep and memory.

7-112.   Ruthie did a survey among her classmates comparing the time spent playing video games to the time spent studying. The scatterplot of her data is shown at right.

Playing Video Games

a.   What association can you make from her data?

b.   Use an ordered pair (x, y) to identify any outliers.

7-113.   Sao can text 1500 words per hour. He needs to text a message with 85 words. He only has 5 minutes between classes to complete the text. Can he do it in 5 minutes?

7-114.   Where would the point $(11, -18)$ be after each transformation described below?

a.   Reflect $(11, -18)$ across the x-axis, and then reflect that point across the y-axis.

b.   Translate $(11, -18)$ 5 units to the right and 3 units down.

7-115.   This problem is a checkpoint for solving equations with fractions and decimals (Fraction Busters). It will be referred to as Checkpoint 7.

Solve each equation or system of equations.

a. $\frac{1}{5}x + \frac{1}{3}x = 2$

b. $x + 0.15x = \$2$

c. $\frac{x+2}{3} = \frac{x-2}{7}$

d. $y = \frac{2}{3}x + 8$
       $y = \frac{1}{2}x + 10$

Check your answers by referring to the Checkpoint 7 materials located at the back of your book.

If you needed help solving these problems correctly, then you need more practice. Review the Checkpoint 7 materials and try the practice problems. Also, consider getting help outside of class time. From this point on, you will be expected to do problems like these quickly and easily.

Chapter 7 Closure   What have I learned?

Reflection and Synthesis

The activities below offer you a chance to reflect
about what you have learned during this chapter.
As you work, look for concepts that you feel very
comfortable with, ideas that you would like to learn
more about, and topics you need more help with.

①   SUMMARIZING MY UNDERSTANDING

This section gives you an opportunity to show what you know about certain
math topics or ideas. In this case, you will be solidifying some of your ideas
about slope.

Obtain the Chapter 7 Closure GO
Resource Page (pictured at right) from
your teacher. Follow the directions
below to demonstrate your
understanding of slope.

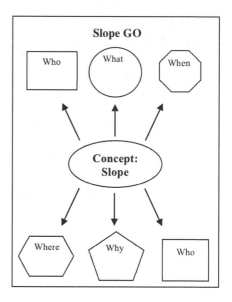

Part 1:   Answer the question provided
in each section of the Slope
GO. On the resource page,
work with your team to write
six "Who, What, When,
Where, Why, How?"
questions about slope.

Part 2:   Follow your teacher's
directions to pair up with
students in another team and
trade GO questions to answer.

Part 3:   Be ready to contribute your team's ideas to a class discussion. On
your own paper, make note of new ideas about slope.

②   WHAT HAVE I LEARNED?

Doing the problems in this section will help you to evaluate which types of problems you feel comfortable with and which ones you need more help with.

Solve each problem as completely as you can. The table at the end of this closure section provides answers to these problems. It also tells you where you can find additional help and where to find practice problems like them.

CL 7-116.   Graph the following data on a scatterplot.

a. Does the graph show either a positive or a negative association?

b. Does there appear to be a connection between height and spelling ability?

c. Does greater height cause better spelling ability?

d. What other factors could create the association you see?

Height (Inches)	Test Scores (Percent)
24	3
56	86
72	98
49	50
18	0
36	12
70	90
66	81
61	75
34	25
59	80
57	77
64	88

CL 7-117.   Complete the table and find the rule.

x	6	$\frac{1}{2}$	−6	8	−12	3	$\frac{2}{3}$
y				18		3	

CL 7-118.   For the following examples, tell whether there is positive association, negative association, or no association.

   a.   The number of inches of rain per hour and the height of water in a reservoir.

   b.   The amount of food a person eats and how many pets he or she has.

   c.   The height of a tree and the amount of nutrients it gets.

   d.   The number of hours spent hiking in the mountains and the amount of water left in your water bottle.

CL 7-119.   Answer the following questions for the graph at right.

   a.   What is the slope of the line?

   b.   What is the y-intercept?

   c.   What is a rule for the line?

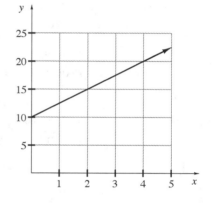

CL 7-120.   Solve the following equations.

   a. $0.75x - 0.5 = x + 1.5$

   b. $x - 2 = -\frac{1}{6}x + \frac{1}{3}$

   c. $3(x+2) - 3 = 3x - 2$

   d. $5(x-1) = 5(2x-3)$

CL 7-121.   Ryan and Janelle are driving from different locations to meet at Mammoth Lakes. When they each stopped for lunch, they called each other on their cell phones. Ryan had traveled 245 miles in $3\frac{1}{2}$ hours. Janelle had driven 260 miles in 4 hours.

   a.   How fast was each person driving?

   b.   If Janelle originally started 575 miles from Mammoth Lakes and continues traveling at the same rate (from part (a)), how many more hours will it take her to arrive at her destination?

330

CL 7-122.   Graph a line that goes through the points $(-2, 1)$ and $(4, -2)$.

     a.   What is the slope of the line?

     b.   Graph a line that is parallel to this line.
         What is the slope of the parallel line?

CL 7-123.   Describe a set of transformations that will move
              Triangle A on the graph at right to match up with
              Triangle B.

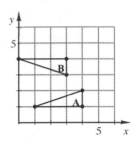

CL 7-124.   For each of the problems above, do the following:

    •   Draw a bar or number line that represents 0 to 10.

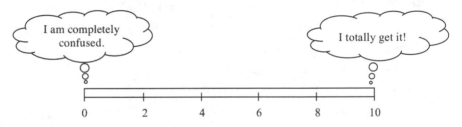

    •   Color or shade in a portion of the bar that represents your level of
        understanding and comfort with completing that problem on your own.

If any of your bars are less than a 5, choose *one* of those problems and do
one of the following tasks:

    •   Write two questions that you would like to ask about that problem.

    •   Brainstorm two things that you DO know about that type of problem.

If all of your bars are a 5 or above, choose one of those problems and do one
of these tasks:

    •   Write two questions you might ask or hints you might give to a student
        who was stuck on the problem.

    •   Make a new problem that is similar and more challenging than that
        problem and solve it.

③   WHAT TOOLS CAN I USE?

You have several tools and references available to help support your learning – your teacher, your study team, your math book, and your Toolkit, to name only a few. At the end of each chapter you will have an opportunity to review your Toolkit for completeness as well as to revise or update it to better reflect your current understanding of big ideas.

The main elements of your Toolkit should be your Learning Log, Math Notes, and the vocabulary used in this chapter. Math words that are new to this chapter appear in bold in the text. Refer to the lists provided below and follow your teacher's instructions to revise your Toolkit, which will help make it a useful reference for you as you complete this chapter and as you work in future chapters.

Learning Log Entries
- Lesson 7.1.3 – Associations
- Lesson 7.2.3 – Slope and Steepness
- Lesson 7.3.1 – Line From Data Points
- Lesson 7.3.2 – Describing Association

Math Notes
- Lesson 7.1.1 – Circle Graphs
- Lesson 7.1.2 – Line of Best Fit
- Lesson 7.1.3 – Describing Association – Part 1
- Lesson 7.2.4 – Slope of a Line
- Lesson 7.2.5 – Proportional Equations
- Lesson 7.3.2 – Describing Association – Part 2

Mathematical Vocabulary

The following is a list of vocabulary found in this chapter. Some of the words you have been seen in previous chapters. The words in bold are the words new to this chapter. Make sure that you are familiar with the terms below and know what they mean. For the words you do not know, refer to the glossary or index. You might also add these words to your Toolkit so that you can reference them in the future.

association	**categorical variable**	**central angle**
circle graph	**cluster**	**constant of proportionality**
form	**frequency table**	**lattice point**
line of best fit	linear equation	**linear (non-linear) form**
negative association	**negative slope**	**positive association**
positive slope	**outlier**	**simple interest**
slope	**strength (of an association)**	unit rate
$y = mx + b$	y-intercept	

Answers and Support for Closure Problems
What Have I Learned?

Note: MN = Math Note, LL = Learning Log

Problem	Solution	Need Help?	More Practice
CL 7-116.	a. Yes, positive b. Yes c. No d. The short people may be young and have not yet learned to spell.	Lessons 7.1.2 and 7.1.3 MN: 7.1.3 and 7.3.2 LL: 7.1.3	Problems 7-15, 7-16, 7-17, 7-18, 7-24, and 7-25

Problem	Solution	Need Help?	More Practice

CL 7-117.

6	$\frac{1}{2}$	−6	8	−12	3	$\frac{2}{3}$
12	−4.5	−24	18	−42	3	−4

$y = 3x - 6$

Lesson 4.1.4

MN: 4.1.7

Problems 7-77 and 7-89

CL 7-118.

a. positive association

b. no association

c. positive association

d. negative association

Lesson 7.3.2

MN: 7.1.3 and 7.3.2

LL: 7.1.3 and 7.3.2

Problems 7-16, 7-18, 7-26, 7-29, 7-72, 7-89, 7-100, 7-102, 7-103, and 7-112

CL 7-119.

a. 2.5

b. 10

c. $y = 2.5x + 10$

Lessons 7.2.2 and 7.2.3

MN: 7.2.4

LL: 7.2.3 and 7.3.1

Problems 7-77 and 7-89

CL 7-120.

a. $x = -8$

b. $x = 2$

c. no solution

d. $x = 2$

Lessons 2.1.8 and 2.1.9

MN: 2.1.8 and 2.1.9

LL: 2.1.9

Problems 7-9, 7-33, 7-63, 7-74, and 7-106

CL 7-121.

a. Ryan: 70 mph, Janelle: 65 mph

b. About 4.85 hours or 4 hours and 51 minutes

Lessons 7.2.2 and 7.3.1

Problems 7-43, 7-45, and 7-87

CL 7-122.

a. Slope $= -\frac{1}{2}$

b. Lines will vary but should have a slope of $-\frac{1}{2}$.

Lesson 7.2.1

LL: 7.3.1

Problems 7-35, 7-77, and 7-93

CL 7-123.

One possible answer is to reflect over the line $y = 2$ and then slide up 1 and left 1.

Lesson 6.1.1

MN: 6.1.3

LL: 6.1.3

Problems 7-11, 7-34, 7-83, and 7-114

Exponents and Functions

CHAPTER 8

In previous chapters you have investigated relationships that have a constant rate and can be represented as lines on a graph. Other relationships do not change at the same rate all of the time. In Section 8.1, you will investigate patterns of non-linear growth in tables, graphs, and expressions.

Following this work, you will look for patterns that will help you simplify complicated expressions with exponents. You will also learn how to represent very large and very small numbers more easily using scientific notation.

Finally, in this chapter, you will learn what a function is. You will explore several non-linear functions and learn how to describe them completely.

In this chapter, you will learn how to:

➢ Calculate compound interest.

➢ Determine whether a relationship grows linearly or exponentially.

➢ Rewrite expressions using exponents and scientific notation.

➢ Perform operations with numbers written in scientific notation.

➢ Determine if a relation is a function by looking at its table or graph.

Guiding Questions

Think about these questions throughout this chapter:

How is it changing?

What patterns can I see?

Is it a function?

How can I describe it?

Chapter Outline

Section 8.1 You will learn about compound interest and use patterns of growth to write expressions. You will analyze the patterns in tables, graphs, and expressions to compare linear and exponential growth.

Section 8.2 You will learn new ways to rewrite numbers and expressions involving exponents. You will also learn how to perform operations with these numbers and expressions.

Section 8.3 This section is devoted to special relationships called functions. You will learn how to distinguish functions from other relationships by examining their graphs and tables. Finally, you will investigate a variety of functions and learn how to describe them completely.

Total Interest Earned	Money Owed
0	1000
20	1020
40	1040
60	1060

$3^5 \cdot 3^2 = 3^7$

8.1.1   Is the graph linear?

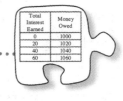

Patterns of Growth in Tables and Graphs

Have you ever noticed that the sun rises earlier and sets later in the summer than it does in the winter? If you live north of the equator, you may have noticed that in December you often wake up for school while it is still dark. However, if you wake up at the same time of day in May, the sun is shining. The number of hours of sunlight in any one place changes during the year, unless you live directly at the equator. This is because the earth's tilt changes in comparison to the sun. The number of hours of daylight is approximately equal to the number of hours of darkness at just two times of year: the fall equinox and the spring equinox.

If you compared the average number of hours of daylight to the time of year on a graph, you would be able to see a pattern in how the number of hours of daylight changes. Today you will explore situations, tables, and graphs that change in different ways and build strategies for visualizing different patterns of growth. As you work with your team, ask each other these questions:

How does this grow?

What happens when one measurement changes?

How can we see the pattern of growth in the table?

8-1.   With your team, discuss each of the comparisons described below. Consider how the measurements are related and visualize what each relationship would look like on a graph. Sketch your predictions after you discuss your ideas with your team.

a.   The month of the year compared to the average daily hours of sunlight in the Northern Hemisphere.

b.   The number of months money has been invested compared to the total balance for a bank account that earns simple interest.

c.   The cost of an item that has had its price repeatedly increased by 50%.

d.   The length of the base of a rectangle that has an area of 24 square centimeters compared to its height.

8-2.   Now that you have predicted what different graphs will look like, you will investigate how some of the measures are related. To start, consider this situation:

Oscar puts $1000 of principal in a bank account that earns 2% simple interest each month. He wants to track how his money is growing over time.

Oscar is using the formula at right to calculate how much interest he will earn on investments that are earning simple interest. He knows that simple interest is paid only on the original amount that was deposited (the principal). For an amount of money that was invested for two months, he wrote the equation below.

$$I = 1000(0.02)(2) = \$40.00$$

> **Formula for Simple Interest**
>
> $I = Prt$ where $P = $ Principal
> $I = $ Interest
> $r = $ Rate

a.   On the Lesson 8.1.1A Resource Page, complete the table to show the interest Oscar has earned after 1, 2, 3, 4, and 5 months. How do you find his new balance each month?

Months	Total Interest Earned	Bank Balance
0	$0	$1000
1		

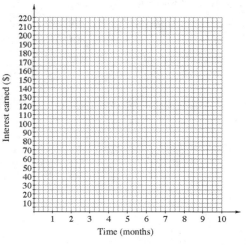

b.   Make a graph comparing months and interest on the resource page.

c.   What patterns do you notice in the table and the graph? How can you see each pattern in the other representations (situation, table, graph)?

d.   Use the patterns you have found to predict how long it will take before Oscar has $1800 in the bank. Justify your prediction.

e.   Compare your graph from part (b) to the sketch you made in part (b) of problem 8-1. Did you predict that the graph would be a straight line? Explain why your prediction was correct, or any changes you would make and why.

8-3.   PROFIT, PROFIT, PROFIT

Anita bought a special baseball card for $8.00. Later, she decided to sell it, but she wanted to make a profit. She added 50% to the price she paid and sold the card to Brandon. When he decided to sell it, he also wanted to make a profit, so he added 50% to the price he paid for the card and sold it to Casey. Casey increased the price by 50% and sold the card to Eli, who increased the price another 50% when he sold it to Fernanda.

a. On the Lesson 8.1.1B Resource Page, make a table and a graph of the new price after 1, 2, 3, 4, and 5 exchanges. How do you find the new price at each exchange?

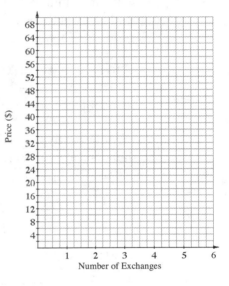

Exchanges	Increase in Price	New Price
0	$0	$8
1		

b. What patterns do you notice in the table and the graph? Is the graph a straight line? How can you justify your conclusion based on the table or the graph?

c. How does the graph you made in this problem compare to your sketch from part (c) of problem 8-1? Did you predict that the graph would curve?

d. How much did Fernanda pay for the baseball card?

8-4.   In problems 8-2 and 8-3, one graph made a straight line while the other curved.

a. How was the situation that created a straight line changing (growing)?

b. Growth that creates a straight line shows constant change and is called **linear growth**. What made the graph in problem 8-3 curve? How did the growth show in the table and in the graph?

8-5.   Guillermo was studying the two different situations below. He knows that one is represented by a line on a graph but that the other is represented by a curve.

The Basketball Tournament: The first round of a basketball tournament starts with 16 teams that each play one game. The eight winning teams move on to Round 2, and the other teams are done competing. The tournament continues in this way until Round 4, the finals, where the last two teams play to determine the champion.

The Basketball Tournament	
Round	Number of Teams Left
1	16
2	8
3	4
4	2

Finishing Homework: You have 16 problems to finish at home tonight. You can finish 4 problems in 10 minutes.

Help Guillermo by explaining how you see the situations above changing over time. For each situation:

Finishing Homework	
Time Spent Working	Problems Left to Complete
0	16
10	12
20	8
30	4

a.   Describe to Guillermo how you see the values in the table changing.

b.   Explain whether the change is constant from one row to the next.

8-6.   Guillermo graphed the points for each table in problem 8-5 and sketched a trend line for each graph to show the pattern in the points. But he forgot to label his axes. Decide which graph matches the basketball tournament data and which graph matches the homework data. Explain how you know that they match.

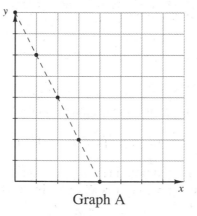

Graph A

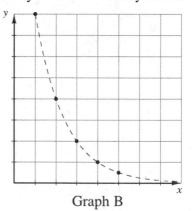

Graph B

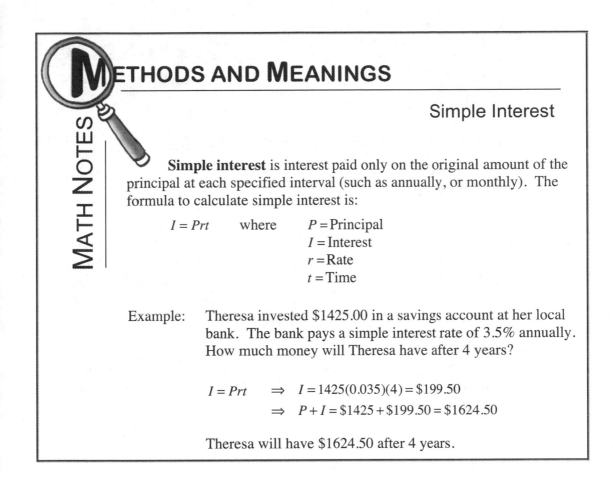

METHODS AND MEANINGS

Simple Interest

Simple interest is interest paid only on the original amount of the principal at each specified interval (such as annually, or monthly). The formula to calculate simple interest is:

$$I = Prt \quad \text{where} \quad \begin{aligned} P &= \text{Principal} \\ I &= \text{Interest} \\ r &= \text{Rate} \\ t &= \text{Time} \end{aligned}$$

Example: Theresa invested $1425.00 in a savings account at her local bank. The bank pays a simple interest rate of 3.5% annually. How much money will Theresa have after 4 years?

$$I = Prt \quad \Rightarrow \quad I = 1425(0.035)(4) = \$199.50$$
$$\Rightarrow \quad P + I = \$1425 + \$199.50 = \$1624.50$$

Theresa will have $1624.50 after 4 years.

8-7.   Cassandra is calculating how much interest she will earn on investments that are earning simple interest. She knows that simple interest is paid only on the original amount that was deposited (the principal). For one amount of money that was invested for three years, she wrote the equation
$$I = 500(0.025)(3) = \$37.50 .$$
Use what you know about simple interest to answer the following questions. Refer to the Math Notes box for this lesson if you need additional information.

a.   In Cassandra's equation, identify the principal, interest, rate, and time.

b.   Use this formula to calculate how much interest you would earn if you deposit $200 for 5 years at an annual (yearly) simple interest rate of 4%.

8-8. Which is a better deal? Sabrina wants to buy a new digital camera. The one she wants is currently on sale for $300. She could borrow the money at a monthly interest rate of 4% simple interest and pay it off after 6 months. Her other option is to work for 6 months and then pay cash, but the camera will no longer be on sale and will cost $350.

Which option will cost her the least money? Include calculations to justify your advice.

8-9. Mighty Max started the wrestling season weighing 135 pounds. By the time the season ended, he weighed 128 pounds. What was the percent decrease in his weight? That is, what was his decrease in weight as a percent of his starting weight?

8-10. Use the Distributive Property to rewrite each of the following expressions as a product. This process of rewriting a sum as a product is also called **factoring**. It is called *factoring* because you are writing the expression as multiplication of *factors*.

a. $4x + 8$ 　　　　 b. $-45 - 5x$ 　　　　 c. $7x - 21$

8-11. The school counselors are worried about the study habits of students who are involved in a lot of after-school activities. They randomly selected students at the school and gathered the following data. Consider the number of activities the independent variable.

| # OF STUDENTS | Hours Spent Studying Per Week | |
Hours of After-School Activities Per Week	Less Than 8 Hours	Eight or More Hours
Less Than 5 Hours	29	19
Five or More Hours	14	36

a. Make a relative frequency table.

b. Is there an association between the amount of time spent studying and number of after-school activities?

8-12. Find the lengths of the missing sides on the similar shapes at right.

15 mm

22 mm

54 mm

z

y　33 mm

40 mm

x

8.1.2 How can I describe the growth?

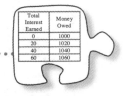

Total Interest Earned	Money Owed
0	1000
20	1020
40	1040
60	1060

Compound Interest

So far in this course you have studied simple interest, which only pays interest on the amount invested. It might be used for informal loan arrangements made between parents and children or between friends. However, banks and other financial institutions calculate interest in a different way. They commonly use **compound interest**. You will learn more about this type of interest in this lesson.

In the last lesson, you explored how simple interest increases a bank balance. That growth can be seen in a table and a graph. You also saw that in another situation, where prices grow by 50% each time they increase, the amount added is not constant. In this lesson, you will learn about compound interest and how to create an expression to describe this non-linear growth. Continue to ask these focus questions in your team:

What patterns do we see?

How can we show the connection?

8-13.   Ms. Hartley won $20,000 in the lottery! She decided to spend half of it right away, and invest the other half of the money for her retirement.

The interest rate on the account Ms. Hartley chose is 5%. She calculated that after 10 years, based on simple interest, her account balance should be $15,000. However, the banker told her that after 10 years the account balance would be $16,289.

A financial adviser explained to her that the bank is paying her **compound interest**. That means that the bank is calculating the interest each year on the total of the principal and any interest she has earned so far, rather than just the $10,000. If Ms. Hartley leaves the money in the account for 30 years, her $10,000 will grow to more than $40,000.

To help Ms. Hartley see the difference between simple interest and compound interest, her adviser made the following tables for her.

Simple Interest		Compound Interest	
Years of Teaching	Account Balance	Years of Teaching	Account Balance
0	$10,000	0	$10,000
5	$12,500	5	$12,763
10	$15,000	10	$16,289
15	$17,500	15	$20,789
20	$20,000	20	$26,533
25	$22,500	25	$33,864
30	$25,000	30	$43,219

a.   Explain how you see the interest growing in the simple-interest table.

b.   Explain how the interest grows in the compound-interest table.

c.   After 30 years, how does the simple-interest balance compare to the balance in the compound-interest table?

8-14.   Compound interest is calculated on all of the money in
an account at specific points in time. Each time interest
is calculated, it is based on both the principal amount
and any interest that was earned before. This is similar
to how the price of the baseball card grew in problem
8-3. In that situation, each price increase was based on
what the seller paid, not on what the card originally cost.

Mariana's grandfather invested $500 for her college
tuition in a savings account when she was born. The
account pays 5% compound interest every year.

a.   On the Lesson 8.1.2 Resource Page, complete
the middle column of the table to show the
account balance each year after the money was
deposited. How do you find the new balance
each year?

b.   Use the information in this column to fill in the
"Total Interest Earned" column in the table on
the resource page. This will show the total
interest earned since year 0 after any number of
years. How do you calculate the total interest
earned?

Time (years)	Balance ($)
0	500
1	525
2	551.25
3	
4	
5	
6	

·1.05
·1.05

c.   On the resource page, make a graph of the year
and total interest earned. Work with your team
to show the growth in both the table and the graph.

   • What patterns do you see on the graph and in the table?

   • How does the interest increase?

8-15.   Mariana is curious how much money will be in her account when she is 18 and
         graduates from high school. She went back to the table she had created. As she
         looked at the numbers in the first two columns (years and balance), she noticed
         a pattern that she thought she could rewrite into a shortcut. Study the table and
         her work.

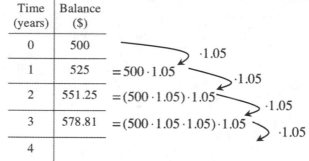

Time (years)	Balance ($)	
0	500	
1	525	$= 500 \cdot 1.05$
2	551.25	$= (500 \cdot 1.05) \cdot 1.05$
3	578.81	$= (500 \cdot 1.05 \cdot 1.05) \cdot 1.05$
4		

a.   As Mariana works down the table to fill in entries, what changes in
     Mariana's calculations? What patterns do you see in her work?

b.   In Mariana's calculation for 2 years, what does $(500 \cdot 1.05)$ represent? What
     is $(500 \cdot 1.05)$ equal to?

c.   How could you rewrite Mariana's balance at the end of any year in terms of
     the principal, $500? In words, generalize the pattern you see in the table.

d.   Based on this pattern, describe how you would find
     Mariana's balance after 18 years *without* first finding her
     balance at 17 years. Then, use your calculator to find out
     her balance in year 18.

8-16.   The pattern you described in words in part (c) of problem 8-15 can be rewritten
         in symbols using an exponent. For example, $4 \cdot 4 \cdot 4 \cdot 4 \cdot 4$ can be rewritten using
         an exponent like this:

$$4 \cdot 4 \cdot 4 \cdot 4 \cdot 4 = 4^5$$

         Here, 4 is the **base** and 5 is the **exponent** (sometimes called a power). 4^5 is
         read, *"Four raised to the fifth power"* or *"Four multiplied by itself 5 times."*

a.   Write the numbers you multiplied in part (d) of problem 8-15 as an
     expression using an exponent.

b.   Write an expression to represent this situation:

     A comic book is purchased for $6. It is resold 7 times, and each time it is
     resold the seller charges 15% more than he or she paid for it.

8-17.   Simplify each expression.

   a. 5^3 b. 3^5 c. $\left(\frac{2}{3}\right)^4$ d. $(0.8)^3$

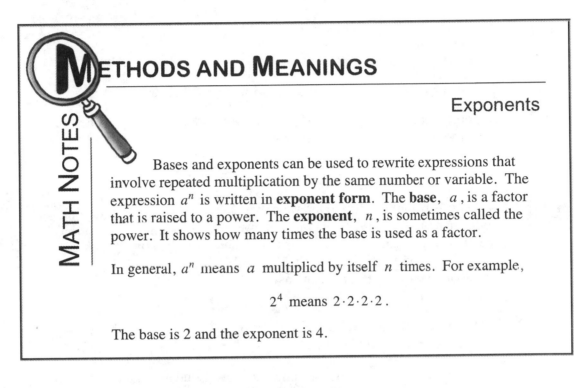

METHODS AND MEANINGS

Exponents

Bases and exponents can be used to rewrite expressions that involve repeated multiplication by the same number or variable. The expression a^n is written in **exponent form**. The **base**, a, is a factor that is raised to a power. The **exponent**, n, is sometimes called the power. It shows how many times the base is used as a factor.

In general, a^n means a multiplied by itself n times. For example,

$$2^4 \text{ means } 2 \cdot 2 \cdot 2 \cdot 2.$$

The base is 2 and the exponent is 4.

Review & Preview

8-18.   Rachel has been given $1000 to put into a savings account. She earns 2% simple interest every month. Rachel hopes to buy a car in two years. Help Rachel determine whether she will have enough money if the car will cost $1500.

8-19.   Copy and complete the table at right for powers of 10.

   a.   Use the pattern in the completed table to decide how many zeros 10^7 will have. How many zeros will 10^{23} have?

   b.   How would you tell someone to write 10^{50}? Do not actually write the number; just write a sentence telling someone how he or she would write it.

Powers of 10	Standard Form
10^0	
10^1	10
10^2	100
10^3	
10^4	
10^5	

8-20. Jack noticed a sale on his favorite model of All-Terrain Vehicle (ATV). The salesperson said the company was cutting the price for that weekend, so Jack got an 8% discount.

a. If the usual price of the ATV was $4298, estimate how much the discount will be. Explain your reasoning.

b. Calculate the amount Jack did pay with the 8% discount.

c. If the store sold three of the ATVs that weekend, how much money was saved by the three customers combined?

8-21. The choir is planning a trip to the water park, and the parents are trying to determine how much to charge each child. The cost to use a school bus is $350. Complete the table at right, graph your results, and then answer parts (a) and (b) below.

Number of Students on the Trip	Bus Cost per Student ($)
10	
15	
20	
35	

a. Think back to your work with proportions. Is this a proportional relationship?

b. Is there an association between the number of students and the cost per student? If so, describe it. Consider the form, direction, and outliers in your description.

8-22. Simplify each expression.

a. $-\frac{4}{5}+\frac{7}{12}$ 　　 b. $\frac{5}{9}+(-\frac{1}{4})$ 　　 c. $-\frac{3}{7}\cdot\frac{11}{12}$ 　　 d. $-1\frac{2}{3}\cdot\frac{4}{5}$

8-23. Graph these points on a coordinate grid and connect them to make a triangle: $(0,1),(3,2),(2,4)$. Then:

- Dilate the shape by multiplying each coordinate by 2.

- List the coordinates of the new vertices.

What do you notice about the sides of the two shapes?

8.1.3   What patterns can I see?

Linear and Exponential Growth

Patterns in tables, graphs, and expressions give clues about the kind of growth that is being represented. Today, you will work with your team to identify whether a table, graph, or situation represents simple interest or compound interest based on the kind of growth that is shown. You will also compare the different kinds of interest in situations to see which one is a better deal. By the end of this lesson, you should be able to answer these questions:

> What are the patterns in the tables, graphs, and expressions for each kind of interest?

> What are the differences between the two kinds of interest?

> How does the pattern relate to how the amounts are growing?

8-24.   John needs to borrow $250. Moneybags Municipal Bank will charge him 8% simple interest each week to borrow the money. Scrooge Savings will charge him 6% compound interest each week. With your team, help John decide which loan is the better choice.

a.   Make a table for each bank. The tables should show the amount John owes after each week for 12 weeks.

b.   Graph both tables on the same set of axes.

c.   Which bank will charge him more if he pays the loan back in 12 weeks? Should he choose the same bank if he plans to pay back the loan in just 4 weeks?

d.   Simple interest is an example of **linear growth**, and compound interest is an example of **exponential growth**. Talk with your team about how you could explain to someone else the difference between the two kinds of growth.

Chapter 8: Exponents and Functions

8-25. The table at right represents the balance in Devin's bank account for the last five months. Has Devin been earning simple interest or compound interest? How do you know?

Time (months)	Balance ($)
0	257.50
1	263.25
2	269.00
3	274.75
4	280.50
5	286.25

8-26. Imari borrowed money from her uncle to buy a new bicycle. She made the graph at right to show how much interest she will need to pay him if she pays back the loan at different points in time.

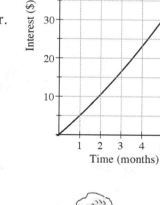

a. About how much interest will Imari owe her uncle if she pays him back in 3 months? When will she owe him $40 in interest?

b. Is Imari's uncle charging her simple or compound interest? Justify your answer. How would the graph be different if he was charging her the other type of interest (simple or compound)?

8-27. Tom has a choice between borrowing $250 from his grandmother, who will charge him simple interest, or borrowing $250 from the bank, which will charge him compound interest at the same percentage rate. He plans to pay off the loan in 8 months. He wrote the two expressions below to figure out how much he would owe for both loan options.

$$250(1.02)^8 \qquad\qquad 250 + 8(5.00)$$

a. What percent interest will he be charged? Where can you see the rate (percent) in each expression?

b. Which expression represents the amount he would owe his grandmother? Which one represents what he would owe the bank?

c. Evaluate each expression. Should he borrow the money from his grandmother or from the bank?

8-28.   **Additional Challenge:** Four years ago, Spencer borrowed $50 from his cousin, who charged him simple interest each year. If Spencer pays his cousin back $62 today, what annual interest rate did his cousin charge? Could you figure this out if he had been charged compound interest instead?

8-29.   LEARNING LOG

How can you describe the differences between simple and compound interest? In your Learning Log, write down what each kind of interest looks like in a table, on a graph, and in an expression. Be sure to answer the questions given at the beginning of the lesson (reprinted below). Title this entry "Simple and Compound Interest" and include today's date.

What are the patterns in the tables, graphs, and expressions for each kind of interest?

What are the differences between the two kinds of interest?

How does the pattern relate to how the amounts are growing?

$\bigcirc$ ETHODS AND MEANINGS

MATH NOTES

Compound Interest

Compound interest is interest paid on both the original principal (amount of money at the start) and the interest earned previously.

The formula for compound interest is: $A = P(1+r)^n$

where A = total amount including previous interest earned,
P = principal,
r = interest rate for each compounding period, and
n = number of time periods

Example: Theresa has a student loan that charges a 1.5% monthly compound interest rate. If she currently owes $1425.00 and does not make a payment for a year, how much will she owe at the end of the year (12 months)?

$$A = P(1+r)^n \Rightarrow A = 1425(1+0.015)^{12}$$
$$\Rightarrow 1425(1.015)^{12} = 1425 \cdot 1.1956 = \$1703.73$$

Theresa will owe $1703.73 after 12 months (1 year).

8-30.   Read this lesson's Math Notes box about compound interest, and then answer the questions below.

    a.   What does the $(1+r)$ represent in the formula? Why are the two quantities added together?

    b.   If Melanie invests \$2500 at a 3% interest rate compounded annually, how much will she have at the end of four years?

8-31.   Simplify each exponential expression.

    a. 2^4 b. 3^6 c. 25^3

    d. 4^2 e. 9^3 f. 5^6

    g.   What patterns do you see between the expressions in parts (a) through (f) that have equivalent simplified forms?

8-32.   Copy and complete the table at right.

8-33.   Write and solve an equation to solve the following problem. Be sure to define your variable and to state your answer in a complete sentence.

Jen, Carrie, and Fran are each thinking of a number. When you add their numbers together you get 207. Jen's number is 9 more than Carrie's, and Fran's number is 3 less than Jen's number. What is Fran's number?

Exponent Form	Factored Form	Standard Form
2^3	$2 \cdot 2 \cdot 2$	8
3^3		
	$4 \cdot 4 \cdot 4$	
		125
6^3		
7^3		
	$8 \cdot 8 \cdot 8$	
9^3		

8-34.   Rotate the triangle at right 90° clockwise about the origin. State the coordinates of the new vertices.

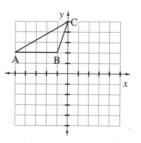

8-35.   Daniel has \$1200 in the bank. He is earning 3.5% compound interest each month. How much money will he have in the bank in one year? Is this example of linear or non-linear growth?

8.2.1 How can I rewrite it?

$$3^5 \cdot 3^2 = 3^7$$

Exponents and Scientific Notation

Earlier in this chapter you worked with expressions for interest problems. You could rewrite them in simpler ways by using multiplication in place of repeated addition, and by using exponents in place of repeated multiplication. Rewriting expressions in different forms can be a powerful tool for simplifying expressions and seeing patterns. In this lesson, you will develop strategies for how to rewrite expressions using exponents.

8-36. Is 3^5 the same as $3 \cdot 5$? Explain.

8-37. Exponents allow you to rewrite some multiplication problems in a simpler form. Some exponent expressions can also be simplified. Complete the table below on the Lesson 8.2.1 Resource Page, or copy and complete it on your own paper. Expand each expression into factored form and then rewrite it with new exponents as shown in the example.

Original Form	Factored Form	Simplified Exponent Form
$5^2 \cdot 5^5$	$(5 \cdot 5) \cdot (5 \cdot 5 \cdot 5 \cdot 5 \cdot 5)$	5^7
$2^2 \cdot 2^4$		
$3^7 \cdot 3^2$		
$x^3 \cdot x^5$		
$x^3 y^2 \cdot xy^2$		
$7^2 \cdot x^3 \cdot 7 \cdot x^2$		
$2 \cdot x^4 \cdot 3 \cdot xy^2$		

a. Work with your team to compare the bases and exponents of the original form to the base and exponent of the simplified exponent form. Write a statement to describe the relationships you see.

b. Visualize how you would expand $20^{12} \cdot 20^{51}$ in your mind. What would this expression be in a simplified exponent form? Describe your reasoning.

c. One study team rewrote the expression $10^3 \cdot 5^4$ as 50^7. Is their simplification correct? Explain your reasoning.

A and

8-38. When you multiply, the order of the factors does not matter. That means that you will get the same answer when multiplying $3 \cdot 2 \cdot 3$ as you would if you were multiplying $2 \cdot 3 \cdot 3$. This is the Commutative Property of Multiplication that you learned about in Chapter 2.

    a. Check that $2 \cdot 10$ is equal to $10 \cdot 2$. Is it also true that $2 \div 10$ is equal to $10 \div 2$?

    b. Write the expression $5^2 \cdot x^4 \cdot 5x$ in factored form. Explain how the Commutative Property of Multiplication helps you simplify the expression to $5^3 \cdot x^5$.

    c. Write the expression $3w^3 \cdot 3w^2 \cdot 3w \cdot 3$ in simplified exponent form.

                                 $3w^6$

8-39. Multiplying a number by 10 changes the number in a special way. Simplify each expression below without using a calculator. As you work, pay attention to how the number changes when you multiply it by powers of 10.

    a. $9.23 \cdot 10$ b. $9.23 \cdot 10^2$ c. $9.23 \cdot 10^3$ d. $9.23 \cdot 10^4$

8-40. Talk with your team about any patterns you see in your answers in problem 8-39.

    a. Based on those patterns, what do you think $9.23 \cdot 10^7$ would be? Why?

    b. Use the patterns you have found to find the product for each expression without using your calculator.

        i. 78.659×10^2 *ii.* 346.38×10^5

    c. With your team, write a statement describing in general how you can quickly multiply by powers of 10. You may want to include information about where the decimal point moves after multiplying the number by a power of 10 or why you have to add zeros. Work with your team to write a clear explanation for why this pattern works.

8-41.   When astronomers describe distances in space, often the numbers are so large that they are difficult to write. For example, the diameter of the sun is approximately one million, three hundred ninety thousand kilometers, or 1,390,000 km. To make these large numbers easier to write, astronomers and other scientists use **scientific notation**. In scientific notation, the diameter of the sun is:

$$1.39 \times 10^6 \text{ km}$$

a.   Rewrite 10^6 as a single number without an exponent. What happens when you multiply 1.39 by this number?

b.   In scientific notation, the mass of the sun is approximately 1.99×10^{30} kg. What does this number mean? Discuss with your team how to rewrite this number without scientific notation, and then write it.

8-42.   Scientific notation requires that one factor is a power of 10, and the other factor is a number greater than or equal to 1 but less than 10. For example, 2.56×10^5 is correctly written in scientific notation, but 25.6×10^4 is not. Scientific notation also uses the symbol "×" for multiplication instead of "·" or parentheses. None of the numbers below is correctly written in scientific notation. Explain why each one does not meet the criteria for scientific notation, and then write it using correct scientific notation.

a. 25.6×10^{15} b. 5.46×100 c. 0.93×10^8

2.56

8-43.   Write each number below in scientific notation.

a.   370,000,000   b.   48,710,000,000

8-44.   Scientific notation makes large numbers easier to write. It also provides you with quick information about the sizes of the numbers. For example, Pluto and Haumea are both dwarf planets. Pluto has a mass of 1.305×10^{22} kilograms, and Haumea has a mass of 4.006×10^{21} kilograms.

Without rewriting the mass of each planet, can you tell which of these dwarf planets is larger? Explain your reasoning.

8-45.   Without using a calculator, estimate how many times bigger the
         larger dwarf planet is than the smaller one in problem 8-44.

8-46.   LEARNING LOG

         In your Learning Log, explain to someone who missed
         today's class what scientific notation is and the difference
         between 3^8 and 3×10^8. Title this entry "Scientific
         Notation" and label it with today's date.

8-47.   Rewrite each of the expressions below in a simpler form using exponents.

         a. $4 \cdot 4 \cdot 5 \cdot 5 \cdot 5$ b. $3 \cdot 3 \cdot 3 \cdot 3 \cdot 3 \cdot y \cdot y$ c. $(6x)(6x)(6x)(6x)$

8-48.   Calculate the following products without using a calculator.

Factors	Product
6.5901×10^2	
0.6893×10^7	
5.86×10^4	
0.092×10^3	

8-49.   Graph the following points on a coordinate grid: $(1,1)$, $(4,1)$, and $(3,4)$.

         Connect the points. Then translate the points three units right and three units
         up. What are the coordinates of the vertices of the new triangle?

8-50.   Scientists consider the average growth rate of kelp (a sea plant) to be an indicator of the health of marine plants. They also consider the average weight (mass) of crabs that live in kelp beds to be an indicator of the health of the marine animals. But they want to know if there is an association between the health of sea plants (kelp) and the health of sea animals (crab).

Marine biologists collected data from different parts of the world and created the following relative frequency table. They considered the average growth rate of kelp as the independent variable.

% CRABS		Average Mass of Crabs (kg)			
		< 0.25	0.25 – 0.49	0.50 – 0.75	> 0.75
Average Growth Rate of Kelp (cm/day)	< 5	66%	34%	0%	0%
	≥ 5	12%	49%	35%	4%

Is there an association between the health of sea plants and the health of sea animals?

8-51.   Enrollment in math courses at Kennedy High School in Bloomington, Minnesota is shown in the pie chart at right. (If you are unfamiliar with pie charts, refer to the glossary for assistance.) If there are 1000 students enrolled in math courses, approximately how many students are enrolled in Algebra? In Geometry? In Calculus?

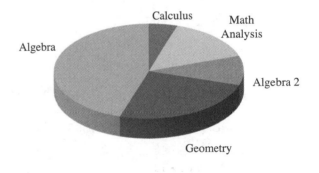

8-52.   Determine the compound interest earned on $220 invested at 3.25% compounded annually for 6 years.

8-53.   Which number is greater, 3.56×10^4 or 1.9×10^6? Explain how you know.

8-54.   Write the following numbers in scientific notation.

   a.   370,000,000   b.   7,600

8-55.   Simplify each expression.

   a. 6^5 b. $\left(\frac{2}{3}\right)^3$ c. $(2+3)^4$ d. $2(-\frac{1}{2}+\frac{3}{4})^3$

8-56.   Consider the equation $7 = 3x - 5$.

   a.   Stanley wants to start solving the equation by adding 5 to both sides, while
        Terrence first wants to subtract 7 from both sides. Will both strategies
        work? Is one strategy more efficient than the other?

   b.   Solve $7 = 3x - 5$. Show your steps.

8-57.   Examine the table below.

x	0.5	0	2	4	5
y	−0.5	−2	4	10	13

   a.   What is the rule for the table?

   b.   Explain the strategy you used to find the rule.

8-58.   Graph the equation $y = -2x^2 - 4x$. Start by making an $x \rightarrow y$ table. Be sure to
         include negative values for x. Does this graph linear or non-linear?

8.2.2 How can I write it in simpler form?

Exponent Rules

In the previous lesson, you expanded expressions written with exponents into factored form and then rewrote them in simpler form. You also looked at ways to rewrite very large numbers in scientific notation to compare them more easily.

In this lesson, you will continue to develop ways to rewrite expressions using exponents. Use the questions below to focus discussion in your study team.

What part of the expression is being raised to a power?

What are the factors?

How can we rewrite the expression to have fewer terms?

8-59.　Rewrite each expression below in a simpler form.

a.　$10^2 \cdot x^3 \cdot 10 \cdot y$　　　b.　$20^3 \cdot 20^8$　　　c.　$x^2 y^2 z^2 \cdot x^3 z^5$

8-60.　Erin wants to rewrite the expression $5^2 x^2 \cdot 5^4 x^3$ in simpler form. She started by expanding the expression like this:

$$5 \cdot 5 + x \cdot x + 5 \cdot 5 \cdot 5 \cdot 5 + x \cdot x \cdot x$$
$$25 + x^2 + 625 + x^3$$

Do you agree with her work so far? Work with your team to complete the problem or, if you do not agree, to write Erin a note explaining how to correct her work and find the correct simplification.

8-61.   When a number is raised to a power, and then raised to a power again, the result follows a consistent pattern. Complete the table below on the Lesson 8.2.2 Resource Page, or copy and complete it on your own paper. Expand each expression into factored form and then rewrite it with new exponents as shown in the example.

Original Form	Factored Form	Simplified Exponent Form
$(5^2)^5$	$(5 \cdot 5)(5 \cdot 5)(5 \cdot 5)(5 \cdot 5)(5 \cdot 5)$	5^{10}
$(2^2)^4$		
$(3^7)^2$		
$(x^3)^5$		
$(x^3y^2)^2$		

a.   Work with your team to describe the pattern between the exponents in the original form and the exponent(s) in the simplified exponent form.

b.   Visualize $(20^3)^8$ written in factored form. What is multiplied? That is, what is the base? How many times is it multiplied? Use the expression you visualized to help you rewrite the expression in simplified exponent form. Describe in detail how you figured out what exponent to use in the simplified exponent form.

8-62.   In problem 8-59, you simplified the expression $20^3 \cdot 20^8$. Compare the factored form you wrote for that expression to the expression you visualized in part (b) of problem 8-61. How are the two expressions different?

8-63.   Heidi is trying to rewrite the two expressions below.

$$(2x)^3 \qquad 2x^3$$

"Are these two ways of writing the same thing? Or do they mean something different?" Heidi wonders.

a.   Rewrite $(2x)^3$ by expanding and then simplifying. What part is being raised to the third power?

b.   Heidi thinks $2x^3$ is the same as $2 \cdot x^3$. Show that she is correct by expanding the expression.

c.   Are $(2x)^3$ and $2x^3$ equivalent? Explain why or why not.

8-64.   AJ was trying to simplify the exponent expression $\frac{5^7}{5^3}$. He started by writing out the factored form. Once he saw the factors he recognized a Giant One in his work.

   a.   Copy AJ's expression on your paper and write out the factored form. Where did he see a Giant One?

   b.   Work with your study team to use the Giant One to simplify and rewrite AJ's expression. What is the result?

8-65.   Expand each expression below into factored form. Then rewrite it in simplified exponent form.

   a. $\frac{2^4}{2^2}$ b. $\frac{3^4}{3^5}$ c. $\frac{y^7}{y^4}$ d. $\frac{x^3y^2}{xy^2}$

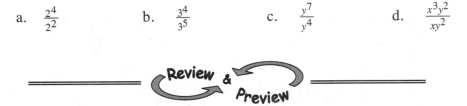

Review & Preview

8-66.   Simplify each expression.

   a. $\frac{3^2 \cdot 5^3 \cdot 8}{3 \cdot 5^3 \cdot 8}$ b. $(3x)^4$ c. $3^3 \cdot 3^5 \cdot (\frac{1}{3})^2$ d. $\frac{7^4 \cdot 9^2}{9^3 \cdot 7^2}$

8-67.   Janet lit a 12-inch candle. She noticed that it was getting an inch shorter every 30 minutes.

   a.   Is the association between the time the candle is lit and the height of the candle positive or negative?

   b.   In how many hours will the candle burn out? Support your answer with a reason.

8-68.   Show the "check" for each of the problems below. Write whether the solution is correct or incorrect.

   a.   For $3x+2 = x-2$, does $x=0$?

   b.   For $3(x-2) = 30+x-2-x+2$, does $x=12$?

8-69.   On graph paper, graph the shape that has coordinates $(-2, -1)$, $(1, 2)$, and $(-2, 3)$.

   a.   Predict the coordinates of the shape after it is translated three units to the right and one unit down. Check your prediction on the graph.

   b.   Dilate the original shape by multiplying both the x- and y-coordinates by 2.

   c.   Reflect the original shape over the y-axis. What are the new coordinates?

8-70.   Solve the equations below for the indicated variable.

   a. $3(2x - 1) + 2y = 5x$ for y

   b. $600x + 200y = 500x$ for x

8-71.   Use $<$, $>$, or $=$ to compare the number pairs below.

   a. 0.183 _____ 0.18

   b. -13 _____ -17

   c. 0.125 _____ $\frac{1}{8}$

   d. -6 _____ -4

   e. 72% _____ $\frac{35}{30}$

   f. -0.25 _____ -0.05

8.2.3 What happens if the exponent is negative?

$3^5 \cdot 3^2 = 3^7$

Negative Exponents

Earlier in this chapter you learned how to write large numbers in scientific notation. Astronomers use those large numbers to measure great distances in space. Not all scientists work with such a large scale, however. Some scientists use very small numbers to describe what they measure under a microscope. In this lesson, you will continue your work with exponents, and then you will turn your attention to using scientific notation to represent small numbers.

8-72. Two of the problems below are correct, and four contain errors. Expand each original expression to verify that it is correct. If it is not, identify the mistake and simplify to find the correct answer.

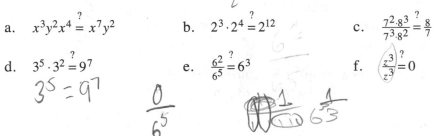

a. $x^3 y^2 x^4 \stackrel{?}{=} x^7 y^2$

b. $2^3 \cdot 2^4 \stackrel{?}{=} 2^{12}$ 2^7

c. $\frac{7^2 \cdot 8^3}{7^3 \cdot 8^2} \stackrel{?}{=} \frac{8}{7}$

d. $3^5 \cdot 3^2 \stackrel{?}{=} 9^7$

$3^5 = 9^7$

e. $\frac{6^2}{6^5} \stackrel{?}{=} 6^3$

$\frac{0}{6^5}$

f. $\left(\frac{z^3}{z^3}\right)^? = 0$

$\frac{1}{6^3}$

8-73. Rewrite each expression in a simpler form using the patterns you have found for rewriting expressions with exponents. If it is reasonable, write out the factored form to help you.

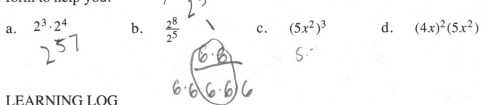

a. $2^3 \cdot 2^4$

2^{57}

b. $\frac{2^8}{2^5}$ 2^3

c. $(5x^2)^3$

$5 \cdots$

d. $(4x)^2 (5x^2)$

$6 \cdot 6$
$6 \cdot 6 \cdot 6 \cdot 6 \cdot 6$

8-74. LEARNING LOG

You have worked with your team to describe ways to rewrite and simplify exponent expressions involving multiplication and division. In your Learning Log, give examples of each kind of expression. Describe in words how to rewrite each one. Include factored and simplified expressions to go with your descriptions. Title this entry "Simplifying Exponent Expressions" and label it with today's date.

8-75.   Salvador was studying microscopic pond animals in science
         class. He read that amoebas were 0.3 millimeters to 0.6
         millimeters in length. He saw that euglenas are as small as
         $8.0 \cdot 10^{-2}$ millimeters, but he did not know how big or small a
         measurement that was. He decided to try to figure out what a
         negative exponent could mean.

   a.   Copy and complete Salvador's calculations at right.
        Use the pattern of dividing by 10 to fill in the missing
        values.

   b.   How is 10^2 related to 10^{-2}?

   c.   What type of numbers did the negative exponents
        create? Did negative exponents create negative
        numbers?

$$10^3 = 1000$$
$$\div 10$$
$$10^2 = 100$$
$$\div 10$$
$$10^1 = 10$$
$$\div 10$$
$$10^0 =$$
$$10^{-1} =$$
$$10^{-2} =$$
$$10^{-3} =$$

8-76.   Ngoc was curious about what Salvador was doing
         and began exploring patterns, too. He completed
         the calculations at right.

   a.   Copy and complete his calculations. Be sure to
        include all of the integer exponents from 5 to –3.

   b.   Look for patterns in his list. How are the values to the
        right of the equal sign changing? Is there a constant
        multiplier between each value?

$$2^5 = 32$$
$$2^4 = 16$$
$$2^3 = 8$$
$$\cdots$$
$$\cdots$$
$$2^{-1} = \tfrac{1}{2}$$
$$2^{-2} =$$
$$2^{-3} =$$

8-77.   In problems 8-75 and 8-76, you saw that 10^0 and 2^0 both simplify to the same
         value. What is it? Do you think that any number to the zero power would have
         the same answer? Explain.

8-78.   Both Ngoc and Salvador are looking for ways to calculate values with negative
         exponents without extending a pattern. Looking at the expression 5^{-2}, they
         each started to simplify differently.

         Salvador thinks that 5^2 is 25, so 5^{-2} must be $\frac{1}{25}$. Ngoc thinks 5^{-2} is $\frac{1}{5^2}$.
         Which student is correct?

8-79. Salvador's first questions about negative exponents came from science class, where he had learned that euglenas measured 8.0×10^{-2} millimeters. Use your understanding of negative exponents to rewrite 8.0×10^{-2} in standard form.

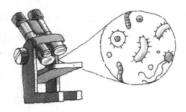

8-80. The probability of being struck by lightening in the United States is 0.000032%, while the probability of winning the grand prize in a certain lottery is 6.278×10^{-7} percent. Which event is more likely to happen? Explain your reasoning, including how you rewrote the numbers to compare them.

8-81. The list below contains a star, a river, and a type of bacteria. Which one is which? Use your understanding of scientific notation to put the three items listed below in order from largest to smallest and identify which is which.

   a. Yangtze measures 6.3×10^5 meters.

   b. Staphylococcus measures 6×10^{-7} meters.

   c. Eta Carinae measures 7.1×10^{17} meters.

8-82. Which of the numbers below are correctly written in scientific notation? For each that is not, rewrite it correctly.

   a. 4.51×10^{-2} b. 0.789×10^5

   c. 31.5×10^2 d. 3.008×10^{-8}

8-83. Create a fraction from these expressions, and then show how you use a Giant One to simplify.

   a. $6^5 \cdot 6^{-3}$ b. $w^5 w^{-2}$ c. $10^{-4} \cdot 10^5$

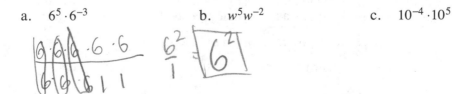

8-84.   Now it is time to reverse your thinking. If negative exponents can create fractions, then can fractions be written as expressions with negative exponents? Simplify the expressions below. Write your answer in two different forms: as a fraction and as an expression with a negative exponent.

a. $\frac{6^3}{6^5}$

b. $\frac{m^5}{m^6}$

c. $\frac{10^2}{10^5}$

8-85.   Rewrite each expression in a simpler form. Visualize the factored form and the Giant One to help you, or write it out if it is reasonable to do so.

a. $(5x^2)^3$

b. $(4x)^2(5x^2)$

c. $\frac{a^2c^{11}}{a^5c^3}$

8-86.   Lamar has a list of 600 pages to read to finish his book for his upcoming book report. He sets a goal to read half of the pages left in his book each day.

a.   How many pages will Lamar have to read the first day to meet his goal? How many will he have left to read after 3 days?

b.   How many pages will he need to read on day 8? With your team, write two different expressions to show how you found your answer.

8-87.   **Additional Challenge:** Alice was simplifying the expressions at right when she noticed a pattern. Each exponent under the radical (square root) sign was two times the exponent of the final answer. She wanted to know more about why this was happening.

$$\sqrt{3^4} = \sqrt{81} = 9 = 3^2$$
$$\sqrt{6^2} = \sqrt{36} = 6 = 6^1$$
$$\sqrt{5^4} = \sqrt{625} = 25 = 5^2$$
$$\sqrt{2^6} = \sqrt{64} = 8 = 2^3$$

a.   Confirm Alice's pattern by simplifying the expression $\sqrt{5^6}$ on your calculator. Can you rewrite your answer as 5 raised to a power?

b.   What does the operation "square root" do to an expression? What operation does it "undo"?

c.   Investigate this pattern using the expression $\sqrt{4^6}$.

- Expand the expression.

- Rewrite 4^6 as an expression raised to the second power.

- Use the square root to "undo" the squaring.

- Write your final answer, and check it on your calculator.

d.   Use that thinking to rewrite each expression below.

i. $\sqrt{7^4}$ ii. $\sqrt{9^8}$ iii. $\sqrt{3^{14}}$

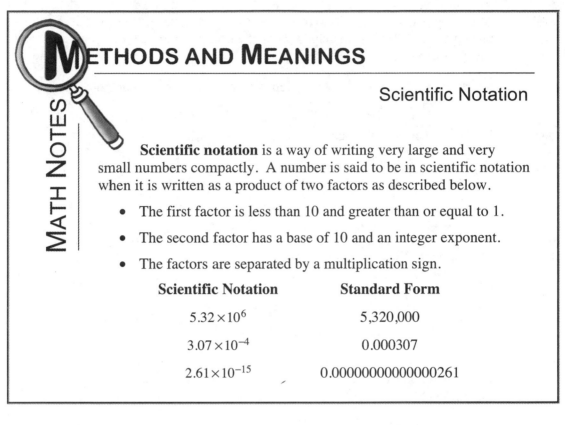

METHODS AND MEANINGS

Scientific Notation

MATH NOTES

Scientific notation is a way of writing very large and very small numbers compactly. A number is said to be in scientific notation when it is written as a product of two factors as described below.

- The first factor is less than 10 and greater than or equal to 1.

- The second factor has a base of 10 and an integer exponent.

- The factors are separated by a multiplication sign.

Scientific Notation	Standard Form
5.32×10^6	5,320,000
3.07×10^{-4}	0.000307
2.61×10^{-15}	0.00000000000000261

Review & Preview

8-88. Decide which numbers below are correctly written in scientific notation. If they are not, rewrite them.

a. 92.5×10^{-2} b. 6.875×10^2 c. 2.8×10 d. 0.83×100^2

8-89. In the table at right, write each power of 10 as a decimal and as a fraction.

a. Describe how the decimals and fractions change as you progress down the table.

b. How would you tell someone how to write 10^{-12} as a fraction? You do not have to write the actual fraction.

Power of 10	Decimal Form	Fraction Form
10^0		
10^{-1}	0.1	$\frac{1}{10}$
10^{-2}		$\frac{1}{100}$
10^{-3}		
10^{-4}		
10^{-5}		

8-90.   Mary wants to have $8500 to travel to South America when she is 21. She currently has $6439 in a savings account earning 4% annual compound interest. Mary is 13 now.

   a.   If Mary does not take out or deposit any money, how much money will Mary have when she is 15?

   b.   Will Mary have enough money for her trip when she is 21?

   c.   If Mary were to graph this situation, describe what the graph would look like.

8-91.   Recall that vertical lines around a number are the symbol for the absolute value of a number. Simplify each expression.

   a. $|6|$ b. $|-17|$ c. $-|-4.5|$

   d. $|2-5|$ e. $|2-3 \cdot 5|$ f. $-2 \cdot |-2|$

8-92.   For each equation below, solve for x. Sometimes the easiest strategy is to use mental math.

   a. $x - \frac{3}{5} = 1\frac{2}{5}$ b. $5.2 + x = 10.95$

   c. $2x - 3.25 = 7.15$ d. $\frac{x}{16} = \frac{3}{8}$

8-93.   Determine the coordinates of each point of intersection without graphing.

   a. $y = 2x - 3$ b. $y = 2x - 5$
         $y = 4x + 1$ $y = -4x - 2$

8-94.   Write each number in scientific notation.

   a.   5467.8   b.   0.0032   c.   8,007,020

8-95.   Simplify each expression using the rules for exponents.

   a. $\frac{3^5}{3^{10}}$ b. $10x^4(10x)^{-2}$ c. $(\frac{1}{4})^3 \cdot (4)^2$ d. $\frac{(xy)^3}{xy^3}$

8-96.   Simplify each expression.

   a. $-\frac{9}{5} \cdot \frac{8}{15}$

   b. $\frac{1}{5} + (-\frac{2}{15}) - (-\frac{4}{9})$

   c. $-\frac{4}{8} \cdot \frac{3}{7} \cdot (-\frac{2}{5})$

   d. $\frac{3}{5} \cdot (-\frac{2}{7}) + (-\frac{5}{7})(\frac{3}{10})$

   e. $-8\frac{1}{9} + 3\frac{5}{6}$

   f. $2\frac{1}{2} \cdot 4\frac{1}{5}$

8-97.   Athletes in the Middle Plains School District regularly receive personal advising on their nutrition. Coaches wondered if the nutritional advising was having an impact, so they divided athletes into two groups. One group received advice and one group did not. After six months, they collected the following data:

# OF ATHLETES	Received Nutrition Advice	Did Not Receive Nutrition Advice
Regularly Ate a Balanced Breakfast	46	39
Often Did Not Eat a Balanced Breakfast	89	73

   a.   Which is the independent variable?

   b.   Make a relative frequency table.

   c.   Is there an association between receiving the nutritional advice and regularly eating a balanced breakfast?

8-98.   Graph the points $X(-3, 5)$, $Y(-2, 3)$, and $Z(-1, 4)$. Connect them to make a triangle.

   a.   Reflect the triangle across the y-axis. What are the new coordinates of point Z?

   b.   Translate the original triangle down 6 units and right 3 units. What are the new coordinates of point Y?

   c.   Dilate the original triangle by multiplying each coordinate by −1. Describe the new shape you create.

8-99. The table below shows the amount of money Francis had in his bank account each day since he started his new job.

Days at New Job	Money in Account
0	$27
1	$70
2	$113
3	$156

a. Write a rule for the amount of money in Francis's account. Let x represent the number of days and y represent the number of dollars in the account.

b. When will Francis have more than $1000 in his account?

8.2.4 How do I compute it?

$$3^5 \cdot 3^2 = 3^7$$

Operations with Scientific Notation

Scientific notation is an application of exponents and the base 10 system. It is very useful when writing very large numbers, like the distance to Alpha Centauri, which is 4.13×10^{16} m, or the radius of the hydrogen atom, which is 5.29×10^{-11} m. But what if you wanted to know how many times larger the distance to Alpha Centauri is than the hydrogen atom? How would you calculate this? What if you wanted to add or subtract two numbers written in scientific notation? In this lesson, you will learn how to do operations with numbers written in scientific notation.

8-100. A typical dwarf sperm whale, the planet's smallest whale species, weighs about 3×10^2 pounds. A blue whale, the planet's largest whale, might weigh about 4.5×10^5 pounds. Estimate about how many times heavier a blue whale is than a dwarf sperm whale, without using a calculator.

1.8m

8-101.   There are about 1.8×10^{21} molecules in one gram of table sugar ($C_{12}H_{22}O_{11}$). A baker uses 8×10^2 grams in a recipe for cinnamon pastries.

a.   How many molecules of sugar does the baker use? Do not use your calculator.

b.   When the baker multiplied, her calculator displayed the answer below.

1.44E24

What do you think her calculator is displaying? Explain.

$\times 10^{24}$

8-102.   Find $(1.75 \times 10^{20})(6.01 \times 10^{14})$ in scientific notation without using a calculator. Then check your answer with your calculator. Write down exactly what your calculator displayed.

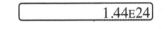

8-103.   The average distance from the sun to the earth is 1.488×10^{11} meters. If the length of the average paperclip is 3×10^{-2} meters, how many paperclips would need to be connected together to reach the sun?

$\frac{3}{100}$

8-104.   Jeremiah wanted to do the following problem. However, he was not sure how to get started, because the numbers were in scientific notation. He knew that if he wrote them out in standard form, without scientific notation, then he could line up the numbers with the same place value and add them together. He does not want to have to do that, though, because he does not want to write all of those zeroes. He is worried that he might just get more confused if he did write them all out. Work with your team to find a way to add the numbers required without first rewriting them in standard form. Here is the problem Jeremiah wanted to solve:

The average distance of each of the first five planets from sun is shown in the table below. Is the distance to Jupiter more or less than the combined distances of the first four planets (Mercury, Venus, Earth, and Mars)?

Planet	Average Distance from the Sun (miles)
Mercury	5.79×10^7
Venus	6.72×10^7
Earth	9.3×10^7
Mars	1.416×10^8
Jupiter	4.836×10^8

8-105.   The United States Department of Agriculture reported in *Vegetables and Melons Outlook* in 2007 that the average American consumes about 7.4×10^3 potato chips in a year. Since Idaho had about 1.5×10^6 people in 2007, how many potato chips would Idaho residents have consumed in 2007? Without using a calculator, make an exact computation and record your answer in scientific notation.

8-106.   One of the giant pyramids of Egypt is made of about 2.4×10^6 carved blocks of stone. If each block weighs approximately 4.95×10^3 pounds, about how many pounds of block make up the pyramid?

8-107.   Simplify.

   a. $1.24 \times 10^3 + 2.3 \times 10^4$ b. $\frac{4 \times 10^5}{8 \times 10^7}$ c. $8.5 \times 10^{10} \cdot 7.6 \times 10^{12}$

8-108.   **Additional Challenge:** The radius of the earth is about 6×10^8 cm.

   a.   The volume of a sphere can be estimated by $V = \frac{88}{21} r^3$, where r is the radius of the sphere. Without using a calculator, estimate the earth's volume in scientific notation.

   b.   Density can be found from $\frac{\text{mass}}{\text{volume}}$. The earth's mass is about 6×10^{24} kg. Without a calculator, estimate the earth's density. Answer in scientific notation.

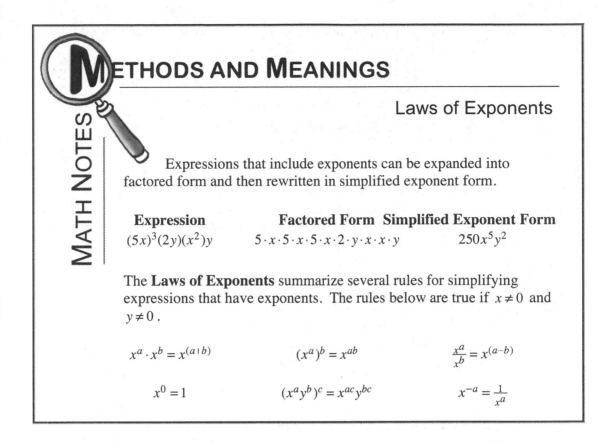

METHODS AND MEANINGS

Laws of Exponents

Expressions that include exponents can be expanded into factored form and then rewritten in simplified exponent form.

Expression	Factored Form	Simplified Exponent Form
$(5x)^3(2y)(x^2)y$	$5 \cdot x \cdot 5 \cdot x \cdot 5 \cdot x \cdot 2 \cdot y \cdot x \cdot x \cdot y$	$250x^5y^2$

The **Laws of Exponents** summarize several rules for simplifying expressions that have exponents. The rules below are true if $x \neq 0$ and $y \neq 0$.

$$x^a \cdot x^b = x^{(a+b)} \qquad (x^a)^b = x^{ab} \qquad \frac{x^a}{x^b} = x^{(a-b)}$$

$$x^0 = 1 \qquad (x^a y^b)^c = x^{ac} y^{bc} \qquad x^{-a} = \frac{1}{x^a}$$

MATH NOTES

Review & Preview

8-109. Compute each product or quotient. Convert the final answer to scientific notation if necessary.

a. $(3 \times 10^2)(2 \times 10^3)$ b. $(2.75 \times 10^{-2})(2.5 \times 10^8)$ c. $\frac{8 \times 10^{12}}{4 \times 10^7}$

8-110. Use the laws of exponents to simplify the following expressions.

a. $(x^2)(x^5)$ b. $\frac{y^7}{y^4}$ c. $x^3 \cdot x^4$

8-111. For the following examples, tell whether there is positive association, negative association, or no association.

   a. The number of inches of rain per hour and the height of water in a reservoir.

   b. The amount of food a person eats and how many pets he or she has.

   c. The height of a tree and the amount of nutrients it gets.

   d. The number of hours spent hiking in the mountains and the amount of water left in your water bottle.

8-112. Silvia has a picture from her trip to the Grand Canyon. The photo is 4 inches tall by 6 inches wide.

   a. She would like to make a larger photo for her wall that is as big as possible. The widest the enlarged photo can be is 48 inches. How tall will the enlarged photo be?

   b. Silvia also wants a wallet-sized photo to carry around and show her friends. She wants it 1.5 inches tall. How wide will it be?

8-113. Since the beginning of school, Steven has been saving money to buy a new MP3 player. His bank balance is represented by the graph below.

   a. According to the graph, about how much money had Steven saved after 2 weeks of school?

   b. About how much money did Steven probably have after 4 weeks of school? How can you tell?

   c. If he keeps saving at the same rate, how much will he have saved by Week 7? Explain how you know.

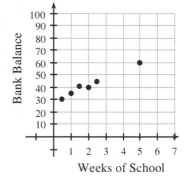

8-114. The science club is selling homemade cookies to raise money for a field trip. The club members know that 12 dozen cookies uses 3 pounds of flour. Use that information to solve each part below.

   a. How much flour is needed for 18 dozen cookies?

   b. How many cookies can be made with 10 pounds of flour?

8.3.1   Can I predict the output?

Functions in Graphs and Tables

Throughout this course, you have used rules that relate two variables to make graphs and find information. An example of such a rule is $y = 5x - 3$. Today you will look more closely at how rules that relate two variables help establish a relationship between the variables.

8-115.   Draw a sketch of an example of each graph described below.

   a.   A graph that neither increases nor decreases.

   b.   A graph that decreases non-linearly.

   c.   A graph that increases linearly and then decreases linearly.

   d.   A graph that is consistently increasing.

8-116.   ARE WE RELATED?

   Examine the table of input (x) and output (y) values below. Is there a relationship between the input and output values? If so, state the relationship.

x	−3	−2	−1	0	1	2	3
y	−16	−10	−4	2	8	14	20

8-117.   FUNCTION MACHINES

A **function** works like a machine. Numbers
are put into the machine one at a time, and
then the rule performs the operation(s) on each
input to determine each output. For example,
when $x = 3$ is put into a machine with the rule
$y = 5x - 7$, the rule multiplies the input, 3, by
5 and then subtracts 7 to get the output, which
is 8. This input and output can be written as an ordered pair: $(3, 8)$. Then it can
be placed on an xy-coordinate graph.

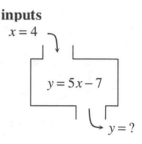

a.   Find the output of the function machine at
       right when the input is $x = 4$.

b.   Likewise, find y when $x = -1$ and $x = 10$.

c.   If the output of this relation is 45, what was
       the input? That is, if $y = 45$, then what is x?
       Is there more than one possible input?

8-118.   Some relationships are special in that they are called **functions**. Below are two
relationships, one of which ($y = x^2 - 2$) is a function and the other,
($x = y^2 - 2$), is not. Look at the graph and table of values below for each
relationship and discuss with your team why you think the relationship in
part (a) is a function and the one in part (b) is not. Use your ideas to create a
definition of a function. Be prepared to share your ideas with the rest of the
class. Use these questions to guide your discussion:

What is similar about the two relationships?

What is different about the two relationships?

What can we predict about the outputs for each relationship for a given input?

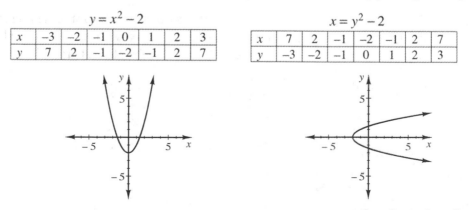

$y = x^2 - 2$

x	–3	–2	–1	0	1	2	3
y	7	2	–1	–2	–1	2	7

$x = y^2 - 2$

x	7	2	–1	–2	–1	2	7
y	–3	–2	–1	0	1	2	3

8-119. Examine each of the relationships below. Compare the inputs and outputs of each relation and decide if the relationship is a function. Explain your reasoning. Use your definition of a function from problem 8-118 to help you justify your conclusion.

a.

x	7	–2	0	4	9	–3	6
y	6	–3	4	2	10	–3	0

b.

x	3	–1	2	0	1	2	9
y	4	–5	9	7	4	–8	2

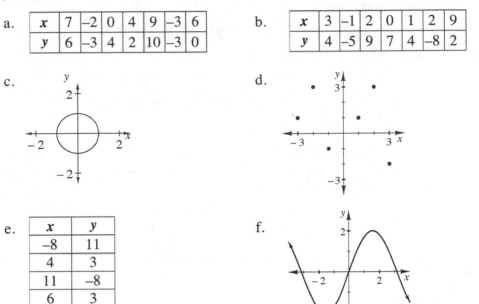

c.

d.

e.

x	y
–8	11
4	3
11	–8
6	3
–8	11

f.

8-120. **LEARNING LOG**

In your Learning Log, describe what it means for a relationship to be a function. How can you describe the differences between graphs of functions and graphs of non-functions? In your Learning Log, give examples of what a function and a non-function look like in a table and on a graph. Title this entry "Functions and Non-Functions" and include today's date.

8-121. For each part below, work with your team to create a graph based on the given information. Do each part on a separate set of axes. If necessary, make a table with sufficient points so that the pattern of the graph is clear.

a.

x	0	1	1	4	4
y	0	1	–1	2	–2

b. $y = |x - 2|$

c. A starting value of 8 and a rate of change of $-\frac{2}{3}$.

d. $xy = 12$

8-122. Use your previous experiences to describe each of the graphs above mathematically and as clearly as possible. Use the questions below to help you get started. Also, as you "read the graph from left to right," tell whether the y-values are increasing, decreasing, or both. Are there any points on the graph where something special happens?

Is it linear or non-linear?

Is it a function or not?

Is the graph discrete or continuous?

How else can I describe the graph?

8-123. Find the relationship between x and y in the table below and write the rule.

x	–2	1	10	4	7		0	5	6
y		1			2401	16		625	

Relationship: y = _______________

MATH NOTES

METHODS AND MEANINGS

Functions

A relationship between inputs and outputs is a **function** if there is no more than one output for each input. A function is often written in a form where y is set equal to some expression involving x. In this " $y=$ " form, x is the input and y is the output. Below is an example of a function.

$$y=(x-2)^2$$

x	–2	–1	0	1	2	3	4	5
y	16	9	4	1	0	1	4	9

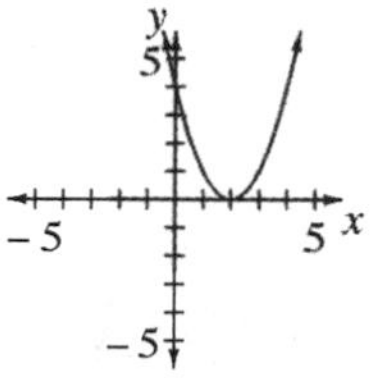

In the example above the value of y depends on x. Therefore, y is called the **dependent variable** and x is called the **independent variable**.

The equation $x^2+y^2=1$ is not a function because there are two y-values (outputs) for some x-values, as shown below.

$$x^2+y^2=1$$

x	–1	0	0	1
y	0	–1	1	0

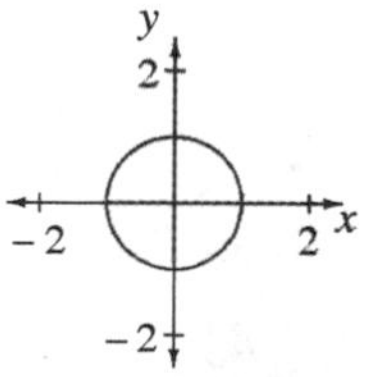

8-124. Find the corresponding inputs or outputs for the following relationships. If there is no solution, explain why not. Be careful: In some cases, there may be no solution or more than one possible solution.

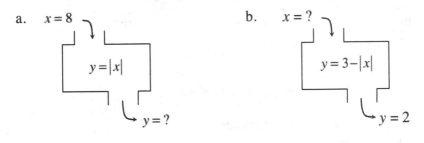

a. $x = 8$

$y = |x|$

$y = ?$

b. $x = ?$

$y = 3 - |x|$

$y = 2$

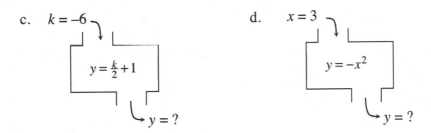

c. $k = -6$

$y = \frac{k}{2} + 1$

$y = ?$

d. $x = 3$

$y = -x^2$

$y = ?$

8-125. Compute each product or quotient. Convert the final answer to scientific notation if necessary.

a. $(6 \times 10^2)(4 \times 10^5)$

b. $(1.75 \times 10^{-2})(8 \times 10^{-8})$

c. $\frac{9 \times 10^5}{4 \times 10^7}$

8-126. Simplify and solve each equation below for x. Show your work and check your answer, if possible.

a. $24 = 3x + 3$

b. $2(x - 6) = y - 14$

c. $3(2x - 3) = 4x - 5$

d. $\frac{3}{4}y = 2x - 6$

8-127. Complete the table.

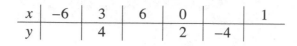

x	−6	3	6	0		1
y		4		2	−4	

a. Find the rule.

b. What is the slope?

c. Is this an example of linear or non-linear growth? Justify your answer.

8-128. The two triangles at right are similar shapes.

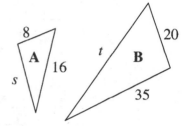

a. What is the scale factor between shape A and shape B?

b. Find the missing sides.

c. If you wanted to make shape A smaller instead of bigger, what is a scale factor you could use?

8-129. Anthony has added a trend line to the scatterplot at right. Do you agree with where he put the line? Explain your reasoning.

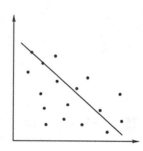

8-130. Find the value of each indicated angle in the following figures. Do not use a protractor. Use the properties of straight and vertical angles to help you.

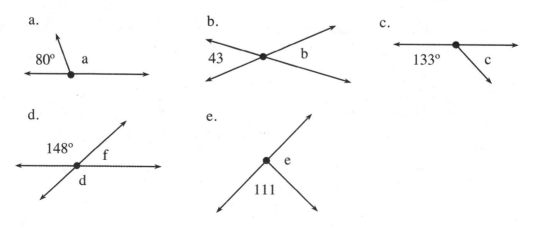

a.

80° a

b.

43 b

c.

133° c

d.

148° f
d

e.

e
111

8-131.   Daniella has $210 in the bank, and her balance is growing at a rate of $3 each month. Lori has $187 in the bank, but her balance is growing at a rate of $4.50 each month. Write a system of equations to find when the girls will have the same amount of money. Be sure to define your variables.

8-132.   A candy store's specialty is taffy. Customers can fill a bag with taffy, and the price is based on how much the candy weighs. The store charges $2 for 10 ounces (oz) of taffy.

   a.   Copy the table below and fill in the missing values. Add three more entries.

Amount of Taffy (oz)	2	5	10	12	15	20
Price ($)			$2			$4

   b.   Graph the values in the table. Let x represent the number of ounces and y represent the price in dollars.

   c.   Is this situation proportional? Explain your reasoning.

   d.   What is the slope of the line you graphed? What information does the slope tell you?

   e.   Write the equation that represents the candy store's pricing.

8-133.   Solve each equation below for the given variable. Be sure to check your solution.

   a. $6x - 11 = 3x + 16$ b. $-2(5 - 3x) + 5 = 9 + 3x$

   c. $\frac{6}{k-2} = 10$ d. $\frac{4}{3x-1} = \frac{2}{x+3}$

8-134.   Compute each product or quotient. Convert the final answer to scientific notation if necessary.

   a. $(2 \times 10^2)(3.2 \times 10^{-5})$ b. $(4 \times 10^2)(2.5 \times 10^{-3})$ c. $\frac{2.5 \times 10^5}{5 \times 10^8}$

8-135. This problem is a checkpoint for transformations.
It will be referred to as Checkpoint 8.

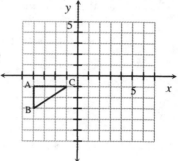

$\triangle ABC$ at right is transformed into $\triangle XYZ$. Tell the
coordinates of the vertices of the new triangle after
each of the following transformations.

a. Translate $\triangle ABC$ 2 units right and 3 units up.

b. Reflect $\triangle ABC$ across the y-axis.

c. Rotate $\triangle ABC$ 90° clockwise about the origin.

d. Dilate $\triangle ABC$ with a scale factor of 2 from the origin.

Check your answers by referring to the Checkpoint 8 materials located at the
back of your book.

If you needed help solving these problems correctly, then you need more
practice. Review the Checkpoint 8 materials and try the practice problems.
Also, consider getting help outside of class time. From this point on, you will
be expected to do problems like these quickly and easily.

Chapter 8 Closure   What have I learned?

Reflection and Synthesis

The activities below offer you a chance to reflect about what you have learned during this chapter. As you work, look for concepts that you feel very comfortable with, ideas that you would like to learn more about, and topics you need more help with.

①   SUMMARIZING MY UNDERSTANDING

This section gives you an opportunity to show what you know about certain math topics or ideas.

THE INTEREST GAME

Today you are going to play a game with your teacher. Your team's goal is to have more money in your account than any other team at the end of the game. You will start with an account balance of $1000. You will record your work and your balances throughout the game on the Chapter 8 Closure Resource Page A. Your team will also need an envelope containing interest rate cards.

To start the game, your teacher will select a card that gives you a time. Record the starting balance and time in the first section on your resource page. Then, as a team, pull a card from the envelope and compute the interest on your account based on the card and the time given to you by your teacher. When you have finished with a card, you will leave it on the desk. Transfer your new account balance to the starting amount in a new section on the resource page. Your teacher will then give you a new time and you will draw another card from your envelope. Your teacher will tell you how many cards to select during the course of the game. While playing the game, ask your teammates the following questions.

- How do we determine compound interest?

- How do we find simple interest?

- How is the interest growing? How can we see this in the interest expression?

Activity continues on next page. →

①   *Activity continued from previous page.*

When playing the Interest Game, you were trying to get the most amount of money in your team account.

a.   What was your final amount?

b.   Did you do more compound-interest or simple-interest problems?

c.   What do you think made the most difference in the amount of money you made, the interest rate or the kind of interest earned (simple or compound)?

②   **WHAT HAVE I LEARNED?**

Doing the problems in this section will help you to evaluate which types of problems you feel comfortable with and which ones you need more help with.

Solve each problem as completely as you can. The table at the end of this closure section provides answers to these problems. It also tells you where you can find additional help and where to find practice problems like them.

CL 8-136.   Rewrite each expression in a simpler form. If it is reasonable, write out the factored form to help you.

a. $3^2 \cdot 3^5$ b. $\frac{4^5}{4^3}$ c. $(3x^2)^4$ d. $(3x^3)(7x^5)$

CL 8-137.   Daniel has \$1200 in the bank. He is earning 3.5% compound interest each month. How much money will he have in the bank in one year?

CL 8-138.   Complete the following table.

Scientific Notation	Standard Form
1.9231×10^3	
	0.00356
	243,700,000
8.149×10^{-6}	

CL 8-139.   Solve each equation or system of equations.

a. $\frac{x+3}{2} = \frac{x-1}{5}$

b. $y = \frac{1}{2}x + 3$
     $y = \frac{1}{3}x - 4$

CL 8-140.   The triangles at right are similar.

a.   Find x.

b.   Find y.

c.   Find the ratio of the perimeters of the two triangles.

CL 8-141.   At a family reunion, each family member recorded his or her age and height.

a.   What kind of association does the scatter plot have?

b.   Copy the scatterplot and draw the trend line.

CL 8-142.   At the farmer's market, Laura bought three pounds of heirloom tomatoes. If the tomatoes are priced at \$8 per five pounds, what did Laura pay for her tomatoes?

CL 8-143.   Matt moved Triangle A on the graph at right to match up with Triangle B in three moves. Follow the steps Matt wrote below. What was his final move?

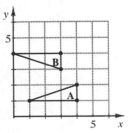

1.   *Slide the triangle up 3 units.*

2.   *Reflect the triangle across the line $y = 4$.*

3.   *?*

CL 8-144.   For each of the problems above, do the following:

- Draw a bar or number line that represents 0 to 10.

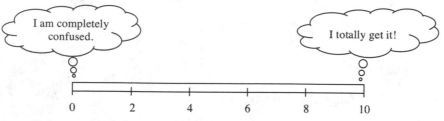

- Color or shade in a portion of the bar that represents your level of understanding and comfort with completing that problem on your own.

If any of your bars are less than a 5, choose *one* of those problems and do one of the following tasks:

- Write two questions that you would like to ask about that problem.
- Brainstorm two things that you DO know about that type of problem.

If all of your bars are a 5 or above, choose one of those problems and do one of these tasks:

- Write two questions you might ask or hints you might give to a student who was stuck on the problem.
- Make a new problem that is similar and more challenging than that problem and solve it.

③   WHAT TOOLS CAN I USE?

You have several tools and references available to help support your learning – your teacher, your study team, your math book, and your Toolkit, to name only a few. At the end of each chapter you will have an opportunity to review your Toolkit for completeness as well as to revise or update it to better reflect your current understanding of big ideas.

The main elements of your Toolkit should be your Learning Log, Math Notes, and the vocabulary used in this chapter. Math words that are new to this chapter appear in bold in the text. Refer to the lists provided below and follow your teacher's instructions to revise your Toolkit, which will help make it a useful reference for you as you complete this chapter and as you work in future chapters.

Learning Log Entries
- Lesson 8.1.3 – Simple and Compound Interest
- Lesson 8.2.1 – Scientific Notation
- Lesson 8.2.3 – Simplifying Exponent Expressions
- Lesson 8.3.1 – Functions

Math Notes

- Lesson 8.1.1 – Simple Interest
- Lesson 8.1.2 – Exponents
- Lesson 8.1.3 – Compound Interest
- Lesson 8.2.3 – Scientific Notation
- Lesson 8.2.4 – Laws of Exponents
- Lesson 8.3.1 – Functions

Mathematical Vocabulary

The following is a list of vocabulary found in this chapter. Some of the words you have been seen in previous chapters. The words in bold are the words new to this chapter. Make sure that you are familiar with the terms below and know what they mean. For the words you do not know, refer to the glossary or index. You might also add these words to your Toolkit so that you can reference them in the future.

base	Commutative Property of Multiplication	
compound interest	**exponent**	**exponential function**
exponential growth	factoring	**function**
interest	linear equation	**linear growth**
linear function	period	principal
relationship	**scientific notation**	simple interest

Answers and Support for Closure Problems
What Have I Learned?

Note: MN = Math Note, LL = Learning Log

Problem	Solution	Need Help?	More Practice
CL 8-136.	a. 3^7 b. 4^2 c. $81x^8$ d. $21x^8$	Lessons 8.2.1, 8.2.2, and 8.2.3 MN: 8.1.2 and 8.2.4 LL: 8.2.3	Problems 8-37, 8-38, 8-47, 8-55, 8-59, 8-65, 8-60, 8-72, 8-73, and 8-85
CL 8-137.	$1813.28	Lesson 8.1.2 MN: 8.1.3	Problems 8-13, 8-14, 8-27, 8-30, and 8-35

Problem	Solution	Need Help?	More Practice
CL 8-138.	<table><tr><th>Scientific Notation</th><th>Standard Form</th></tr><tr><td>1.9231×10^3</td><td>1923.1</td></tr><tr><td>3.56×10^{-3}</td><td>0.00356</td></tr><tr><td>2.437×10^8</td><td>243,700,000</td></tr><tr><td>8.149×10^{-6}</td><td>0.000008149</td></tr></table>	Lessons 8.2.1, 8.2.2, and 8.2.3 MN: 8.2.3 LL: 8.2.1	Problems 8-48, 8-54, 8-84, and 8-88
CL 8-139.	a. $x = -\frac{17}{3}$ b. $y = -18$, $x = -42$	Lessons 2.1.8, 2.1.9, 5.2.2, and 5.2.3 MN: 2.1.8, 2.1.9, 5.2.2, and 5.2.3 LL: 2.1.9	Problems 8-126, 8-131, and 8-133
CL 8-140.	a. 15.75 b. 12.25 c. $\frac{35}{20} = \frac{7}{4}$	Lesson 6.2.2 MN: 6.2.2 and 6.2.6	Problems 8-12, 8-16, and 8-128
CL 8-141.	a. positive association b.	Lessons 7.1.3 and 7.3.2 MN: 7.1.3 and 7.3.2 LL: 7.1.3 and 7.3.2	Problems 8-21, 8-67, 8-111, and 8-129
CL 8-142.	$4.80	Lessons 1.2.1 and 1.2.2 MN: 1.2.2 and 1.2.2 LL: 1.2.1	Problems 8-50, 8-114, and 8-132
CL 8-143.	Slide the triangle left 1 unit.	Lessons 6.1.1 and 6.1.4 MN: 6.1.3 LL: 6.1.3	Problems 8-34, 8-69, 8-98, and 8-135

Angles and the Pythagorean Theorem

9

CHAPTER 9 Angles and the Pythagorean Theorem

This chapter focuses on several important geometry concepts. You will begin to investigate several concepts in this chapter, but you will learn a lot more about them in future courses.

Section 9.1 focuses on angle relationships. The angle relationships you will explore are the ones found with parallel lines and the angles inside and outside of triangles. You will also learn how you can use what you know about angles to decide if a pair of triangles is similar, without even knowing the side lengths!

In Section 9.2, you will focus on the relationships between side lengths in individual triangles. You will learn how to decide if three different lengths will be able to form a triangle and what kind of triangle will be formed. You will use the unique relationship between the side lengths of right triangles to solve problems.

You will also learn some more about numbers. In particular, you will learn the mathematical operation called "square root" and explore how it relates to squaring a number. You will learn how to convert both terminating and repeating decimals to fractions. Finally, you will look at some special numbers called "irrationals."

In this chapter, you will learn how to:

> ➤ Find the measurements of missing angles made by a line that intersects parallel lines.
> ➤ Find unknown angles inside and outside of triangles.
> ➤ Determine if two triangles are similar by looking at their angles.
> ➤ Find missing side lengths of right triangles using the Pythagorean Theorem.
> ➤ Find the square root of a number and identify irrational numbers.
> ➤ Convert terminating and repeating decimals to fractions.

Guiding Questions

Think about these questions throughout this chapter:

How are they related?

Can I make a triangle?

What if it is a right triangle?

What do I know about this triangle?

Chapter Outline

Section 9.1 You will look at angles formed when a third line intersects a set of parallel lines, identifying the relationships between certain pairs of angles. You will also learn about the special relationships between the angles inside and outside a triangle and how to tell if two triangles are similar without knowing anything about their side lengths.

Section 9.2 You will learn how to determine if any three lengths will form a triangle, and, if they do, whether that triangle will be acute, obtuse, or right. You will find missing sides of right triangles using the Pythagorean Theorem. You will also learn about the square root operation and irrational numbers.

9.1.1 How are the angles related?

Parallel Line Angle Pair Relationships

In a previous course you probably learned the vocabulary and considered the relationships created by two intersecting lines. Now you will look at the vocabulary and relationships created by a line that intersects two parallel lines.

9-1.   The box below has some reminders about notation. Read the information, and then use it to complete the following problems.

 Arrowheads at the end of lines indicate that they extend indefinitely. Marks on pairs of lines or segments like **>** and **>>** indicate that the lines (or segments) are **parallel**.

The small box at the point of intersection of two lines or segments indicates that the lines (or segments) are **perpendicular** (that is, form right angles).

In Figure 1 below, line *s* is parallel to line *t*, and line *r* intersects (cuts) line *s* and line *t*. In Figure 2, lines *x* and *y* are *not* parallel, and line *w* intersects lines *x* and *y*. Lines *r* and *w* are called **transversals** because they cut across (intersect) 2 lines. Transversals can also intersect several lines, each at different points.

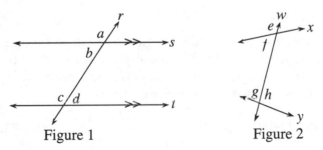

Figure 1   Figure 2

a.   Take a sheet of plain paper (tracing paper is best, but binder paper will work) and place it over ∠*a*. Using a ruler as a guide, make a precise copy of the angle. Slide the copy of ∠*a* to ∠*c* and compare the sizes of the two angles. What do you observe?

b.   Trace a copy of ∠*b* and place it over ∠*d*. What do you observe?

c.   Trace a copy of ∠*e* and place it over ∠*g*. What do you observe?

Problem continues on next page. →

9-1.   *Problem continued from previous page.*

   d.   Trace a copy of ∠*f* and place it over ∠*h*. What do you observe?

   e.   Both figures show two lines that are intersected by a transversal.
        Summarize your findings by describing the relationship between pairs of
        angles and parallel lines cut by a transversal. That is, when the angles are
        congruent, what must be true? And vice versa: If the lines are parallel, then
        what must be true?

9-2.   Your teacher will provide you with a Lesson 9.1.1 Resource Page. On it, you
        will find the figures below. Keep it in an easily accessible place, as you will
        use it in several problems.

        Each figure below shows a pair of <u>parallel</u> <u>lines</u>, *p* and *q*, which are
        intersected (cut) by a third line, *m*. Line *m*, often called a transversal, forms
        several angles at each point of intersection with *p* and *q*. If you need help
        with some of the vocabulary from a previous course, see the Math Notes box in
        this lesson.

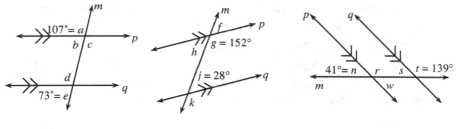

   Figure 1   Figure 2   Figure 3

   a.   Use what you know about straight angles to calculate the measures of these
        angles: *b*, *d*, *f*, *k*, *r*, and *s*. When everyone in your team has completed
        the calculations and agrees with the results, check with your team to be sure
        that everyone agrees that the results are correct.

   b.   Keep in mind that lines *p* and *q* must be parallel as you complete the
        directions below.

        • In Figure 1, compare the measures of angles *a* and *d*, and then
           compare the measures of angles *b* and *e*.

        • In Figure 2, compare the measures of angles *f* and *j*, and then compare
           the measures of angles *g* and *k*.

        • In Figure 3, make similar comparisons for angles *n* and *s*, and then for
           angles *r* and *t*.

Problem continues on next page. →

9-2.   *Problem continued from previous page.*

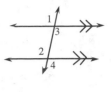

Angles on the same side of two lines and on the same side
of a third line (the transversal) that intersects the two lines
are called **corresponding angles**. In the figure at right,
angles 1 and 2 are corresponding angles, as are angles 3
and 4. Other examples of corresponding angles are on
your resource page: angles *a* and *d* in Figure 1, angles *g*
and *k* in Figure 2, and angles *r* and *t* in Figure 3.

c.   A **conjecture** is an inference or judgment based on incomplete evidence.
Use the definition above and your observations in part (b) to complete the
following conjecture.

   Conjecture: If two parallel lines are cut by a transversal, then pairs of
                corresponding angles are ___.

9-3.   Now focus on a different set of angles on the Lesson 9.1.1 Resource Page.

a.   Use what you know about straight angles and/or vertical angles and your
results from the previous problem to find the measures of angles *c*
(Figure 1), *h* (Figure 2), and *w* (Figure 3).

b.   Compare the measures of the following three pairs of angles.

   •   Figure 1: $m\angle c$ and $m\angle d$

   •   Figure 2: $m\angle h$ and $m\angle j$

   •   Figure 3: $m\angle w$ and $m\angle s$

   How is each pair of angles related?

c.   Read the following definition, and then use it along with your observation
in part (a) to complete the conjecture that follows.

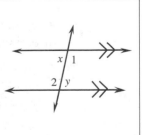

Angles between a pair of lines and on opposite sides
of a transversal are called **alternate interior angles**.
In the figure at right, angles 1 and 2 and angles *x* and
y are examples of *pairs* of alternate interior angles.
Other examples of alternate interior angles are on
your resource page: angles *c* and *d* in Figure 1,
angles *h* and *j* in Figure 2, and angles *w* and *s* in
Figure 3.

   Conjecture: If parallel lines are cut by a transversal, then alternate interior
                angles are _____.

9-4.   Use Figures 1 through 3 on the Lesson 9.1.1 Resource Page from problems 9-2 and 9-3.

a. Examine the pairs of angles b and d, g and j, and r and s on the resource page. If you add the measures of each *pair*, what do you observe?

b. Write a conjecture about two angles on the *same side* of a transversal and are *between* two parallel lines. Note: These are called **same side interior angles**.

Conjecture: The sum of the measures of two interior angles on the same side of a transversal is ____.

Use your conjecture and the figure below right to answer parts (c) and (d).

c. If $m\angle 2 = 67°$, what is $m\angle 5$?

d. If $m\angle 4 = 4x + 23°$ and $m\angle 6 = 3x + 17°$, find $m\angle 4$. Explain your steps.

9-5.   Classify each of the following pairs of angles as corresponding, alternate interior, same side interior, straight, or "none of these."

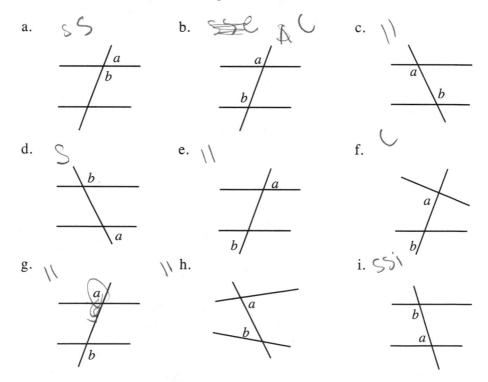

a.   sS

b.

c.

d.   S

e.

f.

g.

h.

i. SSi

j. What condition is necessary to be able to say that the pairs of corresponding angles or alternate interior angles above are equal?

9-6.   Use your conjectures about parallel lines and the angles formed by a transversal to find the measures of the labeled angles. These figures are also on the Lesson 9.1.1 Resource Page. Show the step-by-step procedure you use *and* name each angle conjecture you use (e.g., corresponding, alternate interior, vertical, or straight) to justify your calculation.

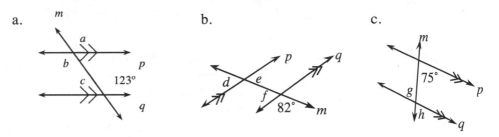

a.   b.   c.

9-7.   LEARNING LOG

What are the angle relationships that you have encountered so far? Answer this question in your Learning Log. Use your geometry vocabulary and include diagrams to show the relationships. Title this entry "Angle Relationships" and label it with today's date.

METHODS AND MEANINGS

Angle Vocabulary

MATH NOTES

It is common to identify angles using three letters. For example, ∠*ABC* means the angle you would find by going from point *A* to point *B* to point *C* in the diagram at right. Point *B* is the **vertex** of the angle (where the endpoints of the two sides meet), and $\overrightarrow{BA}$ and $\overrightarrow{BC}$ are the rays that define it. A **ray** is a part of a line that has an endpoint (starting point) and extends infinitely in one direction.

If two angles have measures that add up to 90°, they are called **complementary angles**. For example, in the diagram above, ∠*ABC* and ∠*CBD* are complementary because together they form a right angle.

If two angles have measures that add up to 180°, they are called **supplementary angles**. For example, in the diagram at right, ∠*EFG* and ∠*GFH* are supplementary because together they form a **straight angle** (that is, together they form a line).

Two angles do not have to share a vertex to be complementary or supplementary. The first pair of angles at right are supplementary; the second pair of angles are complementary.

Supplementary   **Complementary**

Adjacent angles are angles that have a common vertex, share a common side, and have no interior points in common. So angles ∠*c* and ∠*d* in the diagram at right are adjacent angles, as are ∠*c* and ∠*f*, ∠*f* and ∠*g*, and ∠*g* and ∠*d*.

Vertical angles are the two opposite (that is, non-adjacent) angles formed by two intersecting lines, such as angles ∠*c* and ∠*g* in the diagram above right. By itself, ∠*c* is not a vertical angle, nor is ∠*g*, although ∠*c* and ∠*g* together are a pair of vertical angles. Vertical angles always have equal measure.

9-8.   Use the conjectures and definitions in this lesson to solve parts (a) and (b). Each part is a separate problem.

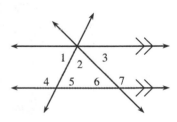

a.   If $m\angle 1 = 63°$, find $m\angle 2$ and $m\angle 3$ by calculation.

b.   If $m\angle 1 = 74°$ and $m\angle 4 = 3x - 18°$, write an equation and find x.

c.   If $m\angle 2 = 3x - 9°$ and $m\angle 1 = x + 25°$, write an equation to find x. Then find $m\angle 2$.

9-9.   If $m\angle 5 = 53°$ and $m\angle 7 = 125°$, find the measures of each numbered angle. Then explain how you found each angle, citing definitions and conjectures that support your steps.

9-10.   Graph the following data as a scatterplot.

Height (Inches)	Test Scores (Percent)
24	3
56	86
72	98
49	50
18	0
36	12
70	90
66	81
61	75
34	25
59	80
57	77
64	88

a.   Does the graph show either a positive or a negative association?

b.   Does there appear to be an association between height and spelling ability?

c.   Does greater height cause better spelling ability?

d.   What other factors could create the association you see?

9-11.   Josue called his father to say that he was almost home. He had traveled 61.5 miles, which was $\frac{3}{4}$ of the way home. Write and solve an equation to calculate the total distance he will travel to get home.

9-12.   Ryan and Janelle are each driving from a different location to meet. When they each stopped for lunch at 12 noon, they called each other on their cell phones. Ryan had traveled 245 miles in $3\frac{1}{2}$ hours. Janelle had driven 260 miles in 4 hours.

If Ryan and Janelle were originally 910 miles apart when they had started driving that morning, at what time will they meet?

9-13.   Determine whether the graphs below are functions or not functions. Explain your reasoning.

a.

b.

c.

d.

e.

f.

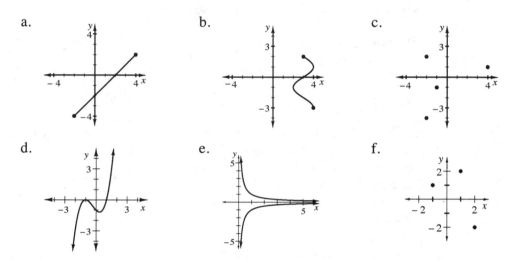

9.1.2 How can I find a missing angle?

Finding Unknown Angles in Triangles

In today's lesson, you will be challenged again to use what you *do* know to determine information that you did *not* previously know, in order to solve problems with variables. You will do an investigation to learn a new geometric relationship for triangles.

9-14.   Quigley was excited about what he had learned about angles. He went home, grabbed his older brother's math book, and tried to find some problems that he could do with angles. He came across the following problem that he wanted to solve.

Solve for x in this figure:

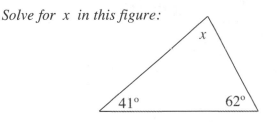

a.   Using what you have learned about angles, can you find the measure of the angle? Why or why not?

b.   Estimate the measure of the angle.

9-15.   TANGLED TRIANGLES

Your teacher will give your team a copy of the Lesson 9.1.2 Resource Page. Cut out the three copies of the triangle.

Your Task: Determine the measure of the missing angle *without* using a protractor. As you work with your team, the following questions might help guide your discussion.

What do we know about angles?

Can we combine the unknown angle with any other angles to create a new angle that we do know?

9-16.   Be prepared to contribute what your team has discovered to a
         whole-class discussion. Your teacher will use a technology
         tool to show what each team has discovered for their triangle.
         Keep track of what each team has found to see if you can find a
         relationship that would allow you to find a missing angle in *any*
         triangle.

9-17.   Now use what you have discovered about the angles in a triangle to find the
         answer to the problem that Quigley was trying to solve in problem 9-14. How
         close was your estimate?

9-18.   Use what you have learned about triangles and angles to write an equation that
         represents each situation. Then find each of the missing angle(s) in the
         triangles below.

a.

b.

9-19.   **Additional Challenge:** Use what you know about triangles and angle
         relationships to find the missing angles in the triangles below.

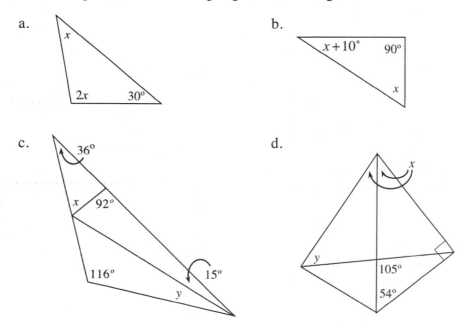

a.

b.

c.

d.

9-20.   LEARNING LOG

Today you explored a fundamental concept about a
triangle and the sum of its angles. In your Learning Log,
state this relationship in your own words and include at
least one example that shows how to use this idea. Title
this entry "Angles in a Triangle" and label it with today's date.

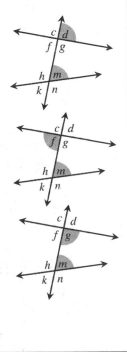

MATH NOTES

METHODS AND MEANINGS

Parallel Lines and Angle Pairs

Corresponding angles lie in the same
position but at different points of intersection of the
transversal. For example, in the diagram at right,
∠*m* and ∠*d* form a pair of corresponding angles,
since both of them are to the right of the transversal
and above the intersecting line. Corresponding
angles are congruent when the lines intersected by
the transversal are parallel.

∠*f* and ∠*m* are **alternate interior angles** because
one is to the left of the transversal, one is to the
right, and both are between (inside) the pair of lines.
Alternate interior angles are congruent when the
lines intersected by the transversal are parallel.

∠*g* and ∠*m* are **same side interior angles** because
both are on the same side of the transversal and both
are between the pair of lines. Same side interior
angles are supplementary when the lines intersected
by the transversal are parallel.

9-21. Find the measure of the missing angle in each triangle below and then classify the triangle as acute, right, or obtuse.

a.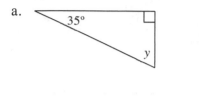

b.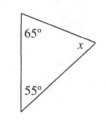

9-22. Find the measures of the angles requested and explain how you found them. Each part is a separate problem.

a. If $m\angle 4 = 61°$, find $m\angle 6$.

b. If $m\angle 1 = 48°$, find $m\angle 8$.

c. If $m\angle 2 = 137°$, find $m\angle 8$.

9-23. Graph the rule $y = 2x - 6$. Create a table if it will help.

9-24. On graph paper, graph the data in the table at right. Is there an association?

Age of Car (years)	Avg. Miles per Gallon
7	28
2	36
5	29
1	42
4	32
10	16
2	39
3	35
8	18

9-25. Tina's rectangular living room floor measures 15 feet by 18 feet.

a. How many square feet of carpet will Tina need to cover the entire floor?

b. The carpet Tina likes is sold by the square yard. How many square yards will she need?

9-26. Solve for y in terms of x. That is, rewrite each equation so that it starts with "$y =$".

a. $6x + 5y = 20$

b. $4x - 8y = 16$

9.1.3 What if the angle is on the outside?

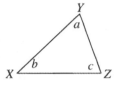

Exterior Angles in Triangles

So far in this section, you have investigated angle relationships in situations with parallel lines and within triangles. In this lesson, you will continue to look at angle relationships. This time, you will investigate the angle relationships on the inside and outside of a triangle.

9-27. Use the diagram at right to name each of the indicated angles below using three letters. Reread the Math Notes box in Lesson 9.1.1 if you need to remember how to do this.

a. $\angle a$ b. $\angle b$ c. $\angle c$

9-28. Read the information below. Then follow the directions that follow.

> **Exterior angles** are formed by extending a side of the triangle. The two angles across the triangle from the exterior angle are called **remote interior angles**. In each figure located below part (a), $\angle A$ and $\angle B$ are remote interior angles with respect to exterior angle $\angle BCD$.

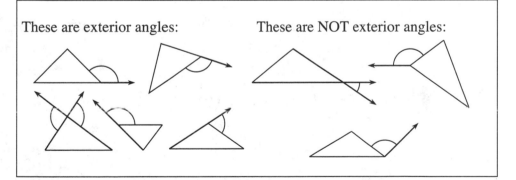

These are exterior angles: These are NOT exterior angles:

a. On the Lesson 9.1.3 Resource Page provided by your teacher, calculate the missing angle measures in each figure and record them in the table. When you have completed the resource page, look for a pattern in the relationship between the measure of $\angle BCD$ (the exterior angle) and the sum of the measures of $\angle A$ and $\angle B$ (the remote interior angles). (Note that $m\angle BCD$ means the *measure* of $\angle BCD$. Similarly, $m\angle A$ means the measure of $\angle A$.)

Problem continues on next page. →

9-28.   *Problem continued from previous page.*

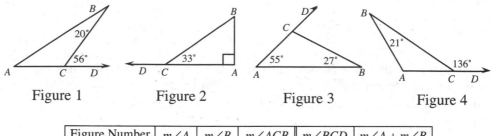

Figure Number	$m\angle A$	$m\angle B$	$m\angle ACB$	$m\angle BCD$	$m\angle A + m\angle B$
1					
2					
3					
4					

b.   Compare your results for $m\angle BCD$ (the exterior angle) and the sum of $m\angle A$ and $m\angle B$ (the remote interior angles) for each figure. Discuss your observations with your team.

c.   Write a conjecture about the relationship of an exterior angle to the two remote interior angles.

9-29.   Calculate the measures of the angles requested. Each part is a separate problem.

a.   If $m\angle 1 = 53°$ and $m\angle 2 = 71°$, find $m\angle 4$.

b.   If $m\angle 2 = 78°$ and $m\angle 4 = 127°$, find $m\angle 1$.

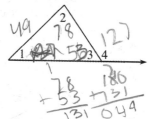

9-30.   Use your conjecture from part (c) of problem 9-28 to solve for x in each figure below.

a.   b.   c.

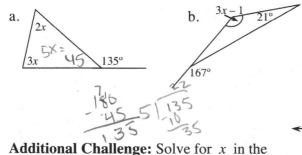

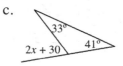

9-31.   **Additional Challenge:** Solve for x in the figure at right.

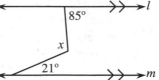

Core Connections, Course 3

9-32.   **LEARNING LOG**

Look back at the entry that you created in Lesson 9.1.1 ("Angle Relationships"). Add to that entry the angle relationships that you learned in this lesson. Use appropriate geometry vocabulary and include diagrams.

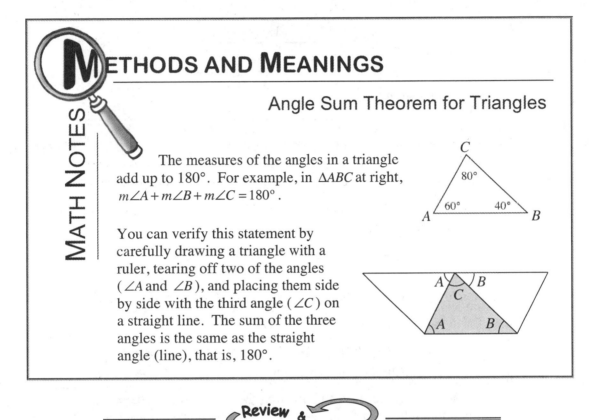

METHODS AND **M**EANINGS

Angle Sum Theorem for Triangles

The measures of the angles in a triangle add up to 180°. For example, in $\triangle ABC$ at right, $m\angle A + m\angle B + m\angle C = 180°$.

You can verify this statement by carefully drawing a triangle with a ruler, tearing off two of the angles ($\angle A$ and $\angle B$), and placing them side by side with the third angle ($\angle C$) on a straight line. The sum of the three angles is the same as the straight angle (line), that is, 180°.

Review & Preview

9-33.   Based on the given information, determine which pairs of lines, if any, are parallel. If none are necessarily parallel, write "none."

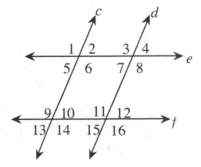

a. $m\angle 2 = m\angle 7$

b. $m\angle 3 = m\angle 11$

c. $m\angle 1 = m\angle 12$

d. $m\angle 13 = m\angle 12$

e. $\angle 6$ and $\angle 7$ are supplementary.

9-34.   In each angle problem below, solve for the variable(s). Write the names of the
         definition(s) and relationship(s) that justify the steps in your solution.

a.   b.   c.

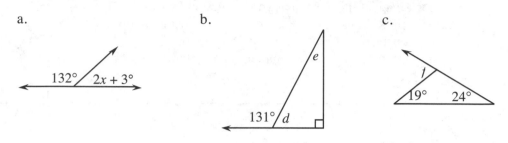

9-35.   Simplify each expression.

a. $\frac{5}{4} \div \frac{7}{16}$ b. $-\frac{10}{13} \cdot \frac{5}{11}$ c. $\frac{9}{11} \div (-\frac{20}{21})$ d. $-\frac{8}{3} \div (-\frac{5}{18})$

9-36.   Simplify and solve each equation below for x. Show your work and check your
         answer.

a. $24 = 3x + 3$ b. $2(x - 6) = x - 14$

c. $3(2x - 3) = 4x - 5$ d. $\frac{3}{4}x = 2x - 5$

9-37.   Joaquin has agreed to lend his younger brother $45 so that he can buy a new
         tank for his pet lizard.

a. Joaquin is charging his brother 2% simple interest per month. If his brother
    pays him back in 6 months, how much will Joaquin get back?

b. If Joaquin's brother instead borrowed the money from a bank at 2%
    compound interest per month, how much would he have to pay the bank at
    the end of 6 months?

9-38.   Martha is saving money to buy a new laptop computer that costs $1800. She
         received $200 for her birthday and has a job where she makes $150 each week.

a. Make a table and a graph for this situation.

b. Explain how you can use the table or graph to predict how many weeks it
    will take Martha to earn enough money to pay for the new computer.

c. Explain how you can tell from both the table and the graph whether this is
    an example of linear or non-linear growth.

9.1.4 Can angles show similarity?

AA Triangle Similarity

In Chapter 6 you learned that you can create similar figures by using dilations. Today you will investigate what happens to the angles in a figure when you enlarge or reduce the figure to create a similar figure.

9-39. ANGLES IN SIMILAR FIGURES

    a. Using a sheet of graph paper and a straightedge, graph the quadrilateral $M(0, 3)$, $N(4, 0)$, $P(2, -2)$, $Q(-2, 1)$.

    b. Enlarge the quadrilateral by a scale factor of 2.

    c. What do you notice about side MN and side $M'N'$? Explain.

    d. What can you say about $\angle M$ and $\angle M'$? Explain your reasoning. Hint: Extend sides MN and QM.

    e. Remember that a conjecture is an inference or judgment based on incomplete evidence. Based on your work in this problem so far, make a conjecture about the angles in similar figures.

    f. Test your conjecture in part (e) using a figure of your own design and a different scale factor. Each team member should create a different figure. Compare your work with your teammates' work. Does your conjecture seem to work always, sometimes, or never?

9-40. Imagine that two pairs of corresponding angles in two triangles are of equal measure. What could you then conclude about the third set of angles? Justify your answer and draw a diagram.

9-41. Use your conjecture from part (e) of problem 9-39 along with your work from problem 9-40 to explain how you can use the angles in a pair of triangles to determine if they are similar. Be sure to include how many angles you need and what needs to be true about them.

9-42. The relationship in the previous problem is called **Angle-Angle Similarity** and is written AA~. The symbol ~ means "similarity" or "is similar to." In the figure at right, is ∆*ABC* ~ ∆*EDC* (that is, is ∆*ABC* similar to ∆*EDC*)? Explain your reasoning.

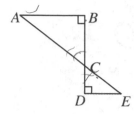

9-43. Eleanor and John were working on a geometry problem together. They knew that in the figure below, line *m* is parallel to side *BC*. They wanted to find the side lengths of each triangle. First they decided that they needed to show that ∆*AED* ~ ∆*ABC*.

Eleanor said, *"This is easy. We have parallel lines, so the triangles are similar by AA~."*

"Hold on a minute!" John replied, *"Which angles are equal?"*

a. Using the diagram at right, name the pairs of equal angles Eleanor sees. Why are they equal?

b. Are the triangles (∆*AED* and ∆*ABC*) similar? Explain.

c. Now that John sees how the triangles are similar, he suggests redrawing them separately as shown at right. *"Look,"* he says, *"Now we just write a proportion."* He suggests the following equation:

$$\frac{3}{3+5} = \frac{x}{x+8}$$

Explain how John came up with this equation.

d. Solve the proportion equation in part (c) for *x* and check you answer.

9-44. LEARNING LOG

What is Angle-Angle Similarity? What does it tell you about a pair of triangles? In your Learning Log, explain the relationship and how you can use it. Be sure to include a diagram. Title this entry "Angle-Angle Similarity" and include today's date.

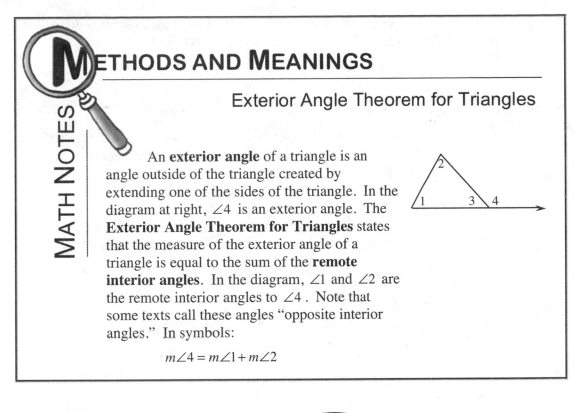
Review & Preview

9-45. △*ABC* is similar to △*DEF* .

a. Find the scale factor from △*ABC* to △*DEF* .

b. Find *x*.

c. Find *y*.

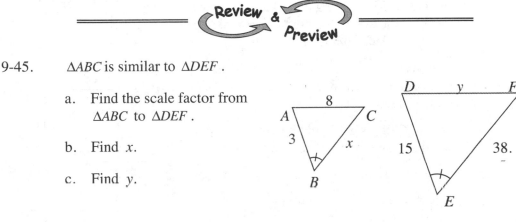

9-46. Sketch an example of each type of graph described below.

a. linear and decreasing

b. non-linear and increasing

9-47. Louis recorded how many times he could jump rope without stopping. Here is his data:

50 15 102 64 29 55 100 97 48 81 61

Find the median, first quartile, and third quartile of his data.

9-48.   Solve the system of equations at right by each of the ways described in parts (a) and (b) below. Then compare your answers in part (c).

   a.   Graph the system on graph paper. Then write its solution (the point of intersection) in (x, y) form.

$$y = -x + 1$$
$$y = 2x + 7$$

   b.   Now solve the system using the Equal Values Method.

   c.   Did your solution in part (b) match your result from part (a)? If not, check your work carefully and look for any mistakes in your algebraic process or on your graph.

9-49.   Use what you know about the angles in a triangle to find x in each diagram below. Show all work. Then classify each triangle as acute, right, or obtuse.

   a. x, $40°$, $80°$

   b. $96°$, $2x$, $x + 12°$

9-50.   This problem is a checkpoint for scatterplots and association. It will be referred to as Checkpoint 9.

Jason is interested in buying a used Panda hybrid car because he heard of its incredible gas mileage. Jason collected data from listings on the Internet.

Age of Car (years)	Listed Cost (in 1000s)
5	20
3	26
4	24
2	29
8	11
9	8
3	25
10	6

   a.   Jason would like to know the typical cost of advertised Pandas. What kind of a graphical display should he use?

   b.   What type of graph should be used to display the relationship between age and cost?

   c.   Make a scatterplot of the data.

   d.   Fully describe the association.

   e.   Draw a line of best fit for the data. Find the equation of the line of best fit.

   f.   Use the equation to predict the expected cost of a 6-year-old car.

   g.   Interpret the slope and y-intercept in context.

Check your answers by referring to the Checkpoint 9 materials located at the back of your book.

If you needed help solving these problems correctly, then you need more practice. Review the Checkpoint 9 materials and try the practice problems. Also consider getting help outside of class time. From this point on, you will be expected to do problems like this one quickly and easily.

9.2.1 What kind of triangle can I make?

Side Lengths and Triangles

Triangles are made of three sides. But can any three lengths make a triangle? Is it possible to predict what kind of triangle – obtuse, acute, or right – three side lengths will make? Today, you will investigate these questions with your team.

9-51.   IS IT A TRIANGLE?

When do three lengths form a triangle? Are there special patterns in lengths that always make obtuse triangles? Or are there combinations of lengths that make right or acute triangles? To investigate these questions, you and your study team will build triangles and look for patterns that will allow you to predict what kind of triangle three lengths will make.

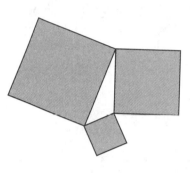

Discussion Points

How can we organize our data?

What other combinations can we make?

What do we expect will happen?

Your Task: Your teacher will provide you with three resource pages for this activity. Carefully cut out each square on the Lesson 9.2.1A Resource Page, shown at right. Using different combinations of three squares, decide if a triangle can be made by connecting the corners of the squares. If you can make a triangle, what kind of triangle is it? (The angle on the Lesson 9.2.1B Resource Page can help you determine if an angle is a right (90°) angle.) Record the side lengths and areas for each combination of squares you try on the Lesson 9.2.1C (or D) Resource Page. Complete the other columns of the chart.

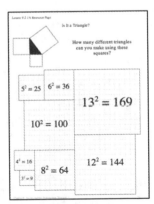

9-52.   Look at your data for the combinations that did *not* form triangles.

- What do you notice about how the three side lengths compare to each other?

- How are the sets of three side lengths that did not form triangles different from the sets of side lengths that *did* form triangles? Be as specific as you can.

When your team has reached a conclusion, copy and complete the two statements below in your Learning Log. Title your entry "Triangle Inequality" and include examples and today's date.

Three side lengths WILL NOT make a triangle if...

Three side lengths WILL make a triangle if...

9-53.   Look at the data that you collected for the acute, obtuse, and right triangles. What patterns do you see between the sum of the areas of the two smaller squares and the area of the larger square that formed the triangles in each row? Copy and complete the sentence starters below in your Learning Log to summarize the patterns that you see. Title the entry "Triangle Side-Length Patterns" and include some examples along with the date.

If three squares have sides that make an acute triangle, *then the sum of the areas of the two small squares...*

If three squares have sides that make an obtuse triangle, *then the sum of the areas of the two small squares...*

If three squares have sides that make a right triangle, *then the sum of the areas of the two small squares...*

9-54.   Use the patterns you found to predict whether each set of lengths below will form a triangle. If a set will form a triangle, state whether the triangle will be acute, obtuse, or right. Justify your conclusion.

a.   5 cm, 6 cm, and 7 cm   b.   2 cm, 11 cm, 15 cm

c.   10 cm, 15 cm, 20 cm   d.   10 cm, 24 cm, 26 cm

e.   1 cm, 3 cm, 9 cm   f.   2 cm, 10 cm, 11 cm

Core Connections, Course 3

9-55.   **Additional Challenge:** Lewis wants to build an obtuse triangle. He has already decided to use a square with an area of 81 square units and a square with an area of 25 square units.

   a.   What area of square could he use to form the third side of his triangle? Explain your reasoning.

   b.   If he makes an acute triangle instead, what size square should he use? Explain your reasoning.

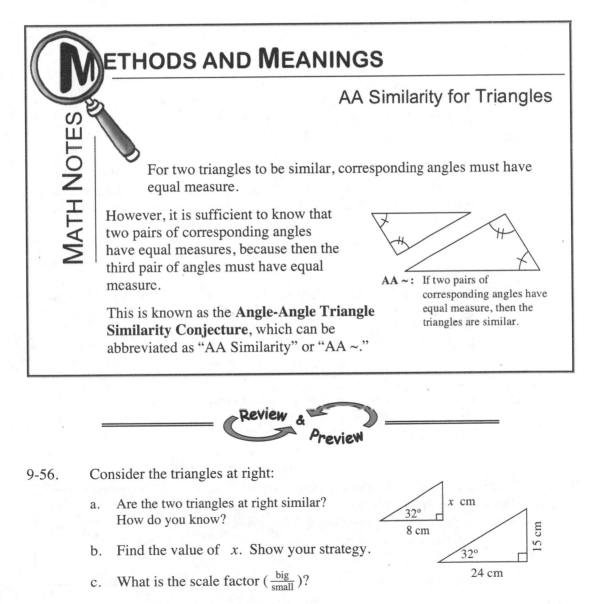

METHODS AND MEANINGS

AA Similarity for Triangles

MATH NOTES

For two triangles to be similar, corresponding angles must have equal measure.

However, it is sufficient to know that two pairs of corresponding angles have equal measures, because then the third pair of angles must have equal measure.

This is known as the **Angle-Angle Triangle Similarity Conjecture**, which can be abbreviated as "AA Similarity" or "AA ~."

AA ~: If two pairs of corresponding angles have equal measure, then the triangles are similar.

Review & Preview

9-56.   Consider the triangles at right:

   a.   Are the two triangles at right similar? How do you know?

   b.   Find the value of x. Show your strategy.

   c.   What is the scale factor ($\frac{big}{small}$)?

   d.   Find the area of each triangle.

9-57.   Jenna is working with three squares. Their areas are 16 cm², 9 cm², and 36 cm². She thinks they will make an obtuse triangle. Do you agree? Explain your reasoning.

9-58.   Copy and complete the following table.

x	5		4		−2	3
y	−17	−5		−2	4	−11

a.   What is the rule?

b.   What is the slope?

9-59.   Write an equation to represent the situation below, and then answer the question.

Ella is trying to determine the side lengths of a triangle. She knows that the longest side is three times longer than the shortest side. The medium side is ten more than twice the shortest side. If the perimeter is 142 cm, how long is each side?

9-60.   Cisco was looking at a table of values for the rule $y = x^2$. She said, "*This table contains* $(0,0)$, *so I think it shows a proportional relationship.*" Is Cisco correct? Why or why not?

9-61.   Solve these equations for x. Check your answers.

a. $2(x + 4.5) = 32$ b. $6 + 2.5x = 21$ c. $\frac{x}{9} = \frac{5}{16}$

9-62.   What kind of triangle will the edges of the squares at right form? What will the side lengths be?

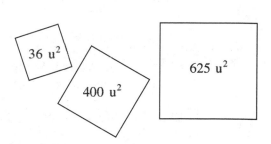

9-63.   Determine by inspection whether the lines in each system below intersect, coincide, or are parallel. Do not actually solve the systems. Justify your reasons.

a. $y = 2x + 3$
     $y = \frac{1}{2}x - 2$

b. $2x + 3y = 6$
     $2x + 3y = 9$

c. $y = \frac{1}{3}x + 2$
     $y = \frac{1}{3}x - 2$

d. $x - 2y = 4$
     $-2x + 4y = -8$

9-64.   Use the graph below to answer the following questions.

a.   What kind of growth does this graph show? How do you know?

b.   What is this graph describing? Write an appropriate title for the graph.

c.   How far from home is the person when the graph starts?

d.   How fast is the person traveling? Explain how you can use the graph to determine the rate of travel.

e.   Write an equation to represent the line on the graph.

9-65.   Eric set up this ratio for two similar triangles:

$\frac{x}{12} = \frac{5}{9}$

He solved the problem and found $x \approx 6.67$. What was his mistake?

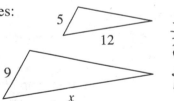

9-66.   If one atom of carbon weighs 1.99×10^{-22} g and one atom of hydrogen weighs 1.67×10^{-27} g, which element weighs more? Explain your choice.

9-67.   Andrea wants to have $9500 to travel to France when she is 22. She currently has $5976 in a savings account earning 5% annual compound interest. Andrea is 14 now.

a.   If she does not take out or deposit any money, how much money will Andrea have when she is 18?

b.   Will Andrea have enough money for her trip when she is 22?

9.2.2 What is special about a right triangle?

Pythagorean Theorem

In Lesson 9.2.1, you saw that for three lengths to form a triangle, they must be related to each other in a special way. Today, you will investigate a special relationship between the side lengths of right triangles. This relationship will allow you to find the length of a missing side.

9-68.   Use your patterns from Lesson 9.2.1 to decide if the squares listed below will form a right triangle.

   a.   Squares with side lengths 6, 8, and 10 meters

   b.   Squares with areas 64 in², 100 in², 144 in²

   c.   Two squares with side length 5 feet and a square with area 50 square feet

   d.   Explain how you know whether three squares will join at their corners to form a right triangle.

9-69.   THE PYTHAGOREAN RELATIONSHIP

   Based on your work so far, if you know the area of three squares, you can tell if they will connect at their corners to form a right triangle. But what if you know that a triangle has a right angle? Will the lengths of the sides be related in this way? Work with your team to look more closely at side lengths of some right triangles.

   a.   On centimeter graph paper, form a right angle by drawing one 5-cm length and one 12-cm length as shown at right. If you do not have centimeter graph paper, then use any graph paper to draw and measure these lengths with a ruler. After drawing the two lengths, create a right triangle by connecting the ends of the two lengths with a third side.

   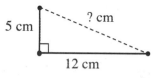

   b.   With a ruler, measure the longest side of the triangle in centimeters and label this length. If you do not have a centimeter ruler or you are using another kind of graph paper, create your triangle using 5 and 7 grid units. Then use an edge of the page and the grid lines as your ruler.

Problem continues on next page. →

9-69.   *Problem continued from previous page.*

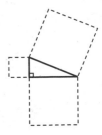

c. Visualize a square connected to each side of the right
    triangle in part (b). On your paper, sketch a picture like
    the one at right. What is the area of each square? Is the
    area of the square that is connected to the longest side
    equal to the sum of the areas of the other two squares?

d. Check this pattern with a new example.

    - Draw a new right angle on the centimeter paper like you did in
      part (a). This time, use 9-cm and 12-cm lengths.

    - Connect the endpoints to create a triangle, and measure the third
      side.

    - Create a sketch for this triangle like the one you created in part (c),
      and find the areas of the squares.

    Is the area of the square that is connected to the longest side equal to the
    sum of the other two areas?

e. The two shortest sides of a right triangle are called the
    legs, and the longest side is called the **hypotenuse**.

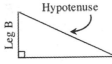

    You previously wrote a statement about the relationship
    between the areas of squares drawn on the sides of a right triangle. Now
    use words to describe the relationship between the *lengths* of the legs and
    the *length* of the hypotenuse.

9-70.   The relationship you described in part (e) of problem 9-69 is called the
         Pythagorean Theorem. It states that in a right triangle, the length of one leg
         squared plus the length of the other leg squared is equal to the length of the
         hypotenuse squared. It can be written as an equation like this:

$$(\text{leg A})^2 + (\text{leg B})^2 = (\text{hypotenuse})^2$$

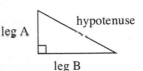

         Use the Pythagorean Theorem to write an equation for
         each diagram below. Then find each missing area.

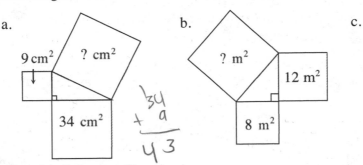

a. 9 cm²   ? cm²
    34 cm²

b. ? m²   12 m²   8 m²

c. 25 ft²   10 ft²   ? ft²

9-71.   In Lesson 9.2.1 you found a relationship between the squares of the sides of triangle and the type of triangle (acute, obtuse, or right). You discovered that if the sum of the squares of the two shortest sides in a triangle equals the square of the length of the longest side, then the triangle is a right triangle. Use this idea to determine whether the lengths listed below form a right triangle. Explain your reasoning.

   a.   15 feet, 36 feet, and 39 feet

   b.   20 inches, 21 inches, and 29 inches

   c.   8 yards, 9 yards, and 12 yards

   d.   4 meters, 7 meters, and 8 meters

9-72.   Find the area of the square in each picture below.

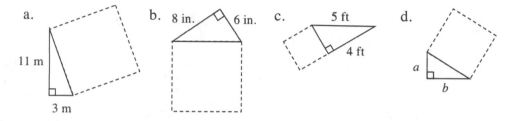

a.   11 m   3 m

b.   8 in.   6 in.

c.   5 ft   4 ft

d.   a   b

9-73.   How long is the missing side of each triangle in parts (b) and (c) of problem 9-72? Be prepared to explain your reasoning.

METHODS AND MEANINGS

Triangle Inequality and Side-Length Patterns

The **Triangle Inequality** establishes the required relationships for three lengths to form a triangle. You can also use these lengths to determine the type of triangle they form — acute, obtuse, or right — by comparing the squares of the lengths of the sides as described below.

For any three lengths to form a triangle, the sum of the lengths of any two sides must be greater than the length of the third side.

For example, the lengths 3 cm, 10 cm, and 11 cm will form a triangle, because:

$$3 + 10 > 11$$
$$3 + 11 > 10$$
$$10 + 11 > 3$$

The lengths 5 m, 7 m, and 15 m will not form a triangle, because $5 + 7 = 12$, and $12 \ngtr 15$.

Acute triangle: The sum of the squares of the lengths of the two shorter sides is greater than the square of the length of the longest side.

Obtuse triangle: The sum of the squares of the lengths of the two shorter sides is less than the square of the length of the longest side.

Right triangle: The sum of the squares of the lengths of the two shorter sides is equal to the square of the length of the longest side.

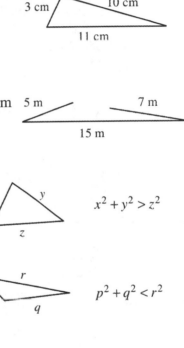

$$x^2 + y^2 > z^2$$

$$p^2 + q^2 < r^2$$

$$a^2 + b^2 = c^2$$

9-74.   If you have 24 square tiles, how many different rectangles can you make? Each rectangle must use all of the tiles and have no holes or gaps. Sketch each rectangle on graph paper and label its length and width. Can you make a square with 24 tiles?

9-75.   Lydia has four straws of different lengths, and she is trying to form a right triangle. The lengths are 8, 9, 15, and 17 units. Which three lengths should she use? Justify your answer.

9-76.   The Wild West Frontier Park now offers an unlimited day pass. For $29.00, visitors can go on as many rides as they want. The original plan charged visitors $8.75 to enter the park, plus $2.25 for each ride. Write an equation to determine the number of rides that would make the total cost equal for the two plans. Solve the equation.

9-77.   a.   Write the rule for the table at right.

b.   What is the slope?

c.   What is the y-intercept?

x	4	$\frac{1}{2}$	−2		−1	7
y	−11		1	−3	−1	

9-78.   Solve for x. Each part is a separate problem.

a.   If $m\angle 1 = 3x - 18°$ and $m\angle 5 = 2x + 12°$, find x.

b.   If $m\angle 3 = 4x - 27°$ and $m\angle 6 = x + 39°$, find x.

c.   If $m\angle 4 = 49°$ and $m\angle 6 = 5x + 41°$, find x.

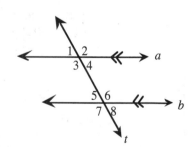

9-79.   Calculate the value of x.

a.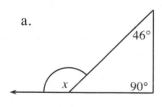

b.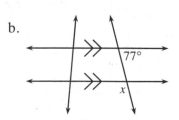

9.2.3 How can I find the side length?

Understanding Square Root

You have developed a way to decide if a triangle is a right triangle by looking at the squares of the side lengths of the triangle. If you already know a triangle is a right triangle, how can the Pythagorean Theorem help you determine the length of a leg or the hypotenuse? Today you and your team will develop new ways to find missing lengths of right triangles.

9-80.   Nikita wants to use the area of the squares in the figure at right to find the lengths of the sides of a right triangle.

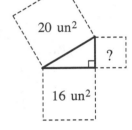

   a.   Find the missing area.

   b.   What are the lengths of the legs of the right triangle in Nikita's diagram? How do you know?

   c.   About how long is the hypotenuse? Are you able to find the length exactly? Explain your reasoning.

9-81.   The numbers 36, 64, 4, 16, 100, 144, 121, and 225 are all examples of **perfect squares**.

   a.   If each of these numbers represents the number of square units in a square, what is the side length of each square?

   b.   Why do you think these numbers are called perfect squares?

9-82.   To find the side length of a square with a particular area, you use an operation called the **square root**. The square root symbol looks like this: $\sqrt{}$. It is also called a **radical sign**.

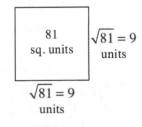

To find the side length of a square with an area of 81 square units, for example, you would write $\sqrt{81}$ and would read it as "the square root of 81." Since $9 \cdot 9 = 81$, then $\sqrt{81} = 9$.

Copy each square root expression below. Rewrite each square root as an equivalent expression without the radical sign. Explain your method for finding the square root of these numbers.

   a. $\sqrt{49}$ b. $\sqrt{121}$ c. $\sqrt{9}$ d. $\sqrt{169}$

9-83.   In problem 9-74, you tried to make a perfect square with
         24 tiles and could not.

    a.   Why was it not possible?

    b.   Estimate the length of a side of a square with an area
         of 24 square units. What two whole numbers is the
         length between?

    c.   Is $\sqrt{24}$ closer to one of the whole numbers or to the other? If you did not
         already do so, estimate to the nearest tenth.

    d.   Multiply your estimate by itself. How close to 24 is your answer? If you
         revised your estimate, how would you change it?

9-84.   Between which two whole numbers is each of the following square roots? To
         which whole number do you think it is closer? Estimate the value of the square
         root to the nearest tenth (0.1). You may find it helpful to create a list of the
         whole numbers from 1 to 17 and their squares to use with this kind of problem.

    a. $\sqrt{40}$ b. $\sqrt{95}$ c. $\sqrt{3}$

    d. $\sqrt{59}$ e. $\sqrt{200}$ f. $\sqrt{154}$

    g.   Describe your method for estimating the approximate value of a square root
         when the number is not a perfect square. Check each estimate for parts (a)
         through (f) on a calculator.

9-85.   ESTIMATING WITH A GRAPH

         In Chapters 6, 7, and 8, you examined the graphs of
         various relationships. What would the relationship
         between the side length of a square and the area of a
         square look like on a graph?

    a.   On the Lesson 9.2.3 Resource Page, complete
         the table for the side lengths and areas. Graph
         the points. Does it make sense to connect them?
         If so, connect them with a smooth curve.

    b.   Describe the relationship between the side length of a square and the area of
         the square. How is it the same or different than other relationships you
         have graphed?

Problem continues on next page. →

9-85. *Problem continued from previous page.*

    c. How can you use the graph to estimate the side length for a square with an area of 24 square units? Does this estimate match your estimate in problem 9-83?

    d. Use your graph to estimate these square roots:

        i. $\sqrt{10}$ *ii.* $\sqrt{15}$ *iii.* $\sqrt{5}$ *iv.* $\sqrt{33}$

9-86. **Additional Challenge:** Nikita wonders, *"What can we say about the square root of a negative number?"* Discuss this question with your team. For example, can you find $\sqrt{-16}$? Write an explanation of your thinking. Be ready to share your ideas with the class.

9-87. LEARNING LOG

What is a square root? How can you estimate a square root? In your Learning Log, write directions for a fifth grader to follow. Explain what a square root is and how to estimate a square root to the nearest tenth. Include examples of perfect squares and non-perfect squares. Title this entry "Square Roots" and label it with today's date.

METHODS AND MEANINGS

Right Triangles and the Pythagorean Theorem

MATH NOTES

A right triangle is a triangle in which the two shorter sides form a right (90°) angle. The shorter sides are called **legs**. The third and longest side, called the **hypotenuse**, is opposite the right angle.

The **Pythagorean Theorem** states that for any right triangle, the sum of the squares of the lengths of the legs is equal to the square of the length of the hypotenuse.

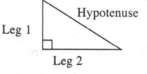

$$(\text{leg 1})^2 + (\text{leg 2})^2 = (\text{hypotenuse})^2$$

Example:

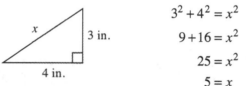

$$3^2 + 4^2 = x^2$$
$$9 + 16 = x^2$$
$$25 = x^2$$
$$5 = x$$

The **converse of the Pythagorean Theorem** states that if the sum of the squares of the lengths of the two shorter sides of a triangle equals the square of the length of the longest side, then the triangle is a right triangle. For example:

Do the lengths 6, 9, and 11 form a right triangle?

$$6^2 + 9^2 \overset{?}{=} 11^2$$
$$36 + 81 \overset{?}{=} 121$$
$$117 \neq 121$$

No, these lengths do not form a right triangle.

Do the lengths 9, 40, and 41 form a right triangle?

$$9^2 + 40^2 \overset{?}{=} 41^2$$
$$81 + 1600 \overset{?}{=} 1681$$
$$1681 = 1681$$

Yes, these lengths form a right triangle.

9-88.   Find the missing length or area.

a.
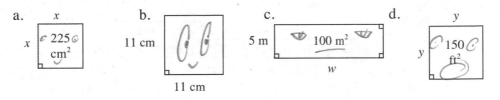

b.   11 cm

11 cm

c.   5 m   100 m²   w

d.   y   150 ft²   y

x   225 cm²   x

9-89.   Determine the positive value that makes each equation true. If the answer is not a whole number, write it as a square root, and then approximate it as a decimal rounded to the nearest tenth.

a.   If $x^2 = 36$, $x = ?$

b.   If $x^2 = 65$, $x = ?$

c.   If $x^2 = 84$, $x = ?$

d.   If $x^2 = 13$, $x = ?$

9-90.   Use the rule $y = -2x + 5$ to answer the questions below.

a.   What is the slope of the line?

b.   Where does the line cross the y-axis?

9-91.   Copy and complete each of the Diamond Problems below. The pattern used in the Diamond Problems is shown at right.

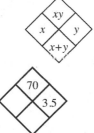

a.   1.5
     0.3

b.   0.2   17

c.   2.6
     0.2

d.   70
          3.5

9-92.   Identify which of the relationships shown below is not a function. Explain your reasoning.

a.

x	3	8	1	9	−1	0
y	12	4	0	4	−3	−8

b.

x	5	2	−1	0	−15	2
y	2	0	−11	8	−25	1

9-93.   Kenneth claims that $(2, 0)$ is the point of intersection of the lines $y = -2x + 4$ and $y = x - 2$. Is he correct? How do you know?

9-94.   Daniel needed to paint his patio, so he made a scale drawing of it. He knows that the width of the patio is 10 feet, but the scale drawing is in inches.

a.   Find the length of the patio in feet.

b.   Find the area of the patio so Daniel knows how much area he needs to paint.

c.   One can of paint covers 125 square feet. How many cans of paint will Daniel need to buy?

9-95.   Juan found that 20 new pencils weigh 12 ounces. How much will 50 new pencils weigh? Show your reasoning.

9-96.   For each diagram below, solve for x. Explain what method you used for each problem.

a. $6x$, $4x + 10°$

b. $5x + 13°$, $3x + 7°$

c. $3x + 5°$, $2x + 18°$, $2x + 17°$

d. x, $30°$

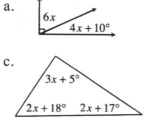

9-97.   Find the surface area and volume of the rectangular prism
         at right.

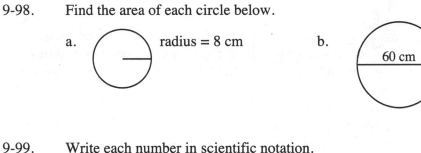

9-98.   Find the area of each circle below.

         a.   radius = 8 cm   b.   60 cm

9-99.   Write each number in scientific notation.

         a.   49.63   b.   0.0000005   c.   3,120,000,000

9.2.4 What kind of number is it?

Real Numbers

Any number that can be written as the ratio of two integers $\frac{a}{b}$ with $b \neq 0$ is called a **rational number**. A rational number can be matched to exactly one point on a number line. There are many other points on the number line, however, for which there is not a corresponding rational number. These numbers are called **irrational numbers**. Numbers such as π, $\sqrt{2}$, and $-\sqrt{5}$ are irrational numbers. The rational numbers and the irrational numbers make up all of the numbers on the number line and together are called the **real numbers**.

In this lesson you will learn how to identify a number as rational or irrational. You will also write decimals as fractions to show that they are rational. Then you will compare these kinds of numbers and place them on the number line.

9-100.   In previous courses, you worked with decimals that repeated and terminated. All of these are called **rational numbers** because they can be written as a ratio, like $\frac{2}{3}$ and $\frac{5}{1} = 5$. Because $\sqrt{9} = 3$, $\sqrt{9}$ is also a rational number.

However, there are some numbers that do not repeat or terminate when they are written as decimals, such as $\sqrt{2}$. Such numbers are called **irrational numbers**. An irrational number cannot be written as a ratio of any two integers. In other words, an irrational number cannot be written as a fraction.

$$\sqrt{2} = 1.41421356237...$$

Use your calculator to find the square root of the following numbers. Decide whether the decimals are rational (having decimals that terminate or repeat) or irrational.

a. $\sqrt{6.25}$ b. $\sqrt{100}$ c. $\sqrt{7}$

9-101.   Do you think that you can decide by looking at it whether a number is rational or irrational? You will explore this idea in parts (a) through (d) below.

a.   Without doing any calculations, which of the numbers below do you think are rational numbers? Which do you think are irrational numbers? Discuss this with your team and make predictions.

$-\frac{5}{9}$ $\sqrt{7}$ $\frac{21}{4}$ $-\sqrt{15}$

π^2 $-\sqrt{76}$ $\frac{730}{99}$ -6.4×10^{-2}

b.   Now use your calculator and write the equivalent decimal for each of the numbers in the list. Were your predictions correct?

c.   What do you notice about the decimal forms of rational numbers compared to irrational numbers?

d.   Is $\sqrt{42.25}$ rational or irrational? Explain your answer.

9-102.   Every rational number can be written as a fraction, that is, as a ratio of two integers. Since 0.78 is described in words as "seventy-eight hundredths," it is not a surprise that the equivalent fraction is $\frac{78}{100}$. Use what you know about place value to rewrite each terminating decimal as a fraction. Check your answers with a calculator.

a.   0.19   b.   0.391   c.   0.001

d.   0.019   e.   0.3   f.   0.524

9-103.   Jessica knows that $0.\overline{57}$ is a rational number, so she should be able to write it as a fraction. She wonders how to rewrite it, though. She started to rewrite it as $\frac{57}{100}$, but she is not sure if that correct. Is $\frac{57}{100}$ equal to $0.\overline{57}$? Be ready to justify your answer.

9-104. To help Jessica with her problem, find the decimal equivalents for the fractions below.

a. $\frac{19}{99}$ b. $\frac{391}{999}$ c. $\frac{3}{9}$

d. $\frac{1}{999}$ e. $\frac{524}{999}$ f. $\frac{19}{999}$

g. What patterns do you see between the fractions and their equivalent decimals? What connections do these fractions have with those you found in problem 9-102? Be ready to share your observations with the class.

h. Use your pattern to predict the fraction equivalent for $0.\overline{24}$. Then test your guess with a calculator.

i. Use your pattern to predict the decimal equivalent for $\frac{65}{99}$. Check your answer with your calculator.

9-105. REWRITING REPEATING DECIMALS AS FRACTIONS

Jessica wants to figure out why the pattern from problem 9-104 works. She noticed that she could eliminate the repeating digits by subtracting, as she wrote at right. This gave her an idea. *"What if I multiply by something before I subtract, so that I'm left with more than zero?"* she wondered. She wrote:

$$0.\overline{57} = 0.575757....$$
$$-0.\overline{57} = -0.575757....$$
$$0 = 0$$

$$10(0.\overline{57}) = 5.75757...$$
$$- (0.\overline{57}) = -0.575757...$$

"The repeating decimals don't make zero in this problem. But if I multiply by 100 instead, I think it will work!" She tried again:

$$100(0.\overline{57}) = 57.575757...$$
$$- (0.\overline{57}) = -0.575757....$$
$$99(0.\overline{57}) = 57.0$$

a. Discuss Jessica's work with your team. Why did she multiply by 100? How did she get 99 sets of $0.\overline{57}$? What happened to the repeating decimals when she subtracted?

b. *"I know that 99 sets of $0.\overline{57}$ are equal to 57 from my equation,"* Jessica said. *"So to find what just one set of $0.\overline{57}$ is equal to, I will need to divide 57 into 99 equal parts."* Represent Jessica's idea as a fraction.

c. Use Jessica's strategy to rewrite $0.\overline{98}$ as a fraction. Be prepared to explain your reasoning.

9-106.   Show that the following repeating decimals are rational numbers by rewriting them as fractions.

   a. $0.\overline{42}$ b. $0.3\overline{12}$ c. $0.1\overline{6}$ d. $0.\overline{8}$

9-107.   Indicate the approximate location of each of the following real numbers on a number line. What can make this task easier? Try to do it without using a calculator.

$$\tfrac{2}{3}, -0.75, \sqrt{8}, -\tfrac{9}{5}, \tfrac{\pi}{3}, 2\tfrac{1}{4}$$

9-108.   Without using a calculator, order the numbers below from least to greatest.

$$\sqrt{102}, 10, 3\pi, \sqrt{99}, 1.1\times10^1, 9.099$$

9-109.   Copy and complete the following sentences.

   a.   The set of all numbers on the number line are called the _____.

   b.   A number that has an equivalent terminating or repeating decimal is called a(n) _____.

   c.   A number that has an equivalent decimal that is non-repeating is called a(n) _____.

   d.   Any number that can be written as a fraction of integers is a(n) _____.

(M)ETHODS AND MEANINGS

The Real-Number System

The **real numbers** include all of the **rational numbers** and **irrational numbers**.

Rational numbers are numbers that can be written as a fraction in the form $\frac{p}{q}$, where p and q are integers and $q \neq 0$. Rational numbers written in decimal form either terminate or repeat. The number 7 is a rational number, because it can be written as $\frac{7}{1}$. The number -0.687 is rational, because it can be written as $-\frac{687}{1000}$. Even $\sqrt{25}$ is rational, because it can be written as $\frac{5}{1}$. Other examples of rational numbers include $-12, 0, 3, \frac{1}{8}, \frac{5}{9}, 0.25$, and $\sqrt{81}$.

Irrational numbers are numbers that cannot be written as fractions. Decimals that do not terminate or repeat are irrational numbers. For example, $\sqrt{3}$ is an irrational number. It cannot be written as a fraction, and when it is written as a decimal, it neither terminates nor repeats ($\sqrt{3} \approx 1.73205080756...$). Other irrational numbers include $\sqrt{2}$, $\sqrt{7}$, and π.

Review & Preview

9-110.   Graph each of the pairs of points listed below and draw a line segment between them. Use the graph to help you find the length of each line segment. State whether each length is irrational or rational.

   a. $(-3,0)$ and $(0,-3)$ b. $(2,3)$ and $(-1,2)$ c. $(3,2)$ and $(3,-3)$

9-111.   Howie and Steve are making cookies for themselves and some friends. The recipe they are using will make 48 cookies, but they only want to make 16 cookies. They have no trouble reducing the amounts of flour and sugar, but the original recipe calls for $1\frac{3}{4}$ cups of butter. Help Howie and Steve determine how much butter they need.

9-112.   Find the perimeter and area of the figure at right. Copy the figure on your paper, and show your work for each of the steps that you use.

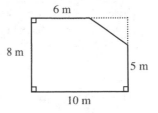

9-113.   Write the following numbers in scientific notation.

   a.   370,000,000

   b.   0.0000000000076

9-114.   Simplify each of the following expressions.

   a. $4x^3y \cdot 3xy^2$

   b. $6a^5b^2 \cdot 3ab^2$

   c. $m^2n \cdot 9mn$

   d. $\dfrac{3^5 \cdot 8 \cdot 5^3}{3^2 \cdot 2^3 \cdot 5^3 \cdot 3^3}$

   e. $\dfrac{m^4 \cdot n}{n^3}$

   f. $\dfrac{9a^4b^2}{15b}$

9-115.   Simplify each numerical expression.

   a. $|5-6+1|$

   b. $-2|-16|$

   c. $|6-2|+|-8-1|$

9-116.   Identify the following numbers as rational or irrational. If the number is rational, show that it can be written as a fraction.

   a. $\sqrt{36}$

   b. $0.\overline{62}$

   c. $\sqrt{92}$

9-117.   Solve each system.

   a. $y = 2x + 1$
        $y = -3x - 4$

   b. $y = \frac{1}{3}x + 4$
        $y = \frac{1}{2}x - 2$

9-118.   For the rule $y = 6 + (-3)x$:

   a.   What is the y-intercept?

   b.   What is the slope?

9-119.   Make a table and graph the rule $y = \sqrt{x-2}$ that includes x-values from -1 to 10. Graph the rule on graph paper.

9-120.   Dawn drove 420 miles in 6 hours on a rural interstate highway. If she maintains the same speed, how far can she go in 7.5 hours?

9-121.   The attendance at the county fair was lowest on Thursday, the opening day. On Friday, 5500 more people attended than attended Thursday. Saturday doubled Thursday's attendance, and Sunday had 3000 more people than Saturday. The total attendance was 36,700. Write and solve an equation to find how many people attended the fair each day.

9.2.5   How can I find missing parts?

Applications of the Pythagorean Theorem

In this section, you have studied different properties of triangles. You have used the Pythagorean Theorem to describe the special relationship between the sides of a right triangle. In this lesson, you will use these ideas to solve a variety of different problems.

9-122.   Ann is measuring some fabric pieces for a quilt. Use the Pythagorean Theorem and your calculator to help her find each of the missing lengths below. Decide whether each answer is rational or irrational. If it is rational, explain whether the decimal repeats or terminates.

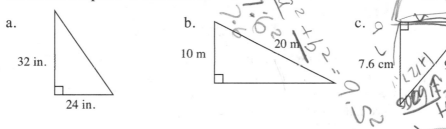

a.

32 in.

24 in.

b.

10 m

20 m

c.

7.6 cm   9.5 cm

9-123.   Coach Kelly's third-period P.E. class is playing baseball. The distance between each base on the baseball diamond is 90 feet. Lisa, at third base, throws the ball to Dano, at first base. How far did she throw the ball? State whether your answer is rational or irrational.

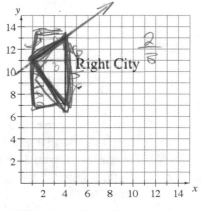

9-124.   As the city planner of Right City, you are responsible to report information to help the Board of Supervisors make decisions about the budgets for the fire and police departments. The board has asked for a report with answers to the following questions. Each grid unit in the figure at right represents 1 mile.

a.   For fire safety, bushes will be cleared along the perimeter of the city. What is the length of the perimeter? Include all of your calculations in your report.

b.   Some people say that Right City got its name from its shape. Is the shape of the city a right triangle? Show how you can tell.

9-125.   Clem and Clyde have a farm with three different crops: a square field of corn, a rectangular field of artichokes, and a right-triangle grove of walnut trees (as shown at right). A fence totally surrounds the farm. Find the total area of Clem and Clyde's land in square miles and tell them how much fencing they need to enclose the outside of their farm.

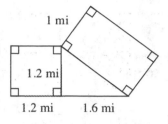

9-126.   Scott and Mark are rock climbing. Scott is at the top of a 75-foot cliff, when he throws a 96-foot rope down to Mark, who is on the ground below. If the rope is stretched tightly from Mark's feet to Scott's feet, how far from the base of the cliff (directly below Scott) is Mark standing? Draw a diagram and label it. Then find the missing length. Is the length irrational?

9-127.   Nicole has three long logs. She wants to place them in a triangle around a campfire to allow people to sit around the fire. The logs have lengths 19, 11, and 21 feet.

   a.   Can she form a triangle with these lengths? If so, what type of triangle (acute, obtuse, or right) will the logs form? Justify your answers.

   b.   Nicole realized she wrote the numbers down incorrectly. Her logs are actually 9, 11, and 21 feet. Will she still be able to surround her campfire with a triangular seating area? If so, will the shape be a right triangle? Justify.

9-128.   LEARNING LOG

The Pythagorean Theorem describes the special relationship that exists between the side lengths of a right triangle. In your Learning Log, describe how the Pythagorean Theorem can be used to find a missing side length on a right triangle. Make up examples in which either the hypotenuse length is missing or a leg length is missing. Be sure to include pictures and describe how you would find each missing length. Title this entry "Pythagorean Theorem" and label it with today's date.

METHODS AND MEANINGS

Squaring and Square Root

When a number or variable is multiplied by itself, it is said to be **squared**. Squaring a number is like finding the area of the square with that number or variable as its side length. For example:

$$6 \cdot 6 = 6^2 = 36 \quad \text{and}$$

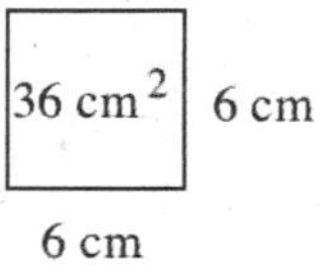

| 36 cm^2 | 6 cm |

6 cm

$$a \cdot a = a^2 \quad \text{and}$$

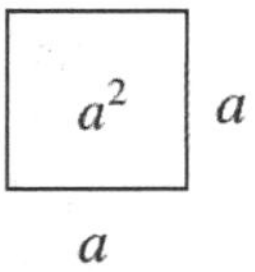

| a^2 | a |

a

The **square root** of a number or variable is the positive factor that, when multiplied by itself, results in the given number. Use a **radical sign**, $\sqrt{}$, to show this operation. If you know the area of a square, then the square root of the numerical value of the area is the side length of that square.

For example, $\sqrt{49}$ is read as, "the square root of 49," and means, "Find the positive number that multiplied by itself equals 49." $\sqrt{49} = 7$, since $7 \cdot 7 = 49$.

By definition, -7 is not the square root of 49 even though $(-7) \cdot (-7) = 49$, since only consider positive numbers are considered to be square roots. No real square region could have a negative side length.

9-129.   On a coordinate grid, draw a triangle with vertices at $(2,6)$, $(2,2)$, and $(5,6)$.

a.   Find the lengths of each side of the triangle. What is the perimeter?

b.   What type of triangle is formed by these points? Justify your answer.

9-130.   Ann lives on the shoreline of a large lake. A market is located 24 km south and 32 km west of her home on the other side of the lake. If she takes a boat across the lake directly toward the market, how far is her home from the market?

9-131.   Change each number below from a decimal to an equivalent fraction. For help with the repeating decimals, review the Math Notes box from Lesson 9.2.4.

a.   0.7   b. $0.\overline{7}$ c.   0.15   d. $0.1\overline{5}$

9-132.   Simplify each of the following expressions.

a. $3\frac{1}{5} \cdot \frac{7}{4}$

b. $5^3 \cdot (-\frac{4}{5})$

c. $2^4 \cdot \frac{5}{8}$

d. $-\frac{1}{2} \cdot 3^2$

e. $-\frac{5}{6} + (\frac{1}{2})^2$

f. $(-\frac{4}{5})^2 - \frac{3}{50}$

g. $(\frac{3}{10})^2 - (-\frac{2}{5})^2$

h. $8^2(-\frac{7}{8}) - \frac{1}{2}$

9-133.   Simplify each expression.

a. $(3x)^4 x^3$

b. $\frac{2^4 \cdot 3}{2^3 \cdot 3^2}$

c. $4^{-3} \cdot 4^2$

9-134.   Identify the type of growth in each table below as linear or non-linear.

a.

x	-2	-1	0	1	2	3
y	-8	-1	0	1	8	27

b.

x	-2	-1	0	1	2	3
y	4	6	8	10	12	14

c.

x	-2	-1	0	1	2	3
y	$\frac{1}{4}$	$\frac{1}{2}$	1	2	4	8

9.2.6 How can I find lengths in three dimensions?

Pythagorean Theorem in Three Dimensions

You have been studying right triangles from a two-dimensional viewpoint. However, often triangles occur in three-dimensional settings. In this lesson, you will build a model, use it to visualize the location of right triangles in a three-dimensional situation, and then make calculations to find the triangle lengths.

9-135. The roof on the Flat Family's house is one large flat rectangle. It is parallel to the ground. The TV antenna is mounted in the center of the roof. Guy wires are attached to the antenna five feet below its highest point, and they are attached to the roof at each corner and at the midpoint of each edge. These wires support the antenna in the wind.

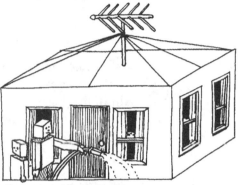

Each guy wire is the hypotenuse of a right triangle. Mr. Flat needs to know how long each wire needs to be to keep the antenna upright. He also needs to find the total amount of wire needed.

a. Build a model of the Flat Family Roof. The model will serve as a reference while your team finds the lengths of the sides of the right triangles in a three-dimensional setting.

  1. For the roof, use a rectangular piece of cardboard. Draw the diagonals of the rectangle to locate the center.

  2. Tape the string guy wires to the antenna (straw). Do not forget to leave a gap that represents the five feet between the strings and the top of the antenna. How many guy wires are there?

  3. Attach the antenna to the center of the roof. Use tape, tie knots, or make slits to anchor your antenna and guy wires to the roof.

b. Locate as many vertical right triangles as you can on your model. How many right triangles did you find?

c. Identify which right triangles are the same size and which are different sizes. How many different-sized right triangles did you find? How many of each size are there?

d. Sketch each of the different-sized right triangles on a different color of paper. Cut out the triangle. Tape the triangle in position on your model.

9-136.   The Flat Family's roof is 60 feet long and 32 feet wide. The TV antenna is 30 feet tall. The wires are attached five feet below the top of the antenna.

   a.   How long must each guy wire be? Show all of your steps to get your solution.

   b.   Mr. Flat needs to buy the wire at his local hardware store. He decides to buy an additional 10% more than the amount that you calculated so that he can attach the wires on each end. How much total wire should he buy? Show all of your work so that Mr. Flat can understand it, and round your answer reasonably.

9-137.   A child's shoe box measures 4" by 6" by 3". What is the longest pencil you could fit into this box? An empty box may help you visualize the various ways you could fit the pencil in the box. If possible, draw a diagram to show the pencil's position. Show your steps.

9-138.   **Additional Challenge:** A fly was sitting on the ground in the back left corner of your classroom. He flew to the ceiling in the opposite corner of the room. How far did he fly if he went in a straight line? Draw a diagram of your classroom, complete with the correct measurements. Write equations. Show your steps.

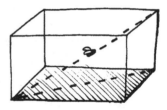

Review & Preview

9-139.   The hypotenuse and one leg of a right triangle are 65 and 60 meters. What is the length of the third side?

9-140.   Find the missing length on this right triangle.

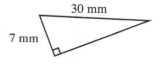

9-141.   Solve these equations for x.

   a. $(x+3.5)2 = 16$ b. $23+5x = 7+2.5x$ c. $3x+4.4 = -(6.6+x)$

9-142.   Simplify each expression.

   a. $\frac{3^5}{3^{10}}$ b. $10x^4(10x)^{-2}$ c. $(\frac{1}{4})^3 \cdot (4)^2$ d. $\frac{(xy)^3}{xy^3}$

9-143.   Complete the table.

   a.   Find the rule.

   b.   What is the slope?

x	−5	1	3	0	8	−2	−1
y	7			2		4	

9-144.   **Additional Challenge:** Use the diagram and your answer to problem 9-138 above. If your classroom measured 30 ft by 30 ft by 10 ft, what distance would the fly travel?

9.2.7 Does it always work?

Pythagorean Theorem Proofs

You have seen that you can find the missing side of a right triangle using the Pythagorean Theorem. To show that it is always true, no matter how long the sides are, it must be proven. There are over 100 different ways to prove this important relationship. Today you will look at two ways to prove the Pythagorean Theorem. As you may remember, the Pythagorean Theorem states that in a right triangle with sides a and b, and hypotenuse c, $a^2 + b^2 = c^2$.

9-145. **PYTHAGOREAN THEOREM PROOF**

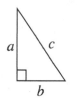

Obtain the Lesson 9.2.7A Resource Page from your teacher. Start by cutting out four copies of the right triangle with legs labeled a, b, and hypotenuse labeled c units.

a. First, arrange the triangles to look like the diagram at right. Draw this diagram on your paper. Explain why the area of the unshaded region is c^2.

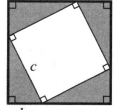

b. Will moving the triangles within the bold outer square change the total unshaded square?

c. Move the shaded triangles to match the diagram at right. In this arrangement, tell why the total area that is unshaded is $a^2 + b^2$.

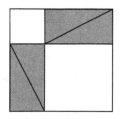

d. Write an equation that relates the unshaded region in part (a) to the unshaded region in part (b).

9-146.   Here is another proof of the Pythagorean Theorem for you to try. Obtain the
        Lesson 9.2.7B Resource Page from your teacher.

        a.   Start with two squares as shown at right. What
             is the total area?

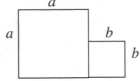

        b.   Use a ruler or another piece of paper to place a
             mark of length b on the bottom left side of the
             larger square. Then draw the dotted lines as
             shown in the diagram at right to create two right
             triangles. How do you know that the legs of
             both triangles are legs a and b? Label each
             hypotenuse c.

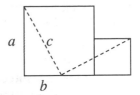

        c.   Cut out the shaded triangles shown in the diagram
             at right. Then work with your team to determine
             how to arrange the shaded triangles and the
             unshaded portion of the original figure to create a
             square. What is the area of the square? How do
             you know?

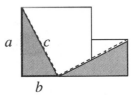

        d.   How does what you have done in this problem prove the Pythagorean
             Theorem?

9-147.   The **converse** of a theorem reverses the evidence and the conclusion. The
        Pythagorean Theorem states that in a right triangle with legs of a and b, and
        hypotenuse c, that $a^2 + b^2 = c^2$.

        a.   State the converse of the Pythagorean Theorem.

        b.   Look back at your work from problem 9-51. What can you conclude about
             a triangle if $a^2 + b^2 = c^2$?

        c.   Why is this not a *proof* of the converse of the Pythagorean Theorem?

9-148.   Graph the points $A\,(-2,2)$ and $B\,(1,-2)$. Then find the distance between them
        by creating a right triangle (like a slope triangle) and computing the length of
        the hypotenuse.

9-149.　Use a graph to find the distance between the points $C\,(-4,-1)$ and $D\,(4,1)$.

9-150.　Jack has a tree in his backyard that he
wants to cut down to ground level. He
needs to know how tall the tree is, because
when he cuts it, it will fall toward his fence.
Jack measured the tree's shadow, and it
measured 20 feet long. At the same time,
Jack's shadow was 12 feet long. Jack is
5 feet tall.

a.　How tall is the tree?

b.　Will the tree hit the fence if the fence is 9 feet away?

9-151.　Examine the diagrams below. What is the geometric relationship between the
labeled angles? What is the relationship of their measures? After you
determine the relationship of their measures, use the relationship to write an
equation and solve
for x.

a.

b.
$4x+150°$

$2x°$

9-152.　On graph paper, graph the system of equations at right.
Then state the solution to the system. If there is not a
solution, explain why not.

$y=-\frac{2}{5}x+1$

$y=-\frac{2}{5}x-2$

9-153. A principal made the histogram at right to analyze how many years teachers had been teaching at her school.

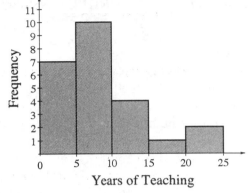

a. How many teachers work at her school?

b. If the principal randomly chose one teacher to represent the school at a conference, what is the probability that the teacher would have been teaching at the school for more than 10 years? Write the probability in two different ways.

c. What is the probability that a teacher on the staff has been there for fewer than 5 years?

9-154. Simplify each expression.

a. $\frac{12}{5} \div \frac{7}{10}$

b. $\frac{9}{4} \div (-\frac{1}{3})$

c. $-\frac{3}{5} \div (-\frac{1}{6})$

Chapter 9 Closure   What have I learned?

Reflection and Synthesis

The activities below offer you a chance to reflect about what you have learned during this chapter. As you work, look for concepts that you feel comfortable with, ideas that you would like to learn more about, and topics with which you need more help.

①   SUMMARIZING MY UNDERSTANDING

This section gives you an opportunity to show what you know about properties of triangles and applying the Pythagorean Theorem, two of the main ideas of this chapter.

Triangular Treasure Hunt

Jasmine and Mason are spending the summer with their Uncle Simon. He lives in an old castle that has many interesting doors, not all of which are rectangles. One day, while looking through the books in the castle library, Jasmine found an unusual piece of paper in a book. *"Look, Mason! This looks like some kind of a treasure map,"* she exclaimed. Mason looked at the paper and read, *"A valuable secret is hidden inside. But beware – danger lurks behind the other doors. Only those who can follow the clues will succeed in the search."* He also saw that it had a series of clues and pictures of triangular doors. Read the clues below and, with your team, help Jasmine and Mason find the secret door and the treasure.

- My sides are not congruent.
- My angles are not congruent.
- I am similar to another door.
- One of my sides is $\sqrt{41}$ units long.

a.   Look at the doors on the Chapter 9 Closure Resource Page.

b.   Using what you have learned in this chapter, decide which door is the secret door. Justify your answer.

c.   List the triangles that were *not* the secret door and justify why each did not fit the clues.

②　　　　WHAT HAVE I LEARNED?

Doing the problems in this section will help
you to evaluate which types of problems you
feel comfortable with and which ones you
need more help with.

Solve each problem as completely as you can.
The table at the end of this closure section provides answers to these
problems. It also tells you where you can find additional help and where to
find practice problems like them.

CL 9-155.　Solve for x.

a.

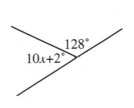

b.

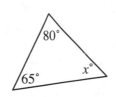

CL 9-156.　Solve for x.

a.

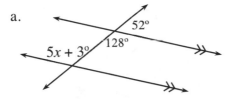

b.

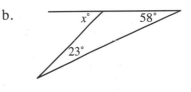

CL 9-157.　Determine the length of side x. Give the answer
in radical form and as a decimal.

CL 9-158.　Simplify the following exponential expressions. Give answers without
negative exponents.

a.　$4^{-3} \cdot 4^7$

c.　$\dfrac{3^7}{3^4}$

b.　$(5x^4)^3$

d.　$(4x^5)(3x^{-8})$

CL 9-159.   Visualize a line that goes through the two points on the graph at right.

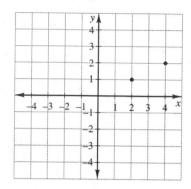

a.   What is the slope of the line?

b.   What is the rule for the line?

CL 9-160.   Casey was building a rectangular pen for his pigs. He has 62 feet of fencing. The length of his pen is 9 feet longer than the width. Write and solve an equation to find the dimensions of the pen.

CL 9-161.   Clay and his friend Lacey are making cookies for the school dance. Clay started early and has already made 3 dozen cookies. He can make an additional 2 dozen cookies an hour. Lacey has not started making cookies yet, but she has a bigger oven and can make 4 dozen cookies an hour. If Lacey starts baking her cookies right away, how long will it take for her to have made as many cookies as Clay? How many cookies will they each have made?

CL 9-162.   Sarah loves to order paperback mystery books. Some of her recent orders are shown in the table below.

# of Books	1	3	1	4	2	5
Total Cost	10.25	18.00	10.25	21.75	14.00	26.25

a.   Draw a scatterplot with this information.

b.   Fully describe the association.

c.   Determine the equation of the line of best fit.

d.   Based on the equation, estimate the total cost of an order of 10 books.

CL 9-163.   For each of the problems above, do the following:

- Draw a bar or number line that represents 0 to 10.

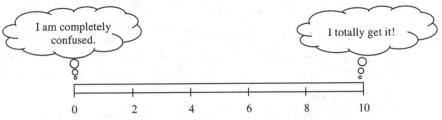

- Color or shade in a portion of the bar that represents your level of understanding and comfort with completing that problem on your own.

If any of your bars are less than a 5, choose *one* of those problems and do one of the following tasks:

- Write two questions that you would like to ask about that problem.
- Brainstorm two things that you DO know about that type of problem.

If all of your bars are a 5 or above, choose one of those problems and do one of these tasks:

- Write two questions you might ask or hints you might give to a student who was stuck on the problem.
- Make a new problem that is similar and more challenging than that problem and solve it.

③ WHAT TOOLS CAN I USE?

You have created or have available to you several tools and references that help support your learning – your teacher, your study team, your math book and your Toolkit to name a few. At the end of each chapter you will have an opportunity to review your Toolkit for completeness as well as to revise or update your Toolkit to better reflect your current understanding of big ideas.

Listed below are the main elements of your Toolkit, Learning Log Entries, Methods and Meanings Boxes, and vocabulary used in this chapter. The words that appear in bold are new to this chapter. Use these lists and follow your teacher's instructions to ensure that your Toolkit is a useful tool as well as a complete reference for you as you complete this chapter and prepare to begin the next one.

Learning Log Entries
- Lesson 9.1.1 – Angle Relationships
- Lesson 9.1.2 – Angles in a Triangle
- Lesson 9.1.4 – Angle-Angle Similarity
- Lesson 9.2.1 – Triangle Inequality
- Lesson 9.2.1 – Triangle Side-Length Patterns
- Lesson 9.2.3 – Square Roots
- Lesson 9.2.5 – Pythagorean Theorem

Math Notes
- Lesson 9.1.1 – Angle Vocabulary
- Lesson 9.1.2 – Parallel Lines and Angle Pairs
- Lesson 9.1.3 – Angle Sum Theorem for Triangles
- Lesson 9.1.4 – Exterior Angle Theorem for Triangles
- Lesson 9.2.1 – AA Similarity for Triangles
- Lesson 9.2.2 – Triangle Inequality and Side-Length Patterns
- Lesson 9.2.3 – Right Triangles and the Pythagorean Theorem
- Lesson 9.2.4 – The Real Number System
- Lesson 9.2.5 – Squaring and Square Root

Mathematical Vocabulary

The following is a list of vocabulary found in this chapter. Some of the words have been seen in previous chapters. The words in bold are the words new to this chapter. Make sure that you are familiar with the terms below and know what they mean. For the words you do not know, refer to the glossary or index. You might also add these words to your Toolkit so that you can reference them in the future.

AA~ (Angle-Angle Similarity)	acute angle
adjacent angles	**alternate interior angles**
complementary angles	**corresponding angles**
exterior angle	**hypotenuse**
leg (of a right triangle)	obtuse angle
parallel	**perfect square**
perpendicular	**Pythagorean Theorem**
radical sign	**remote interior angle**
right angle	**square (of a number)**
square root	supplementary angles
straight angle	**transversal**
vertex	vertical angles

Answers and Support for Closure Problems
What Have I Learned?

Note: MN = Math Note, LL = Learning Log

Problem	Solution	Need Help?	More Practice
CL 9-155.	a. 5 b. 35	Lessons 9.1.2 and 9.1.3 MN: 9.1.2, 9.1.3, and 9.1.4 LL: 9.1.1, 9.1.2, and 9.1.4	Problems 9-14, 9-18, 9-22, 9-28, 9-29, 9-30, 9-33, 9-34, 9-49, 9-78, 9-79, 9-82, 9-151, and 9-154
CL 9-156.	a. 25 b. 81	Lessons 9.1.2 and 9.1.3 MN: 9.1.2, 9.1.3, and 9.1.4 LL: 9.1.1, 9.1.2, and 9.1.4	Problem CL 9-155
CL 9-157.	$\sqrt{176} \approx 13.27$	Lessons 9.2.2, 9.2.3, and 9.2.5 MN: 9.2.3 and 9.2.5 LL: 9.2.3 and 9.2.5	Problems 9-70, 9-122, 9-139, and 9-140
CL 9-158.	a. 4^4 b. $125x^{12}$ c. 3^3 d. $\frac{12}{x^3}$	Lesson 8.2.1 MN: 8.1.2 and 8.2.4 LL: 8.2.3	Problem CL 8-136
CL 9-159.	a. The slope is $\frac{1}{2}$. b. $y = \frac{1}{2}x$	Lesson 7.2.4 LL: 7.3.1	Problems CL 7-122 and 9-90

Problem	Solution	Need Help?	More Practice
CL 9-160.	$2x + 2(x+9) = 62$ OR $4x + 18 = 62$ The dimensions of the pen are 11 feet by 20 feet.	MN: 1.1.3	Problem 9-59
CL 9-161.	In $1\frac{1}{2}$ hours, they will each have made 72 cookies.	Lessons 5.2.2 and 5.2.3 MN: 5.2.2, 5.2.3, and 5.2.4	Problems 9-48, 9-76, and 9-152
CL 9-162.	a. See graph at right. b. Strong positive associaltion c. $y = 4x + 6$ d. $46.00	Lesson 7.1.3 and 7.3.2 MN: 7.1.3 and 7.3.2 LL: 7.1.3 and 7.3.2	Problems 9-10, 9-24, and 9-150

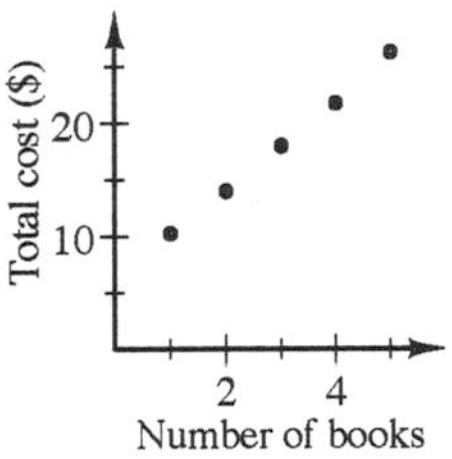

Surface Area and Volume

CHAPTER 10   Surface Area and Volume

The geometry you explored in Chapter 9 focused on triangles and angles. In this chapter, you will continue to explore geometry concepts but now you will focus on surface areas and volumes.

In Section 10.1, you will explore how to find the side length of a cube when you already know the volume. You will measure the surface area and volume of a cylinder, a three-dimensional solid that has a circle as the base. Finally, you will look at the surface areas and volumes of shapes that cannot be sliced into equal layers, such as pyramids, cones, and spheres.

In the course closure and reflection (Section 10.2), you will work with your team to solve challenging problems that allow you to reflect about your learning throughout the course.

In this chapter, you will learn how to:

➢ Find the cube root of a number.

➢ Find the surface areas of cylinders and pyramids.

➢ Find the volumes of non-rectangular shapes, including cylinders, pyramids, cones, and spheres.

Guiding Questions

Think about these questions throughout this chapter:

How much will it hold?

Am I measuring in one, two, or three dimensions?

How are they related?

Chapter Outline

	Section 10.1	You will begin by learning how to find the cube root of a number. Then you will learn how to find the surface areas of cylinders and pyramids and the volumes of cylinders, pyramids, cones, and spheres.
	Course Closure and Reflection (Section 10.2)	You will work with your team to solve challenging problems using your learning from the entire course. You will reflect about your learning and how you have been thinking as you have solved problems this year.

10.1.1 How long is the side?

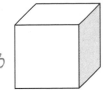

Cube Roots

You have previously calculated the volumes and surface areas of cubes (and, more generally, prisms) using the lengths of the sides. But what if you wanted to reverse this process? In this lesson, you will learn how to determine the length of the side of a cube when you already know the volume. You will learn about a new operation, which is similar to the square-root operation, that will help you do this.

10-1.   Using the cube at right as a model, work with your team to create two problem situations that would require knowing the surface area of the cube. Then make another two problem situations that would require knowing the volume of the cube.

3 feet

10-2.   Find the surface area and the volume of the cube in problem 10-1. Show your steps.

10-3.   A different cube has a side of length 5. Write two expressions that would represent how to find the volume of the cube. One expression should use exponents.

10-4.   Now reverse the process. If you know the volume, how long is the side? Given the volumes of different cubes below, work with your team to find the length of a side of each cube.

   a. 8 un^3 b. 125 m^3 c. 1000 ft^3 d. 40 in.^3

10-5.   In problem 10-4, did you find the solution by guessing and checking, or did you find a special key on your calculator that helped?

10-6.   If s = the length of a side of a cube, then s^3 or "s cubed" represents the volume of the cube. If the volume of the cube is 64 cubic units, write an equation (using s) stating that volume is 64 cubic units.

10-7.   In Chapter 9, you solved equations with squares, such as $x^2 = 16$, by using the square-root operation, $\sqrt{\ }$. To solve equations with cubes, such as $x^3 = 64$, you need an operation that undoes cubing. You need the operation called **cube root**. It uses the symbol $\sqrt[3]{\ }$. Find the cube-root key on your calculator. Different calculators perform this operation in different ways, so figure out how to do this on your calculator and then find $\sqrt[3]{64}$ to get the solution to $x^3 = 64$.

10-8.   If you have not already done so, use the $\sqrt[3]{\ }$ key on your calculator to check your answers for problem 10-4.

10-9.   Just like with perfect squares and square roots, cube roots of perfect cubes are positive integers. Some of them are listed below.

$$\sqrt[3]{0} = 0, \quad \sqrt[3]{1} = 1, \quad \sqrt[3]{8} = 2, \quad \sqrt[3]{27} = 3, \quad \sqrt[3]{64} = 4, \quad \sqrt[3]{125} = 5, \quad \sqrt[3]{216} = 6$$

Cube roots of non-perfect cubes like $\sqrt[3]{40} = 3.419951...$ are irrational numbers. Without a calculator, you can *approximate* the cube root to be between consecutive integers, as you did with square roots. Look at the example below.

$$\sqrt[3]{27} < \sqrt[3]{40} < \sqrt[3]{64}$$
$$3 < \sqrt[3]{40} < 4$$

Approximate each of the following cube roots between consecutive integers. Write each answer in the same way as the above example.

a. $\sqrt[3]{10}$ b. $\sqrt[3]{100}$ c. $\sqrt[3]{52}$ d. $-\sqrt[3]{150}$

10-10.   The office building where Ryan works is made up of two cube-shaped pieces. At lunchtime, Ryan and his other office workers walk around the edge of the building for exercise. If the volume of the larger part is $65,000$ m^3 and the volume of the smaller part is 4000 m^3, what is the distance around the edge of the building?

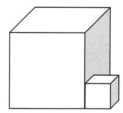

10-11.   LEARNING LOG

How do you find the length of the side of a cube if you know its volume? What is this operation called? In your Learning Log create examples that demonstrate what you know about cube roots and how to find them. Title this entry "Cube Root" and label it with today's date.

Core Connections, Course 3

10-12. Find the cube root of the following numbers. Use your calculator as needed and round any decimal answers to the nearest hundredth. Identify each answer as a rational or irrational number.

    a. 1728   b. 54   c. 0.125

10-13. Given that the volume of a certain cube is 125 cubic inches, find the dimensions given below.

    a. Find the length of one side of the cube.

    b. Find the surface area of the cube.

10-14. Find the area and perimeter of the shape at right. Show your steps.

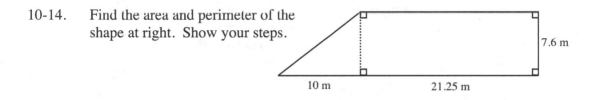

7.6 m

10 m   21.25 m

10-15. Change each number below from a decimal to an equivalent fraction. For help with repeating decimals, review the Math Notes box from Lesson 9.2.4.

    a. 0.72   b. $0.\overline{72}$ c. 0.175   d. $0.1\overline{75}$

10-16. Johanna is planting tomatoes in the school garden this year. Tomato plants come in packs of 6. She needs 80 plants in the garden and already has 28. How many packs of plants will she need?

10-17. Solve the following equations for the given variable.

    a. $3x+(-4)=2y+9$ for y b. $12=\frac{6}{7}x$ for x

    c. $\frac{38}{6}=\frac{x}{18}$ for x d. $\frac{9}{x}=\frac{85}{10y}$ for y

10.1.2 What if the base is not a polygon?

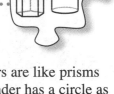

Surface Area and Volume of a Cylinder

Soup cans and rolls of paper towels are examples of **cylinders**. Cylinders are like prisms in many ways. However, a prism has a polygon as its base, while a cylinder has a circle as its base. In this lesson, you will compare the surface areas and volumes of prisms and cylinders.

10-18. COMPARING THE GYM BAGS

The CPM Sports Company is planning a new product line of gym bags. The outside of the bag (without the ends) will be made with a rectangular piece of cloth that is 40 inches by 52 inches. The company is trying to decide whether the end pieces will be squares or circles. CPM designers want to compare the surface area and volume of each bag and consider the advantages and disadvantages of each shape. Your team will help provide data for the designers' decision.

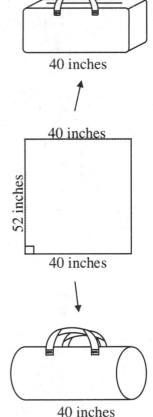

Use a standard piece of paper that measures 8.5 inches on one edge and 11 inches on the other to create a model of each gym bag. To model the square-based prism:

- Fold the paper in half so that the 8.5-inch edges match up, and then unfold.

- Fold each 8.5-inch edge in to the center crease, and then unfold.

- Tape the 8.5-inch edges together to form the **lateral faces** (the faces that are not the bases) of a square-based prism. The open squares at either end are the bases.

Use a new piece of paper to model the cylinder:

- Roll the paper so that one 8.5-inch edge matches up with the other.

- Tape the edges together to form the lateral face of a cylinder. The open circles formed at each end are the bases.

Problem continues on next page. →

10-18.   *Problem continued from previous page.*

Your Task: Using the models for reference, find the surface area and volume of each gym bag. How much fabric will it take to make each bag? How much will each bag hold? Remember that the shorter length on the paper (8.5 inches) models the 40-inch dimension of the cloth, and the longer length (11 inches) models the 52-inch dimension of the cloth. The model you have created is *not* to scale.

Discussion Points

What dimensions will we need to find?

How can we organize our work?

What shape is each surface?

How are prisms and cylinders alike? How are they different?

Further Guidance

10-19.   Focus first on the square-based prism. Sketch the prism on your paper, and then use the dimensions given for the cloth to answer the questions below.

a.   What is the perimeter of the square base? How long is each side of the square base?

b.   What is the surface area of the prism?

c.   Calculate the volume of the prism.

10-20.   Sketch the cylinder on your paper.

a.   On your sketch, label all of the lengths that you know. What shape is the lateral face of the cylinder? This is the face formed by the original piece of paper. Find the area of the lateral face and the area of each base. If you do not have enough information to find the area, list the measurements that you need.

b.   Melissa is looking at the base of the cylinder and realizes that the only measurement she knows is the circumference of the circle. She thinks she can use the circumference to find out other measurements. What is the circumference of this circle? What other lengths can Melissa find using this measurement?

c.   Find the area of each base of the cylinder and then calculate the total surface area.

10-21.   To find the volume of the cylinder, Melissa started by comparing it to a prism. *"To find the volume of a prism, I slice it into equal layers. I wonder if the same method will work for a cylinder?"* she asks. Work with your team to answer Melissa's question. How could a cylinder be sliced into layers? What shape would each layer be? Find the volume of the cylinder.

───────── *Further Guidance* ─────────
section ends here.

10-22.   How does the amount of fabric required to make the cylindrical bag compare to the amount of fabric required to make the square-based-prism bag? How much will each bag hold? Based on this information, which bag style do you think the CPM sports company should make? Explain your reasoning.

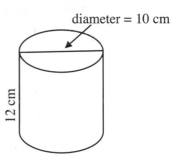

10-23.   Find the surface area and volume of the cylinder at right. Show your work clearly.

10-24.   **Additional Challenge:** Louise calculated the volume of the prism at right to be 702 m^3. She is trying to find the surface area, but she needs help.

   a.   Sketch the shape on your paper and label any lengths that you know. How can you find the lengths of the unlabeled edges?

   b.   What are the length and width of each rectangle?

   c.   What is the total surface area of the shape?

10-25.   LEARNING LOG

With your team, look carefully at how you found the surface area of the cylindrical bag. What measurements did you use to find the area of the base of a cylinder? What measurements did you use to find the lateral area? What measurement is important for both calculations? After your team has discussed these questions, record your ideas in your Learning Log. Title this entry "Surface Area and Volume of a Cylinder" and label it with today's date.

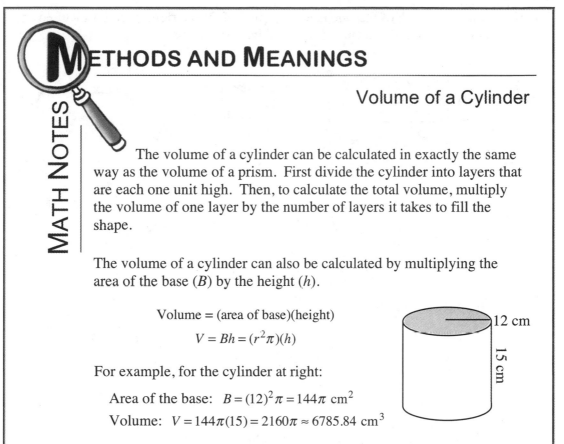

METHODS AND **M**EANINGS

MATH NOTES

Volume of a Cylinder

The volume of a cylinder can be calculated in exactly the same way as the volume of a prism. First divide the cylinder into layers that are each one unit high. Then, to calculate the total volume, multiply the volume of one layer by the number of layers it takes to fill the shape.

The volume of a cylinder can also be calculated by multiplying the area of the base (B) by the height (h).

$$\text{Volume} = (\text{area of base})(\text{height})$$
$$V = Bh = (r^2\pi)(h)$$

For example, for the cylinder at right:

Area of the base: $B = (12)^2\pi = 144\pi$ cm^2

Volume: $V = 144\pi(15) = 2160\pi \approx 6785.84$ cm^3

12 cm

15 cm

Review & Preview

10-26.   Find the area of the base of each cylinder below, and then calculate the volume of each cylinder. Show your steps.

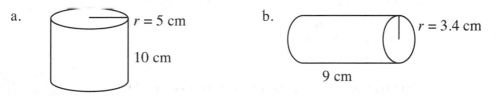

a. $r = 5$ cm

10 cm

b. $r = 3.4$ cm

9 cm

10-27.   What is the volume of a hexagonal-based prism with a height of 12 in. and a base area of 62 in.^{2}? Would the volume be different if the base were a pentagon with an area of 62 in.^{2}? Explain.

10-28.   Find the length of the side labeled x in each of the right triangles pictured below. Identify each answer as a rational or irrational number.

a.   b.   c.

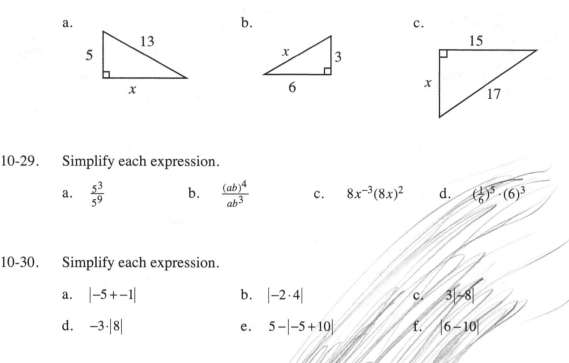

10-29.   Simplify each expression.

a. $\frac{5^3}{5^9}$ b. $\frac{(ab)^4}{ab^3}$ c. $8x^{-3}(8x)^2$ d. $(\frac{1}{6})^5 \cdot (6)^3$

10-30.   Simplify each expression.

a. $|-5+-1|$ b. $|-2 \cdot 4|$ c. $3|-8|$

d. $-3 \cdot |8|$ e. $5-|-5+10|$ f. $|6-10|$

10-31.   Tim wants to invest some money that his grandmother gave him. He has $2000 and can put it in an account with simple interest or an account with compound interest.

a.   The simple interest account has an interest rate of 10%. With this interest rate, what is the total amount in the bank after 5 years?

b.   The compound interest account is also for 5 years (compounded yearly), but it has an interest rate of 8%. Find the total amount that he would have in this account.

c.   Which account is a better investment?

10.1.3 What if the layers are not the same?

Volumes of Cones and Pyramids

Cones and pyramids are three-dimensional objects that have only one base, and that come to a point opposite their base. A **cone** has a circular base. A **pyramid** has a base that is a polygon and lateral faces that are triangles. Today you will be investigating how to use what you know about cylinders and prisms to find the volume of a cone and a pyramid. Questions to keep in mind as you work are:

What is the shape of the base?

How does the shape compare to a cylinder or a prism?

10-32. HOW MUCH SHOULD IT COST?

You have a choice of purchasing a small or a large serving of popcorn at the movies. A small popcorn comes in a cone and costs $1.50, and a large popcorn comes in a cylinder that costs $3.50. Both containers have the same height and have bases with the same circular area. Based on their prices, discuss with your team which container of popcorn you think is a better deal. Be prepared to share your reasons with the class.

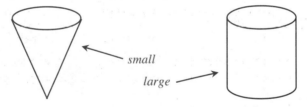

10-33. Your teacher will lead you through a demonstration about the volume of a cone.

a. How are the radius and height of each cone related to the radius and height of each corresponding cylinder?

b. Sketch each cone and cylinder on your paper, and estimate which cone will have a greater volume.

c. How many cones full of rice were needed to fill each corresponding cylinder?

d. Based on the demonstration, describe how the volume of a cone compares to the volume of a cylinder when their heights and base areas are equal.

10-34. Based on the relationship you found in problem
        10-33, determine what a fair price would be for the
        cylinder of popcorn in problem 10-32 if the cone of
        popcorn costs $1.50. At the advertised prices,
        which popcorn is the better deal?

$\times 3 \to 0$

10-35. A different movie theater sells popcorn in the containers shown below. This
        time, the small container is a pyramid priced at $2.50. The large container is a
        prism with the same height and base as the pyramid, and it is priced at $5.50.
        At this theater, which popcorn do you think is a better deal? Be prepared to
        give reasons for your prediction.

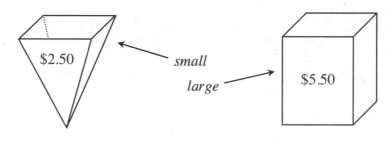

$2.50   small
         large $5.50

10-36. Your teacher will now lead you through another demonstration to help you
        decide if you need to adjust your thinking about the relationship between the
        volume of a pyramid and a prism that have the same base and the same height.
        After you have seen the demonstration with the pyramid and the prism,
        determine which container of popcorn is a better deal. Justify your answer.

10-37. Ann and Dan were trying to find the volume of the
        cone at right. Ann thinks that the cone is 8 inches
        tall, and Dan thinks that the cone is 10 inches tall.
        Write them a note explaining who is correct.

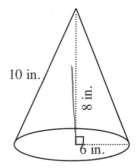

10 in.

8 in.

6 in.

b/c n = bottom to top

side lentr

36 · 3.14

10-38.   Ann, Dan, and Jan calculated the volumes of some shapes and got different answers. Look at their work shown below and make a sketch of the shape that each set of calculations might represent. Why do Dan's and Jan's calculations have the same result even though they look different?

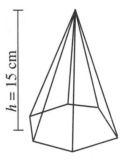

Dan's work: $V = \frac{(4^2\pi)(9)}{3} = 150.8$ cm^3

Ann's work: $V = (4^2\pi)(9) = 452.4$ cm^3

Jan's work: $V = \frac{1}{3}(4^2\pi)(9) = 150.8$ cm^3

10-39.   Find the volume of the pyramid at right. The hexagonal base has an area of 128 cm^2.

$h = 15$ cm

10-40.   LEARNING LOG

If you know the volume of any prism, how can you find the volume of a pyramid that has the same base area and height as the prism? If you know the volume of any cylinder, how can you find the volume of a cone that has the same base area and height as the cylinder? Answer these questions in your Learning Log. Label this entry with today's date, and title it "Volumes of Cones and Pyramids."

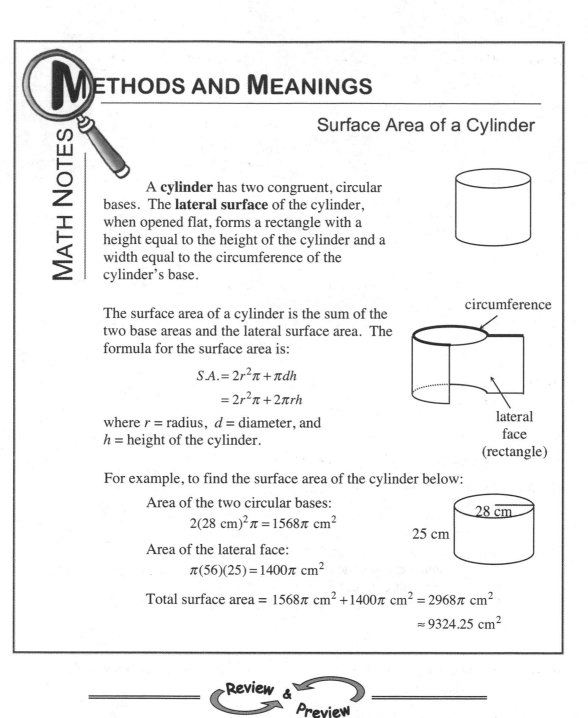

MᴇᴛʜODS AND Mᴇᴀɴɪɴɢs

Surface Area of a Cylinder

A **cylinder** has two congruent, circular bases. The **lateral surface** of the cylinder, when opened flat, forms a rectangle with a height equal to the height of the cylinder and a width equal to the circumference of the cylinder's base.

The surface area of a cylinder is the sum of the two base areas and the lateral surface area. The formula for the surface area is:

$$S.A. = 2r^2\pi + \pi dh$$
$$= 2r^2\pi + 2\pi rh$$

where r = radius, d = diameter, and h = height of the cylinder.

circumference

lateral face (rectangle)

For example, to find the surface area of the cylinder below:

Area of the two circular bases:
$$2(28 \text{ cm})^2 \pi = 1568\pi \text{ cm}^2$$

Area of the lateral face:
$$\pi(56)(25) = 1400\pi \text{ cm}^2$$

Total surface area = $1568\pi \text{ cm}^2 + 1400\pi \text{ cm}^2 = 2968\pi \text{ cm}^2$
$$\approx 9324.25 \text{ cm}^2$$

28 cm

25 cm

Review & Preview

10-41.   Find the volume of the cone shown in problem 10-37.

10-42.   The pyramid at right has a volume of 312 cubic feet. If the prism next to it has the same base area and height, what is its volume? Explain how you know.

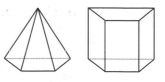

Core Connections, Course 3

10-43. Which table or tables below show a proportional relationship? Justify your answers.

a.

x	5	7	9	–8	0	11	15
y	9	13	17	–17	–19	21	29

b.

x	7	14	91	9	–12	–36	81
y	$2\frac{1}{3}$	$4\frac{2}{3}$	$30\frac{1}{3}$	3	–4	–12	27

c.

x	–3	–10	0	10	5	4	$\frac{1}{2}$	$-\frac{3}{2}$
y	–27	–1000	0	1000	125	48	$\frac{1}{8}$	$-\frac{27}{4}$

10-44. Find the volume of the prism at right. All angles are right angles.

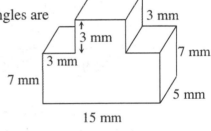

10-45. Graph the points $(-2, 4)$, $(2, 1)$, and $(-2, -2)$ and connect the points to create a triangle.

a. What is the perimeter of the triangle?

b. Translate the triangle up 2 and right 3. What are the new coordinates?

c. What is the perimeter of the triangle after its translation in part (b)?

10-46. a. Make a table for the rule $y = \sqrt{x}$ that includes x-values from –1 to 10. What happened?

b. Graph the rule on graph paper.

c. What kind of growth does the rule show? How do you know?

d. Is this relationship a function? How do you know?

10.1.4 What if it is a three-dimensional circle?

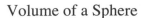

Volume of a Sphere

So far in this chapter you have been finding the volume of three-dimensional solids with circular bases, but what if the object is a three-dimensional circle? A **sphere** is a three-dimensional object shaped like a ball. Every point on the outside of a sphere is the same distance from its center. Today you will use what you have learned about the volume of a cylinder to find the volume of a sphere.

4,186

10-47. Myron's family is putting a pool in their backyard. He is so excited that he wants to figure out how long it will take to fill the pool! He found the blueprints for the pool and recreated the sketches at right, but he is not quite sure how to use them to find the volume of the pool.

What three-dimensional figures does Myron need to be able to find the volume of before he can determine the volume of the pool?

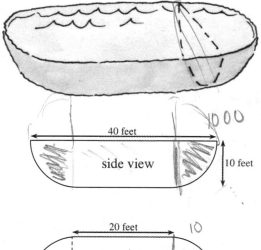

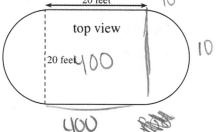

10-48. Your teacher will lead you through a demonstration about the volume of a sphere.

a. How are the diameter of the half sphere related to the diameter and height of the cylinder?

b. How many half spheres full of rice were needed to fill the cylinder to the height of the sphere's diameter?

c. Based on the demonstration, describe how the volume of a full sphere compares to the volume of a cylinder when their heights and diameters are equal.

470

10-49. **VOLUME OF A SPHERE**

What is the formula for the volume of a sphere?
How can you use what your class figured out
about the relationship between the cylinder and
the bowl in problem 10-48 to generalize a
formula for the volume of a sphere?

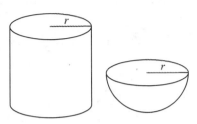

a. If 3 bowls of water completely filled a cylinder in which the diameter was
    the same as the height, how many spheres is this? Write your answer as a
    fraction.

b. Write an equation relating the volume of a sphere and the volume of a
    cylinder.

c. If the height and diameter of the cylinder are equal, write an equation for
    the height of the cylinder using the radius.

d. Use substitution and your equation from part (b) to write an equation for
    the volume of a sphere. Simplify your answer.

10-50. Use what you have learned in the previous problems to help Myron calculate
the volume of the pool in problem 10-47.

10-51. If there is 0.1337 of a cubic foot in 1 gallon, how many gallons of water will it
take to fill Myron's swimming pool completely?

10-52. Since Myron wants to know how long it will take to fill the pool, he needs to
know how fast water flows out of the hose. He gets an empty gallon jug, turns
the water up as high as possible, and finds that it takes 6 seconds to fill the jug.
At this rate, how long will it take to fill the entire pool?

10-53. If a sphere has a volume of 36π ft^3, what is the radius? Work with your team
to write and solve an equation to find the radius of the sphere.

10-54. **LEARNING LOG**

How can you calculate the volume of a sphere? What
information do you need to know? Answer these questions
as an entry in your Learning Log. Include an example that
demonstrates how to find the volume of a sphere. Title the
entry "Volume of a Sphere" and label it with today's date.

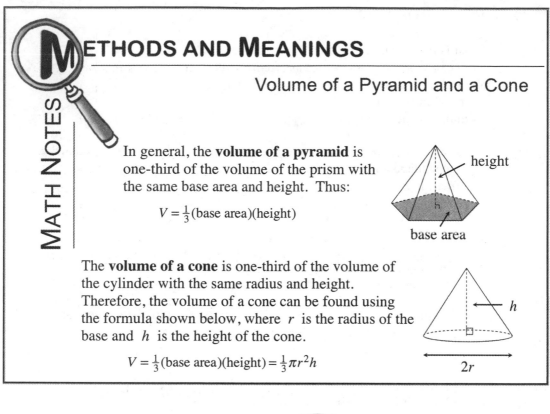

METHODS AND MEANINGS

Volume of a Pyramid and a Cone

MATH NOTES

In general, the **volume of a pyramid** is one-third of the volume of the prism with the same base area and height. Thus:

$$V = \tfrac{1}{3}(\text{base area})(\text{height})$$

The **volume of a cone** is one-third of the volume of the cylinder with the same radius and height. Therefore, the volume of a cone can be found using the formula shown below, where r is the radius of the base and h is the height of the cone.

$$V = \tfrac{1}{3}(\text{base area})(\text{height}) = \tfrac{1}{3}\pi r^2 h$$

Review & Preview

10-55.   Calculate the volume of each sphere described below.

a.   radius = 5 cm

b.   diameter = 3 feet

10-56.   If the volume of a sphere is 113.04 ft^3, write and solve and equation to find the radius.

10-57.   Find the volume of each shape below.

a.   Rectangle-based prism

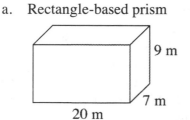

9 m

7 m

20 m

b.   Rectangle-based pyramid

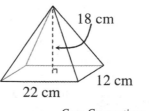

18 cm

12 cm

22 cm

10-58.   a.   Make a table for the rule $y = 2x^3$ that includes x-values from -3 to 3.

b.   Graph the rule on graph paper.

c.   What kind of growth does the rule have? Is the rule a function? Explain your answers.

10-59.   Sarah and three of her friends left her house for a long bike ride on the river bike path. They rode for three hours at 10 miles per hour and then rested for an hour while they ate their lunches. After lunch, they raced each other back to Sarah's house at 15 miles per hour.

a.   Draw a graph that could represent this situation. Place "Time (hours)" on the horizontal axis and "Distance (miles from Sarah's house)" on the vertical axis.

b.   Describe each part of the graph using the following words: linear, nonlinear, decreasing, increasing, and constant.

10-60.   Sherice can fill lemonade cups at a rate of four cups per minute.

a.   How many cups can she fill in 6 minutes?

b.   How many cups can she fill in 10 minutes?

c.   If Sherice fills c cups in t minutes, write an equation that relates c and t.

10-61.   Calculate the value of x.

a.

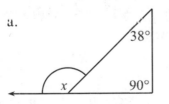

b.

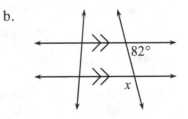

10.1.5 How much will it hold?

Applications of Volume

In this section, you have learned how to find the surface area and the volume of several kinds of solids – cylinders, cones, pyramids, and spheres. These skills can be very useful when solving real-world problems such as the one that you will encounter in this lesson. Use all of what you have learned and work together with your team to accomplish a challenging task!

10-62.   Sam Mallory, the owner of Mallory's Ice Cream Shop, wants to be able to advertise that his cones hold the most ice cream. His cones are made out of circular waffles with a set diameter. His employees cut a wedge-shaped piece from the circle and then fold it into a cone shape. He needs help determining how they can do this to create a cone with the largest volume. You have been hired to help solve this problem.

As you work through the steps below, neatly record your work. When you are finished, you will make a presentation of your findings for the owner.

Your Task: Using the materials provided by your teacher, create cones of various sizes and calculate their volumes. Determine the angle of the removed **sector** (a wedge-shaped piece of the circle) that results in the largest volume. Follow the steps below for creating a cone.

Before you get started, decide on the angle of the sector that each pair in your team will use to create a cone. Repeat the process below using different angles until you think that you have solved the task and found the largest volume possible.

1.   Locate the center of the circle by folding it in half in two different directions. The intersection of the folds is the center of the circle. Place a dot at the center.

2.   Use a ruler to draw a radius of the circle.

3.   Use a protractor to measure the angle of the sector that you chose to be removed. Then use the ruler to draw the second radius for that angle.

4.   Cut out the sector and then tape the edges of the sector together to create a cone.

5.   Use a ruler to make the measurements of the cone that you need and calculate its volume. Record your work.

10-63. Your team needs to present your findings to the owner of the ice-cream shop. Create a stand-alone poster displaying your results and advice for the owner. Be sure to include enough information that someone unfamiliar with the problem will understand your work and how you came to your conclusion. Also be sure to make your poster neat and presentable.

10-64. **Additional Challenge:** Now that the ice-cream-shop owner knows how to create cones with the largest volume, he wants to know how many cones he can make with each tub of ice cream.

He has measured a cylindrical tub and informed you that it has a diameter of 9.5 inches and a height of 10.5 inches. Each waffle cone is created from a circular waffle with a diameter of 5 inches. Then it is packed full and has a half spherical scoop on the top, as shown in the diagram at right.

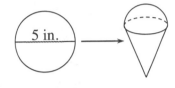

How many cones can the owner create with each tub of ice cream?

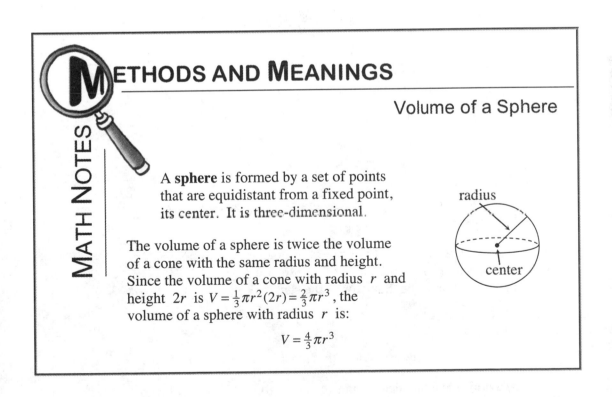

10-65. Find the volume of a sphere with a radius of 620,000 miles. Write your answer using scientific notation.

10-66. Find the volume of the cone.

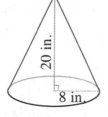

10-67. Graph the points $(0,2)$, $(6,2)$, $(7,4)$, and $(1,4)$ and connect the points in order to create a parallelogram. What is the perimeter of the parallelogram? Is the perimeter a rational or irrational number? How do you know?

10-68. Simplify each of the following expressions.

   a. $(5x^3)^2$ b. $\dfrac{14a^3b^2}{21a^4b^3}$ c. $2m^3n^2 \cdot 3mn^4$

10-69. First decide if the triangles below are similar. Then, if they are similar, use the information in each diagram to solve for x.

   a. 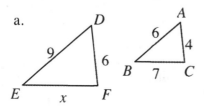   b. Careful!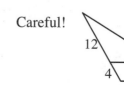

10-70. The label of the Aloha Pineapple Juice can is 7 inches high and has an area of 140 square inches. What is the diameter of the can?

10-71. Sketch an example of a graph that meets the description below.

   a. non-linear and decreasing   b. linear and increasing

Core Connections, Course 3

Chapter 10 Closure   What have I learned?

Reflection and Synthesis

The activities below offer you a chance to reflect
about what you have learned during this chapter.
As you work, look for concepts that you feel very
comfortable with, ideas that you would like to learn
more about, and topics you need more help with.

①   WHAT HAVE I LEARNED?

Doing the problems in this section will help you to evaluate which types of
problems you feel comfortable with and which ones you need more help
with.

Solve each problem as completely as you can. The table at the end of this
closure section provides answers to these problems. It also tells you where
you can find additional help and where to find practice problems like them.

CL 10-72.   Find the surface area and volume of each solid below.

     a.   All angles are right angles.   b.   Right prism with base area = 48 cm²

         7'   4'   15 cm

         18'   14 cm

   12'   8'

          40'   5 cm   5 cm
                                     9 cm

CL 10-73.   Find the surface area and volume of the cylinder   diameter = 8 cm
           at right. Show your work clearly.

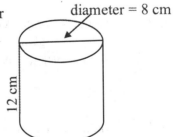

CL 10-74.   Find the volume of a pyramid that has a
           square base with sides of eight inches and
           a height of 12 inches.

CL 10-75.   Ella's cat has climbed up onto the roof of her house and cannot get down! The roof of the house is 24 feet above the ground. The fire department has set up a 28-foot ladder to climb to rescue the cat. The base of the ladder is resting on the ground, and the top of the ladder extends 2 feet beyond the edge of the roof. How far away from the base of the house is the base of the ladder? You may want to draw a diagram to help you solve the problem.

CL 10-76.   Simplify the product or quotient. Be sure your final answer is in scientific notation.

a. $(3.25 \times 10^5)(4 \times 10^3)$

b. $\dfrac{4 \times 10^3}{2 \times 10^{-2}}$

CL 10-77.   If a cube has a volume of 50 cm^3, what is the length of a side?

CL 10-78.   Given the equation of the line $6x - 2y = 10$, complete each of the following problems.

a.   Solve the equation for y.

b.   State the slope of the line.

c.   Graph the line.

CL 10-79.   Two brothers, Martin and Horace, are in their backyard. Horace is taking down a wall on one side of the yard while Martin is building a wall on the other side. Martin starts from scratch and lays 2 bricks every minute. Meanwhile, Horace takes down 3 bricks each minute from his wall. It takes Horace 55 minutes to finish tearing down his wall.

a.   How many bricks were originally in the wall that Horace started tearing down?

b.   Represent this situation with an equation or system of equations. Be sure to define your variable(s).

c.   When did the two walls have the same number of bricks?

CL 10-80.   For each of the problems above, do the following:

- Draw a bar or number line that represents 0 to 10.

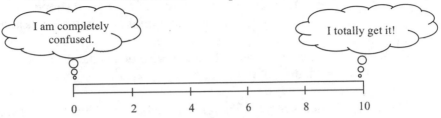

- Color or shade in a portion of the bar that represents your level of understanding and comfort with completing that problem on your own.

If any of your bars are less than a 5, choose *one* of those problems and do one of the following tasks:

- Write two questions that you would like to ask about that problem.
- Brainstorm two things that you DO know about that type of problem.

If all of your bars are a 5 or above, choose one of those problems and do one of these tasks:

- Write two questions you might ask or hints you might give to a student who was stuck on the problem.
- Make a new problem that is similar and more challenging than that problem and solve it.

WHAT TOOLS CAN I USE?

You have several tools and references available to help support your learning – your teacher, your study team, your math book, and your Toolkit, to name only a few. At the end of each chapter you will have an opportunity to review your Toolkit for completeness as well as to revise or update it to better reflect your current understanding of big ideas.

The main elements of your Toolkit should be your Learning Logs, Math Notes, and the vocabulary used in this chapter. Math words that are new to this chapter appear in bold in the text. Refer to the lists provided below and follow your teacher's instructions to revise your Toolkit, which will help make it a useful reference for you as you complete this chapter and prepare to begin the next one.

Learning Log Entries

- Lesson 10.1.1 – Cube Roots
- Lesson 10.1.2 – Surface Area and Volume of a Cylinder
- Lesson 10.1.3 – Volumes of Cones and Pyramids
- Lesson 10.1.4 – Volume of a Sphere

Math Notes

- Lesson 10.1.2 – Volume of a Cylinder
- Lesson 10.1.3 – Surface Area of a Cylinder
- Lesson 10.1.4 – Volume of a Pyramid and a Cone
- Lesson 10.1.5 – Volume of a Sphere

Mathematical Vocabulary

The following is a list of vocabulary found in this chapter. Some of the words you have been seen in previous chapters. The words in bold are the words new to this chapter. Make sure that you are familiar with the terms below and know what they mean. For the words you do not know, refer to the glossary or index. You might also add these words to your Toolkit so that you can reference them in the future.

base (of a prism)	circumference	**cone**
cube (of a number)	**cube root**	**cylinder**
diameter	height	**lateral face**
perfect cube	prism	**pyramid**
radius	**sphere**	square (a number)
square root	surface area	volume

Answers and Support for Closure Problems
What Have I Learned?

Note: MN = Math Note, LL = Learning Log

Problem	Solution	Need Help?	More Practice
CL 10-72.	a. SA = 1512 ft^2, V = 2744 ft^3 b. SA = 572 cm^2, V = 672 cm^3	Lesson 10.1.1	Problems 10-2, 10-27, 10-42, 10-44, and 10-57
CL 10-73.	SA: $128\pi \approx 402.12$ cm^2 V: $192\pi \approx 603.19$ cm^3	Lesson 10.1.2 MN: 10.1.2 and 10.1.3 LL: 10.1.2	Problems 10-18, 10-20, 10-23, and 10-26
CL 10-74.	Volume = 256 in.^{3}	Lesson 10.1.3 MN: 10.1.4 LL: 10.1.3	Problems 10-42 and 10-57
CL 10-75.	The base of the ladder will be approximately 10 feet from the base of the house.	Lessons 9.2.2, 9.2.3, and 9.2.5 MN: 9.2.3 and 9.2.5 LL: 9.2.3 and 9.2.5	Problems 10-14, 10-28, and 10-67
CL 10-76.	a. 1.3×10^9 b. 2×10^5	Lessons 8.2.1, 8.2.3, and 8.2.4 MN: 8.2.3 and 8.2.4 LL: 8.2.1	Problems 8-125, 9-113, 9-114, and 10-65
CL 10-77.	$\sqrt[3]{50} \approx 3.68$ cm	Lesson 10.1.1	Problems 10-4, 10-6, 10-12, and 10-13
CL 10-78.	a. $y = 3x - 5$ b. 3 c. See graph.	Lessons 4.1.4, 5.1.1, and 7.2.1 MN: 5.1.1 and 7.2.3	Problem 9-23, 9-26, 9-58, and 9-77
CL 10-79.	a. $55(3) = 165$ b. Let x = minutes, y = # bricks $\quad y = 2x$ $\quad y = 165 - 3x$ c. In 33 minutes, each wall will have 66 bricks.	Lessons 5.2.2 and 5.2.3 MN: 5.2.2, 5.2.3, and 5.2.4	Problems 8-131, 9-48, and 9-152

10.2.1 How can I find the measurement?

Indirect Measurement

When most people think of measurement, they think of using a ruler or tape measure to find a length. However, during this course you found the measures of objects using other types of information, a process called **indirect measurement**. Today's activity will provide you with opportunities to connect several ways you know for finding measures. As you work with your team, ask the following questions.

$$50 : 7.5$$

How can we visualize it?

$$x : 1.5$$

What information do we need?

$$75 = 1.5x$$

Which strategy should we use?

$$10 = x$$

10-81.   The beautiful young princess of Polygonia is very sad. A mean ogre has locked her into a tower of a castle. She could escape through the window, but it is 50 feet above the ground, a long distance to jump! A moat full of alligators surrounds the tower. Naturally, Prince Charming wants to rescue her.

The prince has some rope. His plan is to use an arrow to shoot one end of the rope up to her window. The princess can then slide down the rope to the other side of the moat, and off they will ride into the sunset.

Help the prince save the princess by answering the questions below.

a.   The prince knows that the closer he is to the tower, the less rope he will need. However, he is not sure how wide the moat is around the castle.

In a book about the castle, the prince found a diagram of the tower and moat. Using his ruler, he found that the window in the diagram is 7.5 inches above the moat, while the farthest edge of the moat is 1.5 inches from the base of the tower. How close to the tower can the prince get? Draw diagrams and show your work.

b.   Before he shoots the arrow, the prince wants to make sure he has enough rope. If he needs an extra 2 feet of rope for tying it to the window frame and holding it on the ground, how long does his rope need to be? Explain.

Problem continues on next page. →

10-81.   *Problem continued from previous page.*

c.   The princess thinks she might fall off the rope if the slope is steeper than $\frac{5}{4}$. The prince plans to attach the rope to the ground at the edge of the moat, and the princess will attach the rope to the window frame 50 feet above the ground.

i.   According to the prince's plan, what would the slope of the rope be? Would it be too steep? Justify your answer.

ii.   Should the princess worry about the prince's plan? How steep would the prince's rope be? Find the angle the rope would make with the ground.
Use a protractor to measure the angle.

d.   If one end of the rope is attached to the window frame and the prince holds his end of the rope 2 feet above the ground, where would the prince need to stand so that the slope of the rope is only $\frac{5}{4}$? If he has a rope that is 62 feet long, will his rope be long enough? Justify your conclusion. Draw a picture and label it with all your measurements.

e.   What if the prince holds his end of the rope 5 feet above the ground? Can he stand in some location so that the rope is not steeper than $\frac{5}{4}$? (The rope is still 62 feet long.) Justify your conclusion.

10-82.   MAKING CONNECTIONS

When you solved this problem, you needed to use what you learned about several different math ideas.

a.   Discuss how you solved the problem with your team.

- Use colors to mark parts of your solution that used particular math ideas. (For example, did you compare portions? Did you solve equations?)

- Label each math idea with words in the margin of your paper.

b.   Contribute your ideas to a class discussion. Did any other teams identify math ideas that you used but did not notice? If so, add them to your notes. Then write each math idea on an index card.

c.   How are these different math ideas connected in this problem? Work with your team and follow your teacher's instructions to make a concept map. Work with your team to find ways to show or explain each of the connections you find.

10-83.   BECOMING MATHEMATICALLY PROFICIENT

During this course, you have been asked lots of different kinds of questions. The purpose of many of the questions is to help you think in new ways.

This book focuses on helping you use some very specific Mathematical Practices. The Mathematical Practices are different ways to approach a mathematics problem, pull it apart, and work on it. They include ways you communicate mathematics to your teammates and teacher. They are what make you a mathematician, not just a number cruncher!

Two of the Mathematical Practices you may have used in this lesson, for example, are **construct viable arguments and critique the reasoning of others** and **use appropriate tools**. Below, you will learn more about what these mean.

a.   With your team, read and discuss the descriptions below.

Construct viable arguments and critique the reasoning of others:

> An important practice of mathematics is to **construct viable arguments and critique the reasoning of others**. In this course, you regularly shared information, opinions, and expertise with your study team. You took turns talking, listening, contributing, arguing, asking for help, checking for understanding, and keeping each other focused.
>
> During this process, you learned to use higher-order thinking. "Critical thinking" is another way to describe "higher-order thinking." It can be difficult to learn, but it is extremely valuable. Learning how to think critically helped you understand concepts more deeply. It allowed you to apply newfound ideas in all sorts of problems, not just the specific concept you happened to be working on.
>
> You and your study teams used higher-order, critical-thinking skills any time you provided clarification, built on each other's ideas, analyzed a problem by breaking it into smaller parts, came to agreement during a discussion, and productively criticized each other's ideas.
>
> Justifying and critiquing was a part of your daily classwork, not an occasional assignment. For each problem, you were expected to communicate your mathematical findings in writing, in oral presentations, or in poster presentations in a clear and convincing manner.

Problem continues on next page. →

10-83. *Problem continued from previous page.*

Use appropriate tools strategically:

> Throughout this course, you had to **use appropriate tools strategically**. In a typical lesson, you had many different tools available to you. Examples of tools include rulers, scissors, diagrams, graph paper, blocks, tiles, and calculators. However, you were not usually told which specific tools to use to solve any particular problem.
>
> Sometimes, different teams decided to use different tools to solve the same problem. Thus, you often shared your solution strategies with the whole class. Frequently, this included a discussion about which tools were most efficient and productive to solve a given problem.
>
> As you continued to do more and more sophisticated mathematics throughout the course, you were introduced to other tools, such as computer applications.

b. How did you **use appropriate tools strategically** when you solved problem 10-81? Be ready to explain your ideas.

c. How did you **construct viable arguments and critique the reasoning of others** while doing problem 10-81? How is **critiquing the reasoning of others** important in problems such as this one?

d. Work with your team to brainstorm other problems in this course in which you **used appropriate tools strategically** and **constructed viable arguments and critiqued the reasoning of others**. Be ready to share your ideas with the class.

10.2.2 How can I figure it out?

Finding Unknowns

Have you ever read a problem and been convinced that you did not have enough information to solve it? Sometimes the relationships just seem too complicated. You may even think it is a trick problem with no logical answer. However, if you persevere, remember all the tools and strategies you have worked with, and try to represent the situation in multiple ways, you may surprise yourself. In this lesson, you will use what you have learned to solve some problems that may at first seem impossible. While you work, keep these questions in mind:

How can we represent it?

What is the best strategy or model for this problem?

Is this like any other problem we have seen?

10-84.   NIFTY NECKLACES

Amber and Melissa were making bead necklaces with one-centimeter wooden beads and longer green glass beads when they stopped to admire each other's work. Amber's necklace had only 11 total beads. She had designed a pattern that alternated 5 green beads with 6 wooden beads, as shown below. Melissa's necklace used 4 green beads and 11 wooden beads in the pattern shown below.

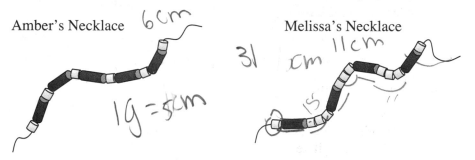

Amber's Necklace

Melissa's Necklace

When they compared their progress, they were surprised to find that the necklaces were exactly the same length!

With your team, figure out the length of each green bead and the total length of each necklace. Be prepared to share your strategies with the class.

10-85. The necklaces are so popular that Amber and Melissa have decided to go into the jewelry business. They have located a supply house that will sell them beads in any color and any length. Help Amber and Melissa fill the orders below by figuring out the necessary bead lengths.

a. Cassie wants a necklace 58 cm long that has 12 of the 1-cm wooden beads arranged with some red beads. Red beads are available in lengths of 3 cm or 4 cm. Find at least two different ways in which Amber and Melissa could fill Cassie's order.

b. Justin wants to order a necklace with the same pattern as Melissa's (one green alternating with three wooden beads, with one wooden bead on each end), but he wants it to be 61 centimeters long. Can his order be filled? If so, sketch a diagram and find out how many beads of each are needed. If not, explain how he could adjust his order.

c. **Additional Challenge:** Leonora wants two necklaces that use the 1-cm wood beads and some other bead of any color or any length. She has created the following designs. The longer necklace will use 24 of the 1-cm wooden beads and just one other bead in the center. The shorter one will use 4 of the other beads, each pair separated by just one of the 1-cm wooden beads. She wants one necklace to be exactly 5 cm shorter than the other. What length of bead should be used for this order?

10-86. MAKING CONNECTIONS

When you solved the previous bead problems, you needed to use your knowledge about several different mathematical ideas.

a. With your team, do the following:

• Use colors to mark parts of your solution that used particular mathematical ideas. (For example, did you measure lengths? Did you draw quadrilaterals?)

• Label each mathematical idea with words in the margin of your paper.

b. Contribute your ideas to a class discussion. Did any other teams identify mathematical ideas that you used but had not noticed? If so, add these to your notes. Then write each mathematical idea on an index card.

c. How are these different mathematical ideas connected in this problem? Work with your team and follow your teacher's instructions to make a concept map. You will need to find ways to show or explain each of the connections you find.

10-87.   BECOMING MATHEMATICALLY
         PROFICIENT

During this course, you have been asked lots of
different kinds of questions. The purpose of
many of the questions is to help you think in
new ways.

This book focuses on helping you use some
very specific Mathematical Practices. The
Mathematical Practices are different ways to
approach a mathematics problem, pull it apart,
and work on it. They include ways you
communicate mathematics to your teammates
and teacher. They are what make you a
mathematician, not just a number cruncher!

Two of the Mathematical Practices you may
have used in this lesson, for example, are **make
sense of problems and persevere in solving
them** and **look for and make use of structure**.
Below, you will learn more about what these mean.

a.   With your team, read and discuss the descriptions below.

Make sense of problems and persevere in solving them:

Making sense of problems and persevering in solving them means
that you can solve realistic problems that are full of different kinds of
mathematics. These types of problems are not routine, simple, or
typical. Instead, they combine lots of math ideas and real-life
situations.

In this course, you made sense of such problems and persevered in
solving them on a daily basis. You carried out investigations that were
not simply "word problems." By making sense of a problem, rather
than being told how to solve it step-by-step, you developed a deeper
understanding of mathematics. You also learned how to carry out
mathematical procedures fluently and efficiently.

In addition to learning and using problem-solving strategies, you had to
stick with challenging problems, trying different strategies and using
all of the resources available to you.

Look for and make use of structure:

> **Looking for and making use of structure** has been an important part of this course. Since you are working to develop a deep, conceptual understanding of mathematics, you often use this practice to bring closure to an investigation. There are many concepts that you have learned by looking at the underlying structure of a math idea and thinking about how it connects to other ideas you have already learned.
>
> One example of when you looked at the underlying structure of a math idea is when you learned to simplify with the "Giant One." The "Giant One" was a structure to use in arithmetic with fractions, where the numerator and denominator are the same, giving you a value of 1.
>
> By being involved in the actual development of math concepts, you gain a deeper understanding of mathematics than you would if you were simply told what they are and how to do related problems.

b. How did you **make sense of problems and persevere in solving them** when you solved problem 10-84? Be ready to explain your ideas.

c. How did you **look for and make use of structure** while doing problem 10-84? How can **looking for and making use of structure** help you do problems like this one?

d. Work with your team to brainstorm other problems in this course in which you **made sense of problems and persevered in solving them** and **looked for and made use of structure**. Be ready to share your ideas with the class.

10.2.3 How is it changing?

Analyzing Data to Identify a Trend

Have you ever tried to figure out whether you could earn enough money to be able to buy something that you want? In this lesson, you will consider the relationship between the time you work and your pay rate as you work with your team to analyze data and make predictions.

10-88. Devon hopes to get a summer job at an amusement park. His goal is to earn enough money during the summer to buy a laptop for $875. He is not sure what pay rate he will be offered, so he asked his friends who work at the same amusement park for information from their last paycheck. The information he gathered is in the table at right.

	Time (hours)	Pay (dollars)
Frieda	21	$200.00
Ben	25	$305.00
Emory	36	$252.00
Si Yun	50	$480.00
Jillian	55	$600.00
Malik	64	$512.00
Dazjon	72	$600.00
Grace	80	$700.00

a. On graph paper, set up a graph, carefully decide how to scale the axes, and graph Devon's data.

b. Find the hourly rate for each of Devon's friends.

c. What is the highest rate per hour one of Devon's friends is earning? What is the lowest rate per hour? Explain how you found your answer.

d. Draw a trend line that represents this data. Use your trend line to help Devon predict how much he will earn. Why does it make sense that the trend line should pass through the origin?

Problem continues on next page. →

Core Connections, Course 3

10-88.   *Problem continued from previous page.*

   e.   Devon hopes to work 4 hours each day. If he works Friday through Sunday
        for 10 weeks, how many hours would he work?

   f.   Based on your trend line, how much money can Devon expect to be paid
        per hour? Show how you found your answer.

   g.   Devon knows that he will need to pay 7.5% tax for his laptop. Will he
        make enough money? Explain how you know.

10-89.   MAKING CONNECTIONS

   When you solved this problem, you needed to use what you learned about
   several different math ideas.

   a.   Discuss how you solved the problem with your team.

        •   Use colors to mark parts of your solution that used particular math
            ideas. (For example, did you calculate volume? Did you use
            transformations?)

        •   Label each math idea with words in the margin of your paper.

   b.   Contribute your ideas to a class discussion. Did any other teams identify
        math ideas that you used but did not notice? If so, add them to your notes.
        Then write each math idea on an index card.

   c.   How are these different math ideas connected in this problem? Work with
        your team and follow your teacher's instructions to make a concept map.
        Work with your team to find ways to show or explain each of the
        connections you find.

10-90.   BECOMING MATHEMATICALLY PROFICIENT

During this course, you have been asked lots of different
kinds of questions. The purpose of many of the questions
is to help you think in new ways.

This book focuses on helping you use some very specific
Mathematical Practices. The Mathematical Practices are
different ways to approach a mathematics problem, pull it
apart, and work on it. They include ways you
communicate mathematics to your teammates and
teacher. They are what make you a mathematician, not
just a number cruncher!

Two of the Mathematical Practices you may have used in this lesson, for
example, are **model with mathematics** and **look for and express regularity in
repeated reasoning.** Below, you will learn more about what these mean.

a.   With your team, read and discuss the descriptions below.

Model with mathematics:

When you **model with mathematics**, you are not wearing fancy
clothes on a runway in New York! Mathematical modeling is what you
do when you work with situations that involve multiple
representations. For example, in this course, you frequently modeled
different relationships and patterns using tables, graphs, equations, and
words or diagrams.

In creating these models, you often first make assumptions, then make
predictions, and finally check to see if your predictions make sense in
the context of the problem.

In situations involving the variability of data, you learned that although
a model may not be perfect, it can still be very useful for describing
data and making predictions. You also found that a calculator or
computer can help you model situations more efficiently than doing the
work by hand.

Look for and express regularity in repeated reasoning:

> **Look for and express regularity in repeated reasoning** means that when you are faced with an investigation of a new mathematical concept, you sometimes look for a simpler or related problem. This strategy can help expand your ability to solve increasingly complex problems.
>
> For example, you **looked for and expressed regularity in repeated reasoning** when you expanded the reasoning for multiplication to develop the rules for exponents.

b. How did **looking for and making use of structure** help you solve problem 10-88? Be ready to explain your ideas.

c. Sometimes you **look for and express regularity in repeated reasoning** to help explain mathematics and to explain your thinking. How did **looking for regularity in repeated reasoning** help you in problem 10-88?

d. Work with your team to brainstorm other problems in this course in which you **looked for and expressed regularity in repeated reasoning** and **looked for and made use of structure**. Be ready to share your ideas with the class.

Core Connections, Course 3
Checkpoint Materials

Notes to Students (and their Teachers)

Students master different skills at different speeds. No two students learn exactly the same way at the same time. At some point you will be expected to perform certain skills accurately. Most of these Checkpoint problems incorporate skills that you should have developed in previous grades. If you have not mastered these skills yet it does not mean that you will not be successful in this class. However, you may need to do some work outside of class to get caught up on them.

Starting in Chapter 1 and finishing in Chapter 9, there are 9 problems designed as Checkpoint problems. Each one is marked with an icon like the one above. After you do each of the Checkpoint problems, check your answers by referring to this section. If your answers are incorrect, you may need some extra practice to develop that skill. The practice sets are keyed to each of the Checkpoint problems in the textbook. Each has the topic clearly labeled, followed by the answers to the corresponding Checkpoint problem and then some completed examples. Next, the complete solution to the Checkpoint problem from the text is given, and there are more problems for you to practice with answers included.

Remember, looking is not the same as doing! You will never become good at any sport by just watching it, and in the same way, reading through the worked examples and understanding the steps is not the same as being able to do the problems yourself. How many of the extra practice problems do you need to try? That is really up to you. Remember that your goal is to be able to do similar problems on your own confidently and accurately. This is your responsibility. You should not expect your teacher to spend time in class going over the solutions to the Checkpoint problem sets. If you are not confident after reading the examples and trying the problems, you should get help outside of class time or talk to your teacher about working with a tutor.

Checkpoint Topics

1. Operations with Signed Fractions and Decimals
2. Evaluating Expressions and Using Order of Operations
3. Unit Rates and Proportions
4. Area and Perimeter of Circles and Composite Figures
5. Solving Equations
6. Multiple Representations of Linear Equations
7. Solving Equations with Fractions ("Fraction Busters")
8. Transformations
9. Scatterplots and Association

Checkpoint 6

Problem 6-109

Multiple Representations of Linear Equations

Answers to problem 6-109:

a:

Figure #	0	1	2	3
# of Tiles	4	6	8	10

b:

x	0	1	2	3
y	7	4	1	−2

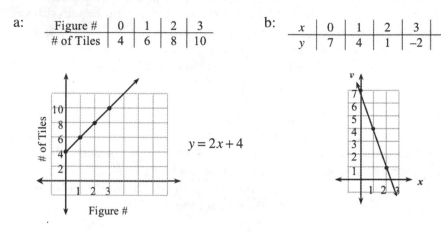

$y = 2x + 4$

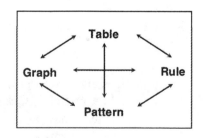

c: $y = 3x + 1$

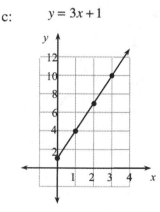

d:

x	0	1	2	3
y	6	4	2	0

$y = -2x + 6$

If you know one representation of a linear pattern, it can also be represented in three other different ways. Linear representations may be written as equations in the form $y = mx + b$ where m is the growth factor and b is the starting value.

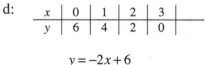

Example 1: Using the pattern at right, create an $x \rightarrow y$ table, a graph, and write the rule as an equation.

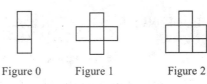

Figure 0   Figure 1   Figure 2   Figure 3

Solution: The number of tiles matched with the figure number gives the $x \rightarrow y$ table. Plotting those points gives the graph. Using the starting value for b and the growth factor for m gives the information to write the equation in $y = mx + b$ form.

Figure # (x)	0	1	2	3
# of Tiles (y)	3	5	7	9

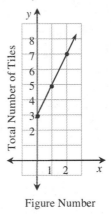

Total Number of Tiles

Figure Number

The starting number is 3 tiles and the pattern grows by 2 tiles each figure so the equation is $y = 2x + 3$.

Example 2: Create an $x \rightarrow y$ table and the rule (equation) based on the graph at right.

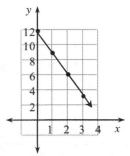

Solution:

Place the given points in a table:

x	0	1	2	3
y	12	9	6	3

The starting value is 12 and the "growth" factor is –3. The equation is:

$y = -3x + 12$

Now we can go back and solve the original problems.

a. Start by making a table from the tile pattern.

Figure #	0	1	2	3
# of Tiles	4	6	8	10

Since the starting value is 4 and the growth factor is 2 the equation is $y = 2x + 4$.

b. Make a table by replacing x in the rule with 0, 1, 2, and then computing y. See the table above. Plot the points from the table to get the graph shown with the given answers.

c. Looking at the table, the y-value changes by 9 when the the x-value changes by 3. Therefore the y-value is changing by 3 when the x-value is changing by 1. A completed table is shown below. Since the starting value is 1 and the growth factor is 3, the table and equation are: See the graph given with the answers.

x	0	1	2	3
y	1	4	7	10

$y = 3x + 1$

d. Again the table above is determined from the points on the graph. Looking at the table, the starting value is 6 and the growth factor is –2 so the equation is $y = -2x + 6$.

x	0	1	2	3
y	6	4	2	0

Here are some more to try. For each situation, complete a Multiple Representations of Linear Equations web by finding the missing $x \rightarrow y$ table, graph, and/or rule. Since there are many possible patterns, it is not necessary to create one.

1.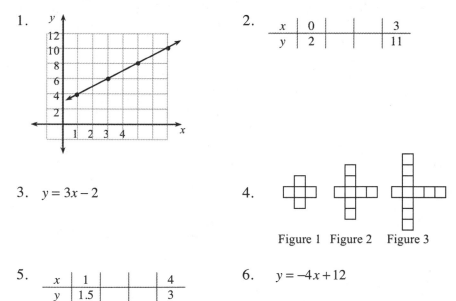

2.

x	0			3
y	2			11

3. $y = 3x - 2$

4.

Figure 1   Figure 2   Figure 3

5.

x	1			4
y	1.5			3

6. $y = -4x + 12$

7.

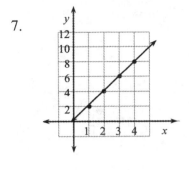

8.

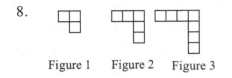

Figure 1   Figure 2   Figure 3

9. $y = -2x + 7$

10.

x	1	2		
y	$4\frac{1}{4}$	$6\frac{1}{2}$		

Answers

1.

x	1	2	3	4
y	4	5	6	7

$y = x + 3$

2.

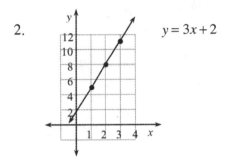

$y = 3x + 2$

3.

x	0	1	2	3
y	−2	1	4	7

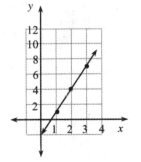

4.

x	0	1	2	3
y	2	5	8	11

$y = 3x + 2$

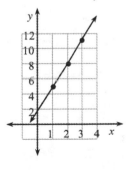

5.

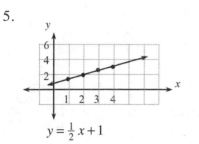

$$y = \tfrac{1}{2}x + 1$$

6.

x	0	1	2	3
y	12	8	4	0

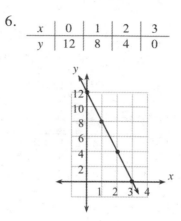

7.

x	0	1	2	3
y	0	2	4	6

$$y = 2x$$

8.

x	0	1	2	3
y	0	3	5	7

$$y = 2x + 1$$

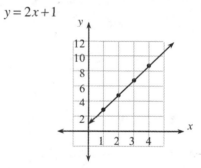

9.

x	0	1	2	3
y	7	5	3	1

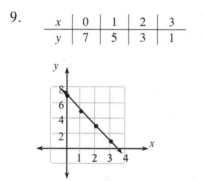

10. $y = \tfrac{3}{4}x + 5$

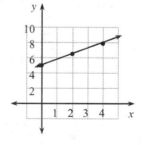

Checkpoint 7

Problem 7-115

Solving Equations with Fractions (Fraction Busters)

Answers to problem 7-115: a: $x = \frac{15}{4} = 3\frac{3}{4}$, b: $x \approx \$1.74$, c: $x = -5$, d: $(12, 16)$

Equations are often easier to solve if there are no fractions. To eliminate fractions from an equation, multiply both sides of the equation by the common denominator.

Example 1: Solve $\frac{1}{2}x + \frac{2}{3} = \frac{3}{4}$

Solution: Start by multiplying both sides of the equation by 12 (the common denominator.) Simplify and then solve as usual.

$$12\left(\tfrac{1}{2}x + \tfrac{2}{3}\right) = 12\left(\tfrac{3}{4}\right)$$
$$6x + 8 = 9$$
$$6x = 1$$
$$x = \tfrac{1}{6}$$

Example 2: Solve $1.1x + 0.35x = 29$

Solution: Two decimal places means that the common denominator is 100. Multiply both sides by 100 and solve as usual.

$$100(1.1x + 0.35x) = 100(29)$$
$$110x + 35x = 2900$$
$$145x = 2900$$
$$x = 20$$

Now we can go back and solve the original problems.

a.
$$\tfrac{1}{5}x + \tfrac{1}{3}x = 2$$
$$15\left(\tfrac{1}{5}x + \tfrac{1}{3}x\right) = 15(2)$$
$$3x + 5x = 30$$
$$8x = 30$$
$$x = \tfrac{30}{8} = \tfrac{15}{4} = 3\tfrac{3}{4}$$

b.
$$x + 0.15x = \$2$$
$$100(x + 0.15x) = 100(\$2)$$
$$100x + 15x = \$200$$
$$115x = \$200$$
$$x \approx \$1.74$$

c.
$$\tfrac{x+2}{3} = \tfrac{x-2}{7}$$
$$21\left(\tfrac{x+2}{3}\right) = 21\left(\tfrac{x-2}{7}\right)$$
$$7(x+2) = 3(x-2)$$
$$7x + 14 = 3x - 6$$
$$4x = -20$$
$$x = -5$$

d.
$$y = \tfrac{2}{3}x + 8$$
$$y = \tfrac{1}{2}x + 10$$
$$\tfrac{2}{3}x + 8 = \tfrac{1}{2}x + 10$$
$$6\left(\tfrac{2}{3}x + 8\right) = 6\left(\tfrac{1}{2}x + 10\right)$$
$$4x + 48 = 3x + 60$$
$$x = 12$$
$$y = \tfrac{2}{3}(12) + 8 = 16$$
$$(12, 16)$$

Here are some more to try. Solve each equation or system of equations.

1. $\frac{1}{6}x + \frac{2}{3}x = 5$

2. $y = 32x + 16$
   $y = 80x + 4$

3. $\frac{6}{15} = \frac{x-2}{40}$

4. $y = \frac{x}{3}$
   $y = \frac{4}{3}x - 9$

5. $\frac{x}{2} - 4 = \frac{x}{3}$

6. $\frac{x}{4} - 3 = \frac{x+4}{6} - 2$

7. $\frac{x}{10} + \frac{5}{12} = 3x - 1$

8. $\frac{2x-2}{6} - \frac{1}{2} = \frac{x}{2} - 2$

9. $0.2x + x = 30$

10. $y = \frac{x}{6} + \frac{1}{4}$
    $y = x - \frac{9}{4}$

11. $y = -3x + 2$
    $y = -\frac{15}{4}x + 3$

12. $x + 3\frac{2}{3} = 2x + \frac{1}{3}$

13. $\frac{x}{2} + \frac{4x}{3} = 2x - 1.5$

14. $\frac{x+1}{4x} = \frac{5}{16}$

15. $y = \frac{1}{3}x + 8$
    $y = -\frac{1}{2}x - 2$

16. $y = 7x + 2$
    $y = 2x - 10\frac{1}{2}$

17. $y = \frac{x}{2} - 1$
    $y = \frac{x+3}{12}$

18. $y = \frac{3}{2}x - 10$
    $y = \frac{x}{3} - \frac{x}{2}$

19. $\frac{x-1}{4} = \frac{7}{8}$

20. $\frac{2}{3}x = x - \frac{10}{3}$

Answers

1. $x = 6$

2. $x = \frac{1}{4}$, $y = 24$

3. $x = 18$

4. $x = 9$, $y = 3$

5. $x = 24$

6. $x = 20$

7. $x = \frac{85}{174}$

8. $x = 7$

9. $x = 25$

10. $x = 3$, $y = \frac{3}{4}$

11. $x = \frac{4}{3}$, $y = -2$

12. $x = 3\frac{1}{3}$

13. $x = 9$

14. $x = 4$

15. $x = -12$, $y = 4$

16. $x = -2\frac{1}{2}$, $y = -15\frac{1}{2}$

17. $x = 3$, $y = \frac{1}{2}$

18. $x = 6$, $y = -1$

19. $x = 4.5$

20. $x = 10$

Checkpoint 8

Problem 8-135

Transformations

Answers to problem 8-135: (Given in the order X, Y, Z) a: $(-2, 2), (-2, 0), (1, 2)$,
b: $(4, -1), (4, -3), (1, -1)$, c: $(-1, 4), (-3, 4), (-1, 1)$, d: $(-8, -2), (-8, 6), (-2, 2)$

Rigid transformations are ways to move an object while not changing its shape or size.
A translation (slide) moves an object vertically, horizontally or both. A reflection (flip)
moves an object across a line of reflection as in a mirror. A rotation (turn) moves an
object clockwise or counterclockwise around a point.

A dilation is a non-rigid transformation. It produces a figure that is similar to the original
by proportionally shrinking or stretching the figure from a point.

**Example 1: Translate (slide) $\triangle ABC$ left six units and down
three units. Give the coordinates of the new $\triangle XYZ$.**

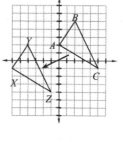

Solution: The original vertices are $A(0, 2)$, $B(2, 5)$, and $C(5, -1)$.
The new vertices are $X(-6, -1)$, $Y(-4, 2)$, and $Z(-1, -4)$.

**Example 2: Reflect (flip) $\triangle ABC$ across the x-axis to get $\triangle PQR$.
Give the coordinates of the new $\triangle PQR$.**

**Now reflect (flip) $\triangle ABC$ across the y-axis to get $\triangle XYZ$. Give the
coordinates of the new $\triangle XYZ$.**

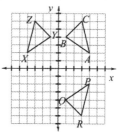

Solution: The key is that the reflection is the same distance from the
axis as the original figure. For the first reflection the points are
$P(4, -2)$, $Q(1, -4)$, and $R(3, -6)$. For the second reflection the
points are $X(-4, 2)$, $Y(-1, 4)$, and $Z(-3, 6)$.

**Example 3: Rotate (turn) $\triangle ABC$ counterclockwise 90° about
the origin to get $\triangle MNO$. Give the coordinates of the new
$\triangle MNO$. Then rotate $\triangle MNO$ counterclockwise another 90° to
get $\triangle XYZ$. Give the coordinates of the new $\triangle XYZ$.**

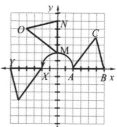

Solution: After the first 90° rotation, the coordinates of $A(2,0)$, B
$(6,0)$, and $C(5, 4)$ became $M(0, 2)$, $N(0, 6)$, and $O(-4, 5)$. Note
that each original point (x, y) became $(-y, x)$. After the next 90° rotation, the coordinates
of the vertices are now $X(-2, 0)$, $Y(-6, 0)$, and $Z(-5, -4)$. After the 180° rotation each of
the points (x, y) in the original $\triangle ABC$ became $(-x, -y)$. Similarly a 270°
counterclockwise rotation or a 90° clockwise rotation about the origin takes each point
(x, y) to the point $(y, -x)$.

Example 4: Dilate (enlarge/reduce) △*ABC* **by a scale factor of**
$\frac{1}{2}$ **from the origin to get** △*XYZ* **. Give the coordinates of the**
new △*XYZ* **.**

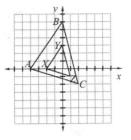

Solution: Multiplying the coordinates of the vertices of △*ABC* by
the scale factor gives the coordinates of the vertices of the new
△*XYZ* . They are *X* (−2,0), *Y* (0,3) and *Z* (1,−1).

Now we can go back and solve the original problems.

a. Sliding the triangle two units to the right and three units up increases the *x*-values by 2
and the *y*-values by 3. See the answers above.

b. Reflecting the triangle across the *y*-axis changes the *x*-values to the opposite and keeps
the *y*-values the same. See the answers above.

c. Rotating the triangle 90° clockwise moves the triangle into the second quadrant. The
original *y*-value becomes the new *x*-value and the opposite of the original *x*-value
becomes the *y*-value. See the answers above.

d. Dilating the triangle by a scale factor of two multiplies all of the coordinates by two.
See the answers above.

Here some more to try. For the following problems, refer to the figures below:

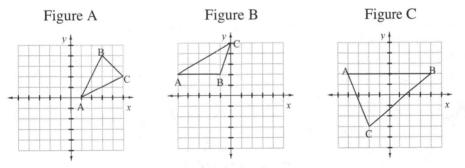

Figure A   Figure B   Figure C

State the new coordinates after each transformation.

1. Translate figure A left 2 units and down 2 units.

2. Rotate figure C 180° counterclockwise about the origin.

3. Reflect figure B across the *y*-axis.

4. Reflect figure B across the *x*-axis.

5. Translate figure A right 4 units and up 1 unit.

6. Reflect figure C across the *y*-axis.

7. Rotate figure B 270° counterclockwise about the origin.

8. Translate figure C left 1 unit and up 2 units.

9. Rotate figure A 90° clockwise about the origin.

10. Reflect figure B across the line $y = 3$.

11. Dilate figure B by a scale factor of 3.

12. Rotate figure A 180° counterclockwise about the origin.

13. Translate figure B 4 units down and 4 units to the right.

14. Dilate figure A by a scale factor of 4.

15. Rotate figure C 90° clockwise about the origin.

16. Reflect figure A across the y-axis.

17. Dilate figure C by a scale factor of $\frac{1}{2}$.

18. Translate figure C 3 units right and 2 units down.

19. Rotate figure C 180° about the origin clockwise.

20. Dilate figure A by a scale factor of 2.

Answers

1. $(-1, -2), (1, 2), (3, 0)$

2. $(4, -2), (-4, -2), (2, 3)$

3. $(5, 2), (1, 2), (0, 5)$

4. $(-5, -2), (-1, -2), (0, -5)$

5. $(5, 1), (7, 5), (9, 3)$

6. $(4, 2), (-4, 2), (2, -3)$

7. $(2, 5), (2, 1), (5, 0)$

8. $(-5, 4), (3, 4), (-3, -1)$

9. $(0, -1), (4, -3), (2, -5)$

10. $(5, 4), (1, 4), (0, 1)$

11. $(-15, 6), (-3, 6), (0, 15)$

12. $(-1, 0), (-3, -4), (-5, -2)$

13. $(-1, -2), (3, -2), (4, 1)$

14. $(4, 0), (12, 16), (20, 8)$

15. $(2, 4), (2, -4), (-3, 2)$

16. $(-1, 0), (-3, 4), (-5, 2)$

17. $(-2, 1), (2, 1), (-1, -1.5)$

18. $(-1, 0), (7, 0), (1, -5)$

19. $(4, -2), (-4, -2), (2, 3)$

20. $(2, 0), (6, 8), (10, 4)$

Checkpoint 9

Problem 9-50

Scatterplots and Association

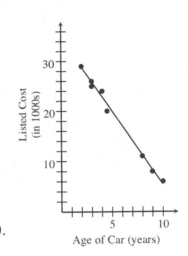

Answers to problem 9-50:

a: box plot

b: scatterplot

c: See graph at right.

d: strong linear negative association

e: $y = -3x + 35$

f: $17,000

g: A slope of –3 means the car is losing $3000 in value each year, y-intercept of 35 means the cost when new was $35,000.

An association (relationship) between two numerical variables on a graph can be described by its form, direction, strength, and outliers. When the association has a linear form, a line a best fit can be drawn and its equation can be used to make predictions about other data.

Example 1: Describe the association in the scatterplot at right.

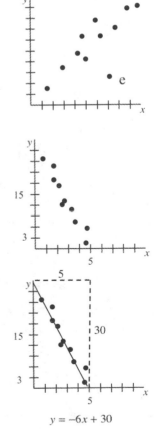

Solution: Looking from left to right, except for point (e), the points are fairly linear and increasing. This is a moderate, positive linear association. Point (e) is an outlier.

Example 2: For the scatterplot, draw a line of best fit and determine the equation of the line.

Solution: Use a ruler or straightedge to draw the line that approximates the trend of the points. If it is not a perfect line, approximately the same number of points will be above and below the line of best fit.

To determine the equation of the line, draw in a slope triangle and determine the ratio of the vertical side to the horizontal side. In this case it is $\frac{-30}{5} = -6$. Estimate the y-intercept by looking at where the line intersects the y-axis. In this case, it is approximately 30. The equation of any non-vertical line may be written in the form $y = mx + b$ where m is the slope and b is the y-intercept.

$$y = -6x + 30$$

Now we can go back and solve the original problem.

a. Since the costs are a single set of data, a box plot is a convenient way to show the distribution.

b. Age and cost are two sets of related data so a scatterplot is appropriate.

c. See the graph given in the answers.

d. Reading from left to right, the scatterplot is decreasing, linear and the points are close to the line of best fit. This is a strong, linear, negative association.

e. Looking at the line of best fit, the slope triangle has a ratio of $-\frac{3}{1}$ and the y-intercept is approximately 35. Placing that information into the equation of a line, $y = mx + b$, yields $y = -3x + 35$.

f. Substituting $x = 6$ into the equation of part (e) yields $y = -3(6) + 35 = 17$, $17,000.

g. Slope represents the rate of change. A rate of change of -3 means that the value is decreasing by 3 units (in this case each unit is $1000) per year. The y-intercept represents the value at year zero or a new car.

Here are some more to try.

In problems 1 through 4, describe the association.

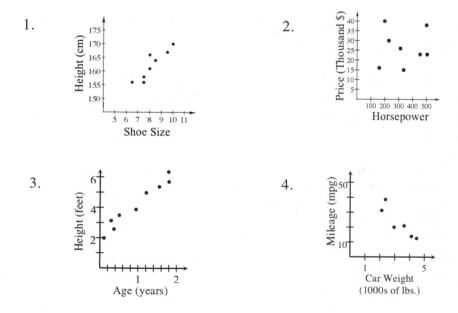

1.

2.

3.

4.

In problems 5 through 8 plot the data, draw a line of best fit, and approximate the equation of the line.

5.

Distance to Airport (mi)	5	10	15	20	25	30
Cost of Shuttle ($)	14	17	21	31	33	40

6.

Exercise/Month (hours)	3	6	9	12	15	18
Rate of Heart Attack/1000	24	21	18	12	6	0

7.

Time Spent Studying (hours)	0	2	2.5	2.8	3	4.5	5
Score on Test	65	70	70	85	80	95	100

8.

Time Since Purchase (hours)	0	2	4	6	8	10
Number of Cookies	24	20	14	11	5	0

Answers

1. strong positive association

2. no association

3. strong positive association

4. strong negative association

5.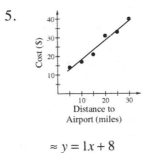

$\approx y = 1x + 8$

6.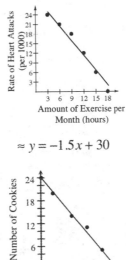

$\approx y = -1.5x + 30$

7.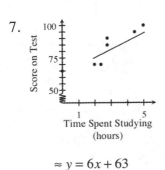

$\approx y = 6x + 63$

8.

$\approx y = 2.4x + 10$

Puzzle Investigator Problems

Dear Students,

Puzzle Investigator problems (PIs) present you with an opportunity to investigate complex, interesting problems. Their purpose is to focus on the process of solving complex problems. **You will be evaluated on your ability to show, explain, and justify your work and thoughts.** Save *all* of your work, including what does not work, in order to write about the processes you used to reach your answer.

Completion of a Puzzle Investigator problem includes four parts:

- **Problem Statement:** State the problem clearly in your own words so that anyone reading your paper will understand the problem you intend to solve.

- **Process and Solutions:** Describe in detail your thinking and reasoning as you work from start to finish. Explain your solution and how you know it is correct. Add diagrams when it helps your explanation. Include what you do that does not work and changes you make along the way. If you do not complete this problem, describe what you <u>do</u> know and where and why you are stuck.

- **Reflection:** Reflect about your learning and your reaction to the problem. What mathematics did you learn from it? What did you learn about your math problem solving strategies? Is this problem similar to any other problems you have done before? If yes, how?

- **Attached work:** Include <u>all</u> your work and notes. Your scratch work is important because it is a record of your thinking. Do not throw anything away.

PI-7.   CUSTOMER SERVICE

Patti the Plumber wants to be ready to repair broken pipes of any whole-number length up to 30 feet long. Unfortunately, her truck has a rack that only allows her to transport 5 pipes. To make new lengths, she can join any pieces end-to-end. Assume her truck can carry pipes of any length.

a.   Patti does not want to cut the pipe on location. Help Patti figure out which five lengths of pipe she should carry in the truck to be able to produce lengths of 1, 2, 3, 4, 5, ..., 29, and 30 feet. Show how Patti can produce each length using one or more of the lengths of pipe you propose.

b.   What is the longest length Patti can produce with her pipes from part (a)?

c.   When solving this problem, Patti remembered a game she used to play as a child. After asking her friend to silently pick a number from 1 to 15, she would then have the friend indicate which cards below had his number on it. She would then instantly know which number her friend had picked. For example, if her friend said his number was on cards B, C, and D, she would quickly know the number was 14. How does this game work? And what is its connection to her problem with pipe lengths?

1	3	5	7
9	11	13	15
17	19	21	23
25	27	29	31

Card A

2	3	6	7
10	11	14	15
18	19	22	23
26	27	30	

Card B

4	5	6	7
12	13	14	15
20	21	22	23
28	29	30	31

Card C

8	9	10	11
12	13	14	15
24	25	26	27
28	29	30	31

Card D

16	17	18	19
20	21	22	23
24	25	26	27
28	29	30	31

Card E

PI-8.   SIERPINSKI TRIANGLES

Fractals are geometric structures developed by repeating a process over and over. A famous example of a fractal is the **Sierpinski Triangle**, shown below. To create this design, start with a triangle, as shown in Figure 1. Then find and connect the midpoints of all of the sides of the triangle, subdividing it into four smaller triangles. Shade all but the central triangle as shown in Figure 1.

Then repeat the process by finding and connecting the midpoints of the shaded triangles of Figure 1. Shade all but the center triangles, as shown in Figure 2. If this process is continued infinitely, the result is the Sierpinski Triangle.

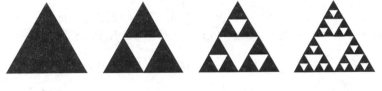

Figure 0   Figure 1   Figure 2   Figure 3

a.   On the PI-8 Resource Page (which can be downloaded at www.cpm.org), shade in the next figure in the sequence.

b.   For Figures 1 through 4, write a fraction to represent the amount of the entire triangle that is shaded. As you work, look for patterns. What is happening to the numerator and denominator of the fraction? What is happening to the amount shaded?

c.   Use your pattern to predict what portion of Figure 5 and Figure 6 in the sequence will be shaded.

d.   The shaded portion of Figure 2 could be written as $\left(\frac{3}{4}\right)^2$. Rewrite the other figures in this form. According to this pattern, what should the value of $\left(\frac{3}{4}\right)^0$ to be? Explain why.

e.   Is there any figure that will have less than 10% shaded? If so, use your pattern to explain how you know.

PI-9.   WEIGHING PUMPKINS

Every year at Half Moon Bay, there is a pumpkin contest to see who has grown the largest pumpkin for that year.

Last year, one pumpkin grower (who was also a mathematician) brought 5 pumpkins to the contest. Instead of weighing them one at a time, he informed the judges, *"When I weighed them two at a time, I got the following weights: 110, 112, 113, 114, 115, 116, 117, 118, 120, and 121 pounds."*

Your Task: Find how much each pumpkin weighed.

PI-10.   MAKING TRACKS!

Vu got a new bicycle for her birthday and
cannot wait to ride it all around her favorite
park. To find out which paths are best, she
wants to ride each of them exactly once,
without repeating any path and without
missing any. When she can do this, it is
called an "Euler" (pronounced "oy-ler") path
after a mathematician who investigated
similar paths.

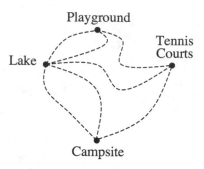

The map of the park is shown at right. Vu needs to decide
where her mother should drop her off to begin her ride.

a.   Is it possible for Vu to ride each trail exactly once without repeating any
     path and without missing any?

     • If it is possible, show all the possible ways for her to do this.

     • If none exist, find a new path you could add to the park to create an Euler
       path.

b.   The park manager is planning to add a parking lot as a new point on the
     map. It will need to be connected to at least one of the other locations in
     the park with a path. Propose a location of a parking lot and at least one
     other path so that the park will have an Euler path. Remember that to be an
     Euler path, it must use all the paths exactly once.

c.   Vu is thinking about going to one of the parks shown below. Which of
     them have Euler paths? Which do not? If an Euler path exists, show where
     Vu could start and stop her ride, and use arrows to show the direction she
     should travel. Look for reasons why some parks have Euler paths and
     others do not.

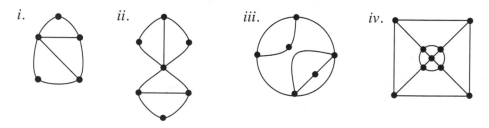

d.   Draw two new parks that have Euler paths and two that do not.

e.   Why do some parks have Euler paths and others do not?

PI-11.   WHAT'S MY NUMBER?

Francesca has a game for you. She decided to show the rules of the game using a flowchart, at right.

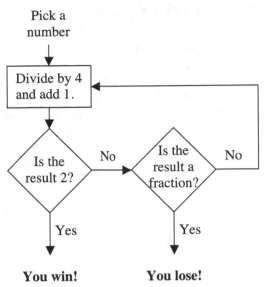

a.   Show that if you start with the number 60, you will lose.

b.   How many starting numbers less than 100 will win? List the possible winning numbers and show how you know they will win.

c.   What if Francesca changed the rules so that you win if you end up with the number 1? What numbers would win?

PI-12.   GOING BANANAS!

This year's harvest from a small, remote banana plantation consists of 3000 bananas. The farmer's camel can carry up to 1000 bananas at a time. The market place where the bananas are sold is 1000 miles away. Unfortunately, the camel eats one banana each and every mile she walks.

Your Task: Of the three thousand bananas harvested, what is the greatest number of bananas the farmer can get to market?

PI-13.   HAPPY NUMBERS

Some numbers have special qualities that earn them a title, such as "square number" or "prime number." This problem will explore another type of number, called "happy numbers."

The number 23 is a happy number. To determine if a number is a happy number, square each of its digits and add.

$$2^2 + 3^2 = 13$$

$$1^2 + 3^2 = 10$$

Repeat this process several times until you get 1, or until you get the same number twice (see below).

$$1^2 + 0^2 = 1$$

When the final answer is 1, the original number is called a **happy number**.

The number 34 is not happy number, as demonstrated below:

Step #1 $3^2 + 4^2 = 25$
Step #2 $2^2 + 5^2 = 29$
Step #3 $2^2 + 9^2 = 85$
Step #4 $8^2 + 5^2 = \mathbf{89}$
Step #5 $8^2 + 9^2 = 145$
Step #6 $1^2 + 4^2 + 5^2 = 42$
Step #7 $4^2 + 2^2 = 20$
Step #8 $2^2 + 0^2 = 4$
Step #9 $4^2 + 0^2 = 16$
Step #10 $1^2 + 6^2 = 37$
Step #11 $3^2 + 7^2 = 58$
Step #12 $5^2 + 8^2 = \mathbf{89}$

Since 89 is repeated, the final answer will be in a never-ending loop and, therefore, will never equal 1. This means that 34 *is not* a happy number.

a.   There are 17 two-digit happy numbers. Find as many as you can. Remember to keep all your work and ideas organized so you can refer back when writing up what you discovered.

b.   Find 5 three-digit happy numbers.

c.   Eve found out that 478 is a happy number. Based on this, what other numbers must be happy numbers? How do you know? Find at least 10 new happy numbers.

PI-14.   MAKING DECISIONS

Carlos wanted to get a part-time job to have
extra money for the holidays. After reading
the advertisement at right, he applied. His
interview went well, and he was offered the
job. He had to choose between the following
two pay scales:

Pay Scale # 1

He would earn $10 per hour.

Pay Scale # 2

On day # 1, he would earn a total of 1¢
On day # 2, he would make a total of 2¢
On day # 3, he would make a total of 4¢

Each day, his salary rate would double
from the day before.

a.   Before starting the problem, guess which pay scale Carlos chose. Explain
     why you think this.

b.   If the store is closed on Thanksgiving (November 27th), and Carlos works
     every day that the store is open through December 24th, make a table that
     shows how much he makes each day using both pay scales.

c.   If you had a job offer like this one, which pay scale would you choose?
     Why?

Glossary

5-D Process An organized method to solve problems. The 5 D's stand for Describe/Draw, Define, Do, Decide, and Declare. This is a problem-solving strategy for which solving begins by making a prediction about the answer or one element of it (a trial), and then confirming whether the result of the trial is correct. If not, information is gained about how close the trial is to the correct value, so that adjustments to the trial value may be made. Being organized is extremely important to the success of this method, as well as writing a usable table. The 5-D Process leads to writing equations to represent word problems. (p. 16)

AA ~ (Triangle Similarity) If two angles of one triangle are congruent to the two corresponding angles of another triangle, then the triangles are similar. For example, given $\triangle ABC$ and $\triangle A'B'C'$ with $\angle A \cong \angle A'$ and $\angle B \cong \angle B'$, then $\triangle ABC \sim \triangle A'B'C'$. You can also show that two triangles are similar by showing that *three* pairs of corresponding angles are congruent (which would be called AAA~), but two pairs are sufficient to demonstrate similarity. (p. 414)

absolute value The absolute value of a number is the distance of the number from zero. Since the absolute value represents a distance, without regard to direction, absolute value is always non-negative. Thus, the absolute value of a negative number is its opposite, while the absolute value of a non-negative number is just the number itself. The absolute value of x is usually written "$|x|$." For example, $|-5| = 5$ and $|22| = 22$.

acute angle An angle with a measure greater than 0° and less than 90°. An example is shown at right.

acute triangle A triangle with all three angle measures less than 90°. (p. 420)

additive identity The number 0 is called the additive identity because adding 0 to any number does not change the number. For example, $7 + 0 = 7$. (p. 74)

Additive Identity Property The Additive Identity Property states that adding zero to any expression leaves the expression unchanged. That is, $a + 0 = a$. For example, $-2 + 0 = -2$. (p. 74)

additive inverse The number you need to add to a given number to get a sum of 0. For example, the additive inverse of –3 is 3. It is also called the opposite. (p. 78)

Additive Inverse Property The Additive Inverse Property states that for every number a there is a number $-a$ such that $a = -a = 0$. For example, the number 5 has an additive inverse of –5; $5 + (-5) = 0$. The additive inverse of a number is often called its opposite. For example, 5 and –5 are opposites. (p. 78)

adjacent angles   For two angles to be adjacent, they must satisfy these three conditions: (1) The two angles must have a common side; (2) They must have a common vertex; and (3) They can have no interior points in common. This means that the common side must be between the two angles; no overlap between the angles is permitted. In the example at right, $\angle ABC$ and $\angle CBD$ are adjacent angles. (p. 396)

algebra   A branch of mathematics that uses variables to generalize the rules of numbers and numerical operations.

algebra tiles   An algebra tile is a manipulative whose area represents a constant or variable quantity. The algebra tiles used in this course consist of large squares with dimensions x-by-x; rectangles with dimensions x-by-1; and small squares with dimensions 1-by-1. These tiles are named by their areas: x^2, x, and 1, respectively. The smallest squares are called "unit tiles." In this text, shaded tiles will represent positive quantities while unshaded tiles will represent negative quantities. (p. 139)

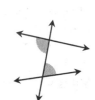

algebraic expression   See *expression*.

alternate interior angles   Angles between a pair of lines that switch sides of a third intersecting line (called a transversal). For example, in the diagram at right the shaded angles are alternate interior angles. If the lines intersected by the transversal are parallel, the alternate interior angles are congruent. Conversely, if the alternate interior angles are congruent, then the two lines intersected by the transversal are parallel. (p. 401)

angle   Generally, an angle is formed by two rays that are joined at a common endpoint. Angles in geometric figures are usually formed by two segments that have a common endpoint (such as the angle shaded in the figure at right). Also see *acute angle*, *obtuse angle*, and *right angle*. (p. 396)

annual   Occurring once every year.

area   For this course, area is the number of square units needed to fill up a region on a flat surface. In later courses, the idea will be extended to cones, spheres, and more complex surfaces. Also see *surface area*.

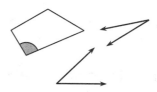

Area = 15 square units

association   A relationship between two (or more) variables. An association between numerical variables can be displayed on a scatterplot, and described by its form, direction, strength, and outliers. Possible association between two categorical variables can be studied in a relative frequency table. Also see *scatterplot*. (p. 290)

Associative Property of Addition   The Associative Property of Addition states that if a sum contains terms that are grouped, then the sum may be grouped differently with no effect on the total, that is, $a+(b+c)=(a+b)+c$. For example, $3+(4+5)=(3+4)+5$. (p. 74)

Associative Property of Multiplication   The Associative Property of Multiplication states that if a product contains terms that are grouped, then the product may be grouped differently with no effect on the result, that is, $a(bc)=(ab)c$. For example, $2\cdot(3\cdot4)=(2\cdot3)\cdot4$. (p. 74)

average   The sum of given values divided by the number of values used in computing the sum. For example, the average of 1, 4, and 10 is $\frac{1+4+10}{3}=5$. See *mean*.

axis (plural: axes)   On a coordinate plane, two number lines that meet at right angles at the origin $(0,0)$. The x-axis runs horizontally and the y-axis runs vertically. (p. 11)

b   When the equation of a line is expressed in $y=mx+b$ form, the constant b gives the y-intercept of the line. For example, the y-intercept of the line $y=-\frac{1}{3}x+7$ is 7. (p. 162)

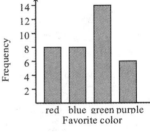

bar graph   A bar graph is a set of rectangular bars that have height proportional to the number of data elements in each category. Each bar stands for all of the elements in a single distinguishable category (such as "red"). Usually all of the bars are the same width and separated from each other. Also see *histogram*.

base of a geometric figure   (a) The base of a triangle: any side of a triangle to which a height is drawn. There are three possible bases in each triangle. (b) The base of a trapezoid: either of the two parallel sides. (c) The base of a parallelogram (including rectangle, rhombus, and square): any side to which a height is drawn. There are four possible bases. (d) The base of a three-dimensional figure. Also see *prism* and *pyramid*.

base of an exponent   When working with an exponential expression in the form b^a, b is called the base. For example, 2 is the base in 2^5. (5 is the exponent, and 32 is the value.) See *exponent*. (p. 347)

box plot   A graphic way of showing a summary of data using the median, quartiles, and extremes of the data.

categorical data   Data that can be put into categories (like what color you prefer, your gender, or the state you were born in), as opposed to numerical data that can be placed on a number line. (p. 324)

center of a circle On a flat surface, the fixed point from which all points on the circle are equidistant. *See* circle. (p. 128)

central angle An angle with its vertex at the center of a circle. (p. 273)

chord A line segment with its endpoints on a circle. A chord that passes through the center of a circle is called a "diameter." *See* circle. (p. 128)

circle The set of all points on a flat surface that are the same distance from a fixed point. If the fixed point (center) is O, the symbol $\odot O$ represents a circle with center O. If r is the length of a circle's radius and d is the length of its diameter, the circumference of the circle is $C = 2\pi r$ or $C = \pi d$. The area of the circle is $A = \pi r^2$. (p. 128)

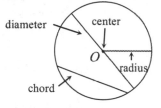

circle graph A way of displaying data that can be put into categories (like what color you prefer, your gender, or the state you were born in). A circle graph shows the proportion each category is of the whole. (p. 276)

Favorite Fruits

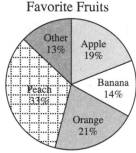

circumference The perimeter (distance around) of a circle. (p. 128)

coefficient (numerical) A number multiplying a variable or product of variables. For example, -7 is the coefficient of $-7x$. (p. 52)

coincide Two graphs coincide if they have all their points in common. For example, the graphs of $y = 2x + 4$ and $3y = 6x + 12$ coincide; both graphs are lines with a slope of 2 and a y-intercept of 4. When the graphs of two equations coincide, those equations share all the same solutions and have an infinite number of intersection points. (p. 210)

combining like terms Combining two or more like terms simplifies an expression by summing constants and summing those variable terms in which the same variables are raised to the same power. For example, combining like terms in the expression $3x + 7 + 5x - 3 + 2x^2 + 3y^2$ gives $8x + 4 + 2x^2 + 3y^2$. When working with algebra tiles, combining like terms involves putting together tiles with the same dimensions. (p. 56)

Commutative Property of Addition The Commutative Property of Addition states that if two terms are added, then the order may be reversed with no effect on the total. That is, $a + b = b + a$. For example, $7 + 12 = 12 + 7$. (p. 66)

Commutative Property of Multiplication The Commutative Property of Multiplication states that if two expressions are multiplied, then the order may be reversed with no effect on the result. That is, $ab = ba$. For example, $5 \cdot 8 = 8 \cdot 5$. (p. 66)

complementary angles Two angles whose measures add up to 90°. Angles T and V are complementary because $m\angle T + m\angle V = 90°$. Complementary angles may also be adjacent, like $\angle ABC$ and $\angle CBD$ in the diagram at far right. (p. 396)

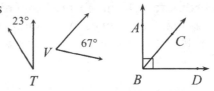

complete graph A complete graph is one that includes everything that is important about the graph (such as intercepts and other key points, asymptotes, or limitations on the domain or range), and that makes the rest of the graph predictable based on what is shown. (p. 124)

compound interest Interest that is paid on both the principal and the previously accrued interest. (p. 351)

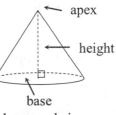

cone A three-dimensional figure that consists of a circular face, called the "base," a point called the "apex," that is not in the flat surface (plane) of the base, and the lateral surface that connects the apex to each point on the circular boundary of the base. (p. 465)

congruent Two shapes are congruent if they have exactly the same shape and size. Congruent shapes are similar and have a scale factor of 1. (p .245)

conjecture An educated guess that often results from noticing a pattern. (p. 240)

constant of proportionality (**k**) In a proportional relationship, equations are of the form $y = kx$, where k is the constant of proportionality. (p. 315)

constant term A number that is not multiplied by a variable. In the expression $2x + 3(5 - 2x) + 8$, the number 8 is a constant term. The number 3 is not a constant term, because it is multiplied by a variable inside the parentheses. (p. 52)

continuous graph For this course, when the points on a graph are connected and it makes sense to connect them, then the graph is continuous. Such a graph will have no holes or breaks in it. This term will be more completely defined in a later course. (p. 105)

converse The converse of a conditional statement can be found by switching the hypothesis (the "if" part) and the conclusion (the "then" part). For example, the converse of "*If P, then Q*" is "*If Q, then P.*" (p. 444)

converse of the Pythagorean Theorem The converse of the Pythagorean Theorem can be used to determine if a triangle is a right triangle. If $(\text{leg \#1})^2 + (\text{leg \#2})^2 = \text{hypotenuse}^2$ then the triangle is a right triangle. (p. 425)

coordinate The number corresponding to a point on the number line or an ordered pair (x, y) that corresponds to a point in a two-dimensional coordinate system. In an ordered pair, the x-coordinate appears first and the y-coordinate appears second. For example, the point $(3, 5)$ has an x-coordinate of 3 and a y-coordinate of 5. See *ordered pair*. (p. 11)

coordinate graph (system) A system of graphing ordered pairs of numbers on a coordinate plane. An ordered pair represents a point, with the first number giving the horizontal position relative to the x-axis and the second number giving the vertical position relative to the y-axis. Also see *ordered pair*. (p. 14)

coordinate plane A flat surface defined by two number lines meeting at right angles at their zero points. A coordinate plane is also sometimes called a "Cartesian Plane." (p. 11)

corresponding angles (a) When two lines are intersected by a third line (called a transversal), angles on the same side of the two lines and on the same side of the transversal are called corresponding angles. For example, the shaded angles in the diagram at right are corresponding angles. Note that if the two lines cut by the transversal are parallel, the corresponding angles are congruent. Conversely, if the corresponding angles are congruent, then the two lines intersected by the transversal are parallel. (p. 401)

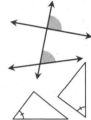

corresponding parts Points, sides, edges, or angles in two or more figures that are images of each other with respect to a transformation. If two figures are congruent, then the corresponding parts of the figures are congruent to each other. See *similar* and *congruent*. (p. 245)

counterexample An example showing that a statement has at least one exception; that is, a situation in which the statement is false. For example, the number 4 is a counterexample to the statement that all even numbers are greater than 7. (p. 194)

cube A polyhedron of six faces, each of which is a square. (p. 457)

cube root In the equation $a = b^3$, the value b that is multiplied by itself three times to give the value a. For example, the cube root of 8 is 2 because $8 = 2 \cdot 2 \cdot 2 = 2^3$. This is written $\sqrt[3]{8} = 2$. (p. 457)

cubic unit A cube, each of whose edges measure 1 unit in length. Volume is measured in cubic units.

cylinder (circular)   A three-dimensional figure that consists of two parallel congruent circular regions (called *bases*) and a lateral surface containing segments connecting each point on the circular boundary of one base to the corresponding point on the circular boundary of the other. (p. 468)

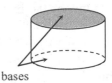
bases

degree   A unit for measuring angles. Usually denoted by ° (the degree symbol). There are 360° in one full rotation.

dependent variable   When one quantity depends for its value on one or more others, it is called the dependent variable. For example, the speed of a car might be related to the amount of force you apply to the gas pedal. Here, the speed of the car is the dependent variable; it depends on how hard you push the pedal. The dependent variable appears as the output value in an $x \rightarrow y$ table, and is usually placed relative to the vertical axis of a graph. You often use the letter y and the vertical y-axis for the dependent variable. When working with functions or relations, the dependent variable represents the output value. In Statistics, the dependent variable is often called the response variable. Also see *independent variable*. (p. 113, 378)

diameter   A line segment drawn through the center of a circle with both endpoints on the circle. The length of a diameter is usually denoted d. Note that the length of a circle's diameter is twice the length of its radius. *See* circle. (p. 128)

dilation   A transformation which produces a figure similar to the original by proportionally shrinking or stretching the figure. In a dilation, a shape is stretched (or compressed) proportionally from a point, called the point of dilation. (p. 239)

direction (of an association)   If one variable in a relationship increases as the other variable increases, the direction is said to be a positive association. If one variable decreases as the other variable increases, there is said to be a negative association. If there is no apparent pattern in the scatterplot, then the variables have no association. When describing a linear association, you can use the slope, and its numerical interpretation in context, to describe the direction of the association. (p. 287)

discrete graph   A graph that consists entirely of separated points is called a discrete graph. For example, the graph shown at right is discrete. Also see *continuous*. (p. 105)

Distributive Property   For any a, b, and c, $a(b + c) = ab + ac$. For example, $10(7 + 2) = 10 \cdot 7 + 10 \cdot 2$. (p. 139)

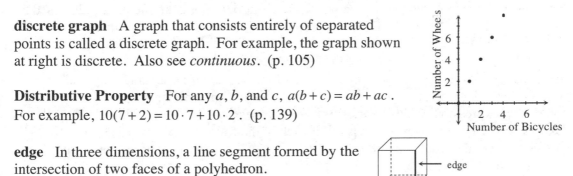

edge   In three dimensions, a line segment formed by the intersection of two faces of a polyhedron.

edge

endpoint   A point that mark the ends of a line segment or ray.

enlarge To make larger. (p. 262)

Equal Values Method A method for solving a system of equations.
To use the equal values method, take two expressions that are each equal to
the same variable and set those expressions equal to each other. For
$$y = -2x + 5$$
$$y = x - 1$$
example, in the system of equations at right, $-2x + 5$ and $x - 1$ each equal y. So you write
$-2x + 5 = x - 1$, then solve that equation to find x. Once you have x, you substitute that
value back into either of the original equations to find the value of y. (p. 205)

equation A mathematical sentence in which two expressions have an "equals" sign ($=$)
between them indicating that they have an equal value. For example, the equation
$7x + 4.2 = -8$ states that the expression $7x + 4.2$ has the value -8. In this course, an
equation is often used to represent a rule relating two quantities.

Equation Mat An Equation Mat puts two Expression Mats side-
by-side to find the value(s) which make the expressions equal.
Legal moves are used to find the value(s) that makes the expressions
equal. For example, the Equation Mat at right represents the
equation $2(x + 1) - 1 = x + 4$. The two sides of the mat are equal
when $x = 3$. Also see *"legal" moves*. (p. 81)

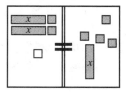

equivalent Two expressions are equivalent if they have the same value. For example,
$2 + 3$ is equivalent to $1 + 4$. Two equations are equivalent if they have all the same
solutions. For example, $y = 3x$ is equivalent to $2y = 6x$. Equivalent equations have the
same graph. (p. 194)

evaluate (an expression) To find the numerical value of. To evaluate an expression,
substitute the value(s) given for the variable(s) and perform the operations according to
the order of operations. For example, evaluating $2x + y - 10$ when $x = 4$ and $y = 3$ gives
the value 1. Also see *expression*. (p. 61)

exponent In an expression of the form b^a, a is called the exponent. For example, in the
expression 2^5, 5 is called the exponent (2 is the base, and 32 is the value). The exponent
indicates how many times to use the base as a multiplier. For example, in 2^5, 2 is used 5
times: $2^5 = 2 \cdot 2 \cdot 2 \cdot 2 \cdot 2 = 32$. For exponents of zero, the rule is: for any number $x \neq 0$,
$x^0 = 1$. (p. 61)

expression An expression is a combination of individual terms separated by plus or
minus signs. Numerical expressions combine numbers and operation symbols; algebraic
(variable) expressions include variables. For example, $4 + (5 - 3)$ is a numerical
expression. In an algebraic expression, if each of the following terms, $6xy^2$, 24, and $\frac{y-3}{4+x}$,
are combined, the result may be $6xy^2 + 24 - \frac{y-3}{4+x}$. An expression does not have an
"equals" sign. (p. 52)

Expression Comparison Mat   An Expression Comparison Mat puts two Expression Mats side-by-side so they can be compared to see which represents the greater value. For example, in the Expression Comparison Mat at right, Mat A represents –3, while Mat B represents –2. Since –2 > –3 Mat B is greater. (p. 64)

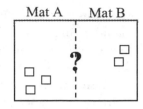

Expression Mat   An organizing tool used to visually represent an expression with algebra tiles. (p. 64)

exterior angle (of a triangle)   When a side of a triangle is extended to form an angle outside of the triangle, that angle is called an exterior angle. The exterior angle is adjacent to the angle inside the triangle. For example, ∠4 in the diagram at right is an exterior angle of the triangle. (p. 409)

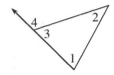

Exterior Angle Theorem   The measure of an exterior angle of a triangle is equal to the sum of the measures of the two remote (non-adjacent) interior angles of the triangle. In the diagram above, m∠1 + m∠2 = m∠4. (p. 409)

face   One of the flat surfaces of a polyhedron, including the base(s). (p. 460)

factor   (1) In arithmetic: when two or more integers are multiplied, each of the integers is a factor of the product. For example, 4 is a factor of 24, because $4 \cdot 6 = 24$.
(2) In algebra: when two or more algebraic expressions are multiplied together, each of the expressions is a factor of the product. For example, x^2 is a factor of $-17x^2y^3$, because $(x^2)(-17y^3) = -17x^2y^3$. (3) To factor an expression is to write it as a product. For example, the factored form of $3x - 18$ is $3(x - 6)$. (p. 52)

Fibonacci numbers   The sequence of numbers 1, 1, 2, 3, 5, 8, 13, …. Each term of the Fibonacci sequence (after the first two terms) is the sum of the two preceding terms. (p. 95)

first quartile (Q1)   The median of the lower half of an ordered set of data is the lower quartile.

flip   See *reflection*.

form (of an association)   The form of an association can be linear of non-linear. The form can contain cluster of data. (p. 920)

formula   An equation that shows a mathematical relationship.

fraction   The quotient of two quantities in the form $\frac{a}{b}$ where b is not equal to 0.

Fraction Busters "Fraction Busting" is a method of simplifying equations involving fractions that uses the Multiplicative Property of Equality to rearrange the equation so that no fractions remain. To use this method, multiply both sides of an equation by the common denominator of all the fractions in the equation. The result will be an equivalent equation with no fractions. For example, when given the equation $\frac{x}{7}+2=\frac{x}{3}$, you can multiply both sides by the "Fraction Buster" 21. The resulting equation, $3x+42=7x$, is equivalent to the original but contains no fractions. (p. 198)

frequency The number of times that something occurs within an interval or data set.

frequency table A table that displays counts, or frequencies, of data. (p. 324)

function A relationship in which for each input value there is one and only one output value. For example, the relationship $y=x+4$ is a function; for each input value (x) there is exactly one output value (y). In terms of ordered pairs (x, y), no two ordered pairs of a function have the same first member (x). (p. 378)

generic rectangle A type of diagram used to visualize multiplying expressions without algebra tiles. Each expression to be multiplied forms a side length of the rectangle, and the product is the sum of the areas of the sections of the rectangle. For example, the generic rectangle at right may be used to multiply $(2x+5)$ by $(x+3)$. (p. 139)

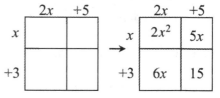

$$(2x+5)(x+3)=2x^2+11x+15$$

area as a product   area as a sum

Giant One A fraction that is equal to 1. Multiplying any fraction by a Giant One will create a new fraction equivalent to the original fraction. (p. 35)

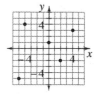

$$\frac{2}{3}\cdot\frac{2}{2}=\frac{4}{6}$$

graph A graph represents numerical information in a visual form. The numbers may come from a table, situation (pattern), or rule (equation or inequality). Most of the graphs in this course show points, lines, and/or curves on a two-dimensional coordinate system like the one at right or on a single axis called a number line (see diagram below right). (p. 124)

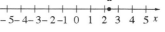

growth One useful way to analyze a mathematical relationship is to examine how the output value grows as the input value increases. You can see this growth on a graph of a linear relationship by using a growth triangle.

growth triangle   A growth triangle is a right triangle drawn on a graph of a line so that the hypotenuse of the triangle is part of the line. The vertical leg length is the change in the y-value (+ 4); the horizontal leg length is the change in the x-value (+ 1). We use the lengths of the legs in the triangle describe the pattern of growth. For example, the diagram at right shows a growth pattern of adding 4 to each y-value for every increase of 1 in the x-value. In a tile pattern, each figure grows by adding 4 tiles.

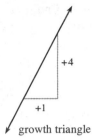

growth triangle

height   (a) Triangle: the length of a segment that connects a vertex of the triangle to a line containing the opposite base (side) and is perpendicular to that line. (b) Trapezoid: the length of any segment that connects a point on one base of the trapezoid to the line containing the opposite base and is perpendicular to that line. (c) Parallelogram (includes rectangle, rhombus, and square): the length of any segment that connects a point on one base of the parallelogram to the line containing the opposite base and is perpendicular to that line. (d) Pyramid and cone: the length of the segment that connects the apex to a point in the plane containing the base of a figure and is perpendicular to that plane. (e) Prism or cylinder: the length of a segment that connects one base of the figure to the plane containing the other base and is perpendicular to that plane.

histogram   A way of displaying data that is much like a bar graph in that the height of the bars is proportional to the number of elements. The difference is that each bar of a histogram represents the number of data elements in a range of values, such as the number of people who weigh from 100 pounds up to, but not including, 120 pounds. Each range of values should have the same width. Also see *bar graph*.

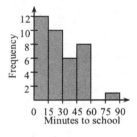

horizontal   Parallel to the horizon. The x-axis of a coordinate graph is the horizontal axis. (p. 310)

horizontal lines   Horizontal lines are "flat" and run left to right in the same direction as the x-axis. Horizontal lines have equations of the form $y = b$, where b can be any number. For example, the graph at right shows the horizontal line $y = 3$. The slope of any horizontal line is 0. The x-axis has the equation $y = 0$ because $y = 0$ everywhere on the x-axis. (p. 310)

hypotenuse   The longest side of a right triangle (the side opposite the right angle). (p. 425)

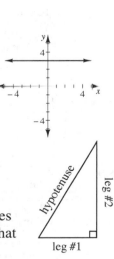

Identity Property of Addition   The Identity Property of Addition states that adding zero to any expression leaves the expression unchanged. That is, $a + 0 = a$. For example, $7 + 0 = 7$, and $-2y + 0 = -2y$. (p. 74)

Identity Property of Multiplication   The Identity Property of Multiplication states that multiplying any expression by 1 leaves the expression unchanged. That is, $a(1) = a$. For example, $437x \cdot 1 = 437x$. (p. 74)

independent variable   When one quantity changes in a way that does not depend on the value of another quantity, the value that changes independently is represented with the independent variable. For example, you might relate the speed of a car to the amount of force you apply to the gas pedal. Here, the amount of force applied may be whatever the driver chooses, so it represents the independent variable. The independent variable appears as the input value in an $x \rightarrow y$ table, and is usually placed relative to the horizontal axis of a graph. You often use the letter x and the horizontal x-axis for the independent variable. When working with functions or relations, the independent variable represents the input value. In Statistics, the independent variable is often called the explanatory variable. Also see *dependent variable*. (p. 11, 378)

indirect measurement   A technique that uses proportionality to determine a measurement when directly measuring the object is not possible. (p. 482)

inequality   An inequality consists of two expressions on either side of an inequality symbol. For example, the inequality $7x + 4.2 < -8$ states that the expression $7x + 4.2$ has a value less than -8.

inequality symbols   The symbol $\leq$ read from left to right means "less than or equal to," the symbol $\geq$ read from left to right means "greater than or equal to," and the symbols $<$ and $>$ mean "less than" and "greater than," respectively. For example, "$7 < 13$" means that 7 is less than 13.

input value   The input value is the independent variable in a relation. Substitute the input value into our rule (equation) to determine the output value. For example, if you have a rule for how much your phone bill will be if you talk a certain number of minutes, the number of minutes you talk is the input value. The input value appears first in an $x \rightarrow y$ table, and is represented by the variable x. When working with functions, the input value is the value put into the function. (p. 14)

integers   The set of numbers $\{\ldots, -3, -2, -1, 0, 1, 2, 3, \ldots\}$.

intercepts   Points where a graph crosses the axes. x-intercepts are points at which the graph crosses the x axis and y-intercepts are points at which the graph crosses the y axis. On the graph at right the x-intercept is $(3, 0)$ and the y-intercept is $(0, 6)$. (p. 124)

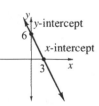

interest   An amount paid which is a percentage of an initial value (principal). For example, a savings account may offer 4% annual interest rate, which means they will pay $4.00 in interest for a principal of $100 kept in the account for one year. (p. 304)

inverse operation   An operation that undoes another operation. For example, multiplication is the inverse operation for division.

irrational numbers   The set of numbers that cannot be expressed in the form $\frac{a}{b}$, where a and b are integers and $b \neq 0$. For example, π and $\sqrt{2}$ are irrational numbers. (p. 429)

lateral face   A (flat) sides of a polyhedron. It is always a polygon. (p. 468)

lattice points   The points on a coordinate grid where the grid lines intersect. The diagram at right shows two lattice points. The coordinates of lattice points are integers. (p. 302)

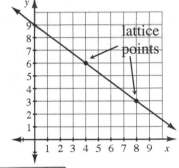

laws of exponents   The laws of exponents studied in this course are: (p. 373)

Law	Examples	
$x^m x^n = x^{m+n}$ for all x	$x^3 x^4 = x^{3+4} = x^7$	$2^5 \cdot 2^{-1} = 2^4$
$\frac{x^m}{x^n} = x^{m-n}$ for $x \neq 0$	$x^{10} \div x^4 = x^{10-4} = x^6$	$\frac{5^4}{5^7} = 5^{-3}$
$(x^m)^n = x^{mn}$ for all x	$(x^4)^3 = x^{4 \cdot 3} = x^{12}$	$(10^5)^6 = 10^{30}$
$x^0 = 1$ for $x \neq 0$	$\frac{y^2}{y^2} = y^0 = 1$	$9^0 = 1$
$x^{-1} = \frac{1}{x}$ for $x \neq 0$	$\frac{1}{x^2} = (\frac{1}{x})^2 = (x^{-1})^2 = x^{-2}$	$3^{-1} = \frac{1}{3}$

legs   The two sides of a right triangle that form the right angle. Note that legs of a right triangle are always shorter than its hypotenuse. (p. 425)

"legal" moves   When working with an Equation Mat or Expression Comparison Mat, there are certain "legal" moves you can make with the algebra tiles that keep the relationship between the two sides of the mat intact. For example, removing an x tile from the positive region of each side of an equation mat is a legal move; it keeps the expressions on each side of the mat equal. The legal moves are those justified by the properties of the real numbers. (p. 72)

like terms   Two or more terms that contain the same variable(s), with corresponding variables raised to the same power. For example, $5x^2$ and $2x^2$ are like terms. See *combining like terms*. (p. 56)

line   A line is an undefined term in geometry. A line is one-dimensional and continues without end in two directions. A line is made up of points and has no thickness. A line may be named with a letter (such as l), but also may be labeled using two points on the line, such as $\overleftrightarrow{AB}$ shown the right.

$$\overleftrightarrow{ \bullet \bullet }$$
$$A \qquad\qquad B$$

line segment   The portion of a line between two points. A line segment is named using its endpoints. For example, the line segment at right may be named either $\overline{AB}$ or $\overline{BA}$.

●————————————●
A B

line of best fit   A line that represents, in general, data on a scatterplot. The line of best fit is a model of numerical two-variable data that helps describe the data. It is also used to make predictions for other data. (p. 282)

linear association   See *association*. (p. 290)

linear equation   An equation in two variables whose graph is a line. For example, $y = 2.1x - 8$ is a linear equation. The standard form for a linear equation is $ax + by = c$, where a, b, and c are constants and a and b are not both zero. Most linear equations can be written in $y = mx + b$ form, which is more useful for determining the line's slope and y-intercept. (p. 189)

lowest common denominator (LCD)   The smallest common multiple of the denominators of two or more fractions. For example, the LCD of $\frac{5}{12}$ and $\frac{3}{8}$ is 24. (p. 192)

m   When the equation of a line is expressed in $y = mx + b$ form, the parameter m gives the slope of the line. For example, the slope of the line $y = -\frac{1}{3}x + 7$ is $-\frac{1}{3}$. (p. 162)

mean   The mean, or average, of several numbers is one way of defining the "middle" of the numbers. To find the average of a group of numbers, add the numbers together then divide by the number of numbers in the set. For example, the average of the numbers $1, 5,$ and 6 is $(1 + 5 + 6) \div 3 = 4$. The mean is generally the best measure of central tendency when there are not outliers in the data set. See *average*.

measure of central tendency   Mean and median are measures of central tendency, reflecting special statistical information about a set of data. See *center (of a data distribution)*.

measurement   For the purposes of this course, a measurement is an indication of the size or magnitude of a geometric figure. For example, an appropriate measurement of a line segment would be its length. Appropriate measurements of a square would include not only the length of a side, but also its area and perimeter. The measure of an angle represents the number of degrees of rotation from one ray to the other about the vertex.

median   The middle number of an ordered set of data. If there is no distinct middle, then the average of the two middle numbers is the median. The median is generally more accurate than the mean as a measure of central tendency when there are outliers in the data set.

model A mathematical summary (often an equation) of a trend in data, after making assumptions and approximations to simplify a complicated situation. Models allow us to describe data to others, compare data more easily to other data, and allow us to make predictions. For example, mathematical models of weather patterns allow us to predict the weather. No model is perfect, but some models are better at describing trends than other models. (p. 492)

multiple representations web An organizational tool used to keep track of connections between the four representations of relationships between quantities emphasized in this course. In this course, four different ways of representing a numerical relationship are emphasized: with a graph, table, situation (pattern), or rule (equation or inequality).

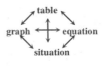

multiplicative identity The number 1 is called the multiplicative identity because multiplying any number by 1 does not change the number. For example, $7(1) = 7$. (p. 74)

Multiplicative Identity Property The Multiplicative Identity Property states that multiplying any expression by 1 leaves the expression unchanged. That is, $a(1) = a$. For example, $437x \cdot 1 = 437x$. (p. 74)

multiplicative inverse The multiplicative inverse for a non-zero number is the number you can multiply by to get the multiplicative identity, 1. For example, for the number 5, the multiplicative inverse is $\frac{1}{5}$; for the number $\frac{2}{3}$ the multiplicative inverse is $\frac{3}{2}$. (p. 78)

non-commensurate Two measurements are called non-commensurate if no whole number multiple of one measurement can ever equal a whole number multiple of the other. For example, measures of 1 cm and $\sqrt{2}$ cm are non-commensurate, because no combination of items 1 cm long will ever have exactly the same length as a combination of items $\sqrt{2}$ cm long. (p. 48)

number line A diagram representing all real numbers as points on a line. All real numbers are assigned to points. The numbers are called the coordinates of the points and the point for which the number 0 is assigned is called the origin. Also see *boundary point*. (p. 18)

obtuse angle Any angle that measures between (but not including) 90° and 180°.

obtuse triangle A triangle with one obtuse angle. (p. 420)

one-dimensional Something that does not have any width or depth. Lines and curves are one-dimensional.

operation A mathematical process such as addition, subtraction, multiplication, division, raising to a power, or taking a root.

opposite (of a number)   The same number but with the opposite sign (+ or −).
The additive inverse. (p. 78)

Order of Operations   The specific order in which certain operations are to be carried out
to evaluate or simplify expressions: parentheses (or other grouping symbols), exponents
(powers or roots), multiplication and division (from left to right), and addition and
subtraction (from left to right). (p. 61)

ordered pair   Two numbers written in order as follows: (x, y). The
primary use of ordered pairs in this course is to represent points in an
xy-coordinate system. The first coordinate (x) represents the distance
from the x-axis. The second coordinate (y) represents the distance from
the y-axis. For example, the ordered pair $(3, 5)$ represents the point
shown in bold at right. (p. 11)

origin   The point on a coordinate plane where the x-axis and y-axis intersect is called the
origin. This point has coordinates $(0, 0)$. The point assigned to zero on a number line is
also called the origin. See *axis*. (p. 11)

outlier   A number in a set of data that is much larger or much smaller than the other
numbers in the set. (p. 322)

output value   The output value is the dependent variable in a relation. When you
substitute the input value into our rule (equation), the result is the output value. For
example, if you have a rule for how much your phone bill will be if you talk a certain
number of minutes, the amount of your phone bill is the output value. The output value
appears second in an $x \rightarrow y$ table, and is represented by the variable y. When working with
functions, the output value is the value that results from applying the rule for the function
to an input value. (p. 14)

parabola   A parabola is a particular kind of
mathematical curve. In this course, a parabola is always
the graph of a quadratic function $y = ax^2 + bx + c$ where a
does not equal 0. The diagram at right shows some
examples of parabolas. The highest or lowest point on
the graph is called the vertex. (p. 109)

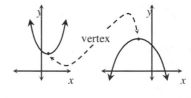

parallel   Two or more straight lines on a flat surface that do not
intersect (no matter how far they are extended) are parallel. The
matching arrows on the parallelogram (see below) indicate that
those segments are parallel. (p. 210)

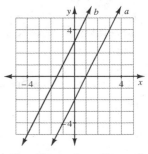

Core Connections, Course 3

parameter In a general equations where x and y represent the inputs and outputs of the function, variables such as b and m, are often referred to as parameters, and they are often replaced with specific values. For example: in the equation $y = mx + b$ representing all lines, the b and m are (variable) parameters that give the slope and y-intercept, while x and y are the independent and dependent variables. (p. 162)

pattern A pattern is a set of things in order that change in a regular way. For example, the numbers $1, 4, 7, 10, \ldots$ form a pattern, because each number increases by 3. The numbers $1, 4, 9, 16, \ldots$ form a pattern, because they are squares of consecutive integers. In this course, you often look at tile patterns, whose figure numbers and areas are represented with a table, a rule (equation), or a graph.

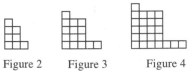

Figure 2   Figure 3   Figure 4

percent (%) A ratio that compares a number to 100. Percents are often written using the "%" symbol. For example, 0.75 is equal to $\frac{75}{100}$ or 75%. (p. 5)

perfect square A number that is the product of an integer and itself. For example, 25 is a perfect square because it is the product of 5 and 5. (p. 422)

perimeter The distance around a figure on a flat surface. (p. 50)

Perimeter =
$5 + 8 + 4 + 6 = 23$ units

perpendicular Two rays, line segments, or lines that meet (intersect) to form a right angle (90°) are called perpendicular. A line and a flat surface may also be perpendicular if the line does not lie on the flat surface but intersects the surface and forms a right angle with every line on the flat surface passing through the point of intersection. A small square at the point of intersection of two lines or segments indicates that the lines form a right angle and are therefore perpendicular. (p. 391)

pi (π) The ratio of the circumference (C) of the circle to its diameter (d). For every circle, $\pi = \frac{\text{circumference}}{\text{diameter}} = \frac{C}{d}$. Numbers such as 3.14, 3.14159, or $\frac{22}{7}$ are approximations of π. (p. 128)

plane A plane is a two-dimensional flat surface that extends without end. It is made up of points and has no thickness.

point An exact location in space. In two dimensions, an ordered pair specifies a point on a coordinate plane. See *ordered pair*.

point of intersection A point of intersection is a point that the graphs of two equations have in common. For example, (3, 4) is a point of intersection of the two graphs shown at right. Two graphs may have one point of intersection, several points of intersection, or no points of intersection. The ordered pair representing a point of intersection gives a solution to the equations of each of the graphs. (p. 197)

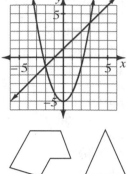

polygon A two-dimensional closed figure of three or more line segments (sides) connected end to end. Each segment is a side and only intersects the endpoints of its two adjacent sides. Each point of intersection is a vertex. At right are two examples of polygons.

portion A part of something; a part of a whole.

portions web The web diagram at right illustrates that fractions, decimals, and percents are different ways to represent a portion of a number. Portions may also be represented in words, such as "four-fifths" or "seven-fourths," or as diagrams. (p. 5)

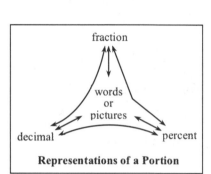

Representations of a Portion

power A number or variable raised to an exponent in the form x^n. See *exponent*.

predicted value (of an association) The dependent (y-value) that is predicted for an independent (x-value) by the best-fit model for an association.

prime number A positive integer with exactly two factors. The only factors of a prime number are 1 and itself. For example, the numbers 2, 3, 17, and 31 are all prime.

principal Initial investment or capital. An initial value. (p. 341, 351)

prism A three-dimensional figure that consists of two parallel congruent polygons (called *bases*) and a vertical surface containing segments connecting each point on each side of one base to the corresponding point on the other base. The lateral surface of a prism consists of parallelograms.

product The result of multiplying. For example, the product of 4 and 5 is 20.

proportion An equation stating that two ratios (fractions) are equal. For example, the equation at right is a proportion. A proportion is a useful type of equation to set up when solving problems involving proportional relationships. (p. 315)

$$\frac{68 \text{ votes for Mr. Mears}}{100 \text{ people surveyed}} = \frac{34 \text{ votes for Mr. Mears}}{50 \text{ people surveyed}}$$

proportional equation   An equation stating that two ratios (fractions) are equal. (p. 313)

proportional relationship   Two values are in a proportional relationship if a proportion may be set up that relates the values. (p. 313)

pyramid   A three-dimensional figure with a base that is a polygon. The lateral faces are formed by connecting each vertex of the base to a single point (the vertex of the pyramid) that is above or below the surface that contains the base. (p. 465)

Pythagorean Theorem   The statement relating the lengths of the legs of a right triangle to the length of the hypotenuse: $(\text{leg \#1})^2 + (\text{leg \#2})^2 = \text{hypotenuse}^2$. The Pythagorean Theorem is powerful because if you know the lengths of any two sides of a right triangle, you can use this relationship to find the length of the third side. (p. 425)

quadrants   The coordinate plane is divided by its axes into four quadrants. The quadrants are numbered as shown in the first diagram at right. When graphing data that has no negative values, sometimes a graph that shows only the first quadrant is used. (p. 11)

4-quadrant graph:

II │ I
───┼───→ x-axis
III │ IV
    ↓ y-axis

1st-quadrant graph:

↑ y-axis
───→ x-axis

quadrilateral   A polygon with four sides. The shape at right is a quadrilateral.

quartile   Along with the median, the quartiles divide a set of data into four groups of the same size. Also see *box plot*.

quotient   The result of a division problem.

radical   An expression in the form $\sqrt{a}$, where $\sqrt{a}$ is the positive square root of a. For example, $\sqrt{49} = 7$. Also see *square root*. (p. 438)

radicand   The expression under a radical sign. For example, in the expression $3 + 2\sqrt{x-7}$, the radicand is $x - 7$. (p. 438)

radius (plural: radii)   A line segment drawn from the center of a circle to a point on the circle. (p. 128)

rate   A ratio comparing two quantities, often a comparison of time. For example, miles per hour. (p. 310)

ratio   A ratio compares two quantities by division. A ratio may be written using a colon, but is more often written as a fraction. For example, the comparison may be made of the ratio of female students in a particular school to the total number of students in the school. This ratio could be written as 1521:2906 or as the fraction shown at right. (p. 262)

$$\frac{1521 \text{ female students}}{2906 \text{ total students}}$$

rational numbers Numbers that may be expressed in the form $\frac{a}{b}$, where a and b are integers and $b \neq 0$. For example, 0.75 is a rational number because 0.75 may be expressed in the form $\frac{3}{4}$. (p. 433)

ray A ray is part of a line that starts at one point and extends without end in one direction. In the example at right, ray $\overrightarrow{AB}$ is part of $\overleftrightarrow{AB}$ that starts at A and contains all of the points of $\overleftrightarrow{AB}$ that are on the same side of A as point B, including A. Point A is the endpoint of $\overrightarrow{AB}$. (p. 396)

A •————————————• *B*

real numbers Irrational numbers together with rational numbers form the set of the real numbers. For example, the following are all real numbers: $2.78, -13267, 0, \frac{3}{7}, \pi, \sqrt{2}$. All real numbers are represented on the number line. (p. 433)

reciprocal The reciprocal of a nonzero number is its multiplicative inverse, that is, the reciprocal of x is $\frac{1}{x}$. For a number in the form $\frac{a}{b}$, where a and b are non-zero, the reciprocal is $\frac{b}{a}$. The product of a number and its reciprocal is 1. For example, the reciprocal of 12 is $\frac{1}{12}$, because $12 \cdot \frac{1}{12} = 1$. (p. 78)

reduce To make smaller. (p. 262)

reflection A transformation across a line that produces a mirror image of the original (pre-image) shape. The reflection is called the "image" of the original figure. The line is called a "line of reflection." See the example at right. Note that a reflection is also sometimes referred to as a "flip." (p. 233)

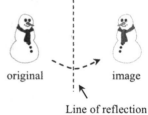

original   image

Line of reflection

relative frequency A ratio or percent. If 60 people are asked, and 15 people prefer "red," the relative frequency of people preferring red is $\frac{15}{60} = 25\%$. (p. 325)

relative frequency table A two-way table in which the percent of subjects in each combination of categories is displayed. (p. 325)

remote interior angles If a triangle has an exterior angle, the remote interior angles are the two angles not adjacent to the exterior angle. Also called "non-adjacent interior angles." (p. 409)

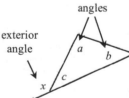

remote interior angles

exterior angle

repeating decimal A repeating decimal is a decimal that repeats the same sequence of digits forever from some point onward. For example, $4.56073073073\ldots$ is a decimal for which the three digits 073 continue to repeat forever. Repeating decimals are always the decimal expansions of rational numbers. (p. 431)

Core Connections, Course 3

right angle An angle that measures 90°. A small square is used to note a right angle, as shown in the example at right.

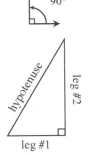

right triangle A triangle that has one right angle. The side of a right triangle opposite the right angle is called the "hypotenuse," and the two sides adjacent to the right angle are called "legs." (p. 425)

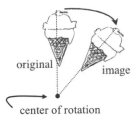

rigid transformations Movements of figures that preserve their shape and size. Also called "rigid transformations." Examples of rigid motions are reflections, rotations, and translations. (p. 233)

rotation A transformation that turns all of the points in the original (pre-image) figure the same number of degrees around a fixed center point (such as the origin on a graph). The result is called the "image" of the original figure. The point that the shape is rotated about is called the "center of rotation." To define a rotation, you need to state the measure of turn (in degrees), the direction the shape is turned (such as clockwise or counter-clockwise), and the center of rotation. See the example at right. Note that a rotation is also sometimes referred to as a "turn." (p. 223)

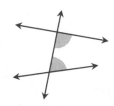

rule A rule is an equation or inequality that represents the relationship between two numerical quantities. A rule is often used to represent the relationship between quantities in a table, a pattern, a real-world situation, or a graph. (p. 93)

same side interior angles Two angles between two lines and on the same side of a third line that intersects them (called a transversal). The shaded angles in the diagram at right are an example of a pair of same-side interior angles. Note that if the two lines that are cut by the transversal are parallel, then the two angles are supplementary (add up to 180°). (p. 401)

scale factor A ratio that compares the sizes of the parts of one figure or object to the sizes of the corresponding parts of a similar figure or object. In this course it is also referred to as the multiplier. (p. 262)

scale (on axes) The scale on an axis tells you what number each successive tick mark on the axis represents. A complete graph has the scale marked with numbers on each axis. Each axis should be scaled so that each interval represents the same amount. (p. 108)

scatterplot   A way of displaying two-variable numerical data where two measurements are taken for each subject (like height and forearm length, or surface area of cardboard and volume of cereal held in a cereal box). To create a scatterplot, the two values for each subject are written as coordinate pairs and graphed on a pair of coordinate axes (each axis representing a variable). Also see *association*. (p. 196)

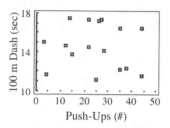

scientific notation   A number is expressed in scientific notation when it is in the form $a \cdot 10^n$, where $1 \le a < 10$ and n is an integer. For example, the number 31,000 can be expressed in scientific notation as $3.1 \cdot 10^4$. (p. 367)

similar figures   Similar figures have the same shape but are not necessarily the same size. For example the two triangles at right are similar. In similar figures, the measures of corresponding angles are equal and the ratio of the corresponding sides lengths are equal. (p. 245)

simple interest   Interest paid on the principal alone. (p. 341)

simplify   To simplify an expression is to write a less complicated expression with the same value. A simplified expression has no parentheses and no like terms. For example, the expression $3 - (2x + 7) - 4x$ may be simplified to $-4 - 6x$. When working with algebra tiles, a simplified expression uses the fewest possible tiles to represent the original expression. (p. 50)

slide   *See* translation.

slope   A ratio that describes how steep (or flat) a line is. Slope can be positive, negative, or even zero, but a straight line has only one slope. Slope is the ratio $\frac{\text{vertical change}}{\text{horizontal change}}$ or $\frac{\text{change in } y \text{ value}}{\text{change in } x \text{ value}}$, sometimes written $\frac{\Delta y}{\Delta x}$. When the equation of a line is written in $y = mx + b$ form, m is the slope of the line. Some texts refer to slope as the ratio of the "rise over the run." A line has positive slope if it slopes upward from left to right on a graph, negative slope if it slopes downward from left to right, zero slope if it is horizontal, and undefined slope if it is vertical. Slope is interpreted in context as the amount of change in the y-variable for an increase of one unit in the x-variable. (p. 310)

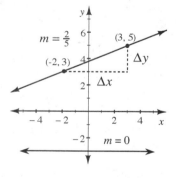

slope-intercept form   A form of a linear equation: $y = mx + b$. In this form, m is the slope and the point $(0, b)$ is the y-intercept. *See* "$y = mx + b$." (p. 189)

solid   A closed three-dimensional shape and all of its interior points. Examples include regions bounded by pyramids, cylinders, and spheres.

solution   The number or numbers that when substituted into an equation or inequality make the equation or inequality true. For example, $x = 4$ is a solution to the equation $3x = 12$ because $3x$ equals 12 when $x = 4$. (p. 136)

solve   To find all the solutions to an equation or an inequality. The solution(s) may be number(s), variable(s), or an expression.

sphere   The set of all points in space that are the same distance from a fixed point. The fixed point is the center of the sphere and the distance is its radius. (p. 470)

Sphere

square (a number)   To square a number means to multiply it by itself, or raise it to the second power. For example, 7 squared is 7^2 or $7 \cdot 7$ which is 49. (p. 438)

square root   A number a is a square root of b if $a^2 = b$. For example, the number 9 has two square roots, 3 and −3. A negative number has no real square roots; a positive number has two; and zero has just one square root, namely, itself. Other roots, such as cube root, will be studied in other courses. Also see *radical*. (p. 438)

square units   The units used to describe the measure of an area in the form of 1×1 unit squares.

standard form of a linear equation   The standard form for a linear equation is $ax + by = c$, where a, b, and c are real numbers and a and b are not both zero. For example, the equation $2.5x - 3y = 12$ is in standard form. When you are given the equation of a line in standard form, it is often useful to write an equivalent equation in $y = mx + b$ form to find the line's slope and y-intercept. (p. 189)

stem-and-leaf plot   A frequency distribution that arranges data so that all digits except the last digit in each piece of data are in the stem, the last digit of each piece of data are the leaves, and both stems and leaves are arranged in order from least to greatest. The example at right displays the data: 49, 52, 54, 58, 61, 61, 67, 68, 72, 73, 73, 73, 78, 82, 83, 108, 112, and 117.

"leaf"

4	9
5	2 4 8
6	1 1 7 8
7	2 3 3 3 8
8	2 3
9	
10	8
11	2 7

"stem"

stoplight icon   The icon (shown at right) will appear periodically throughout the text. Problems that display this icon contain errors of some type. (p. 104)

straight angle   An angle that measures 180°. This occurs when the rays of the angle point in opposite directions, forming a line. (p. 396)

180°

strength (of an association) A description of how much scatter there is in the data away from the line or curve of best fit.

substitution Replacing one symbol with a number, a variable, or another algebraic expression of the same value. Substitution does not change the value of the overall expression. For example, suppose that the expression $13x - 6$ must be evaluated for $x = 4$. Since x has the value 4, 4 may be substituted into the expression wherever x appears, giving the equivalent expression $13(4) - 6$. (p. 61)

supplementary angles Two angles a and b for which $a + b = 180°$. Each angle is called the supplement of the other. In the example at right, angles A and B are supplementary. Supplementary angles are often adjacent. For example, since $\angle LMN$ is a straight angle, then $\angle LMP$ and $\angle PMN$ are supplementary angles because $m\angle LMP + m\angle PMN = 180°$. (p. 396)

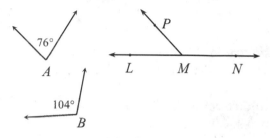

surface area The sum of all the area(s) of the surface(s) of a three-dimensional solid. For example, the surface area of a prism is the sum of the areas of its top and bottom bases, and its vertical surfaces (lateral faces). (p. 468)

system of equations A system of equations is a set of equations with the same variables. Solving a system of equations means finding one or more solutions that make each of the equations in the system true. A solution to a system of equations gives a point of intersection of the graphs of the equations in the system. There may be zero, one, or several solutions to a system of equations. For example, $(1.5, -3)$ is a solution to the system of equations at right; setting $x = 1.5$, $y = -3$ makes both of the equations true. Also, $(1.5, -3)$ is a point of intersection of the graphs of these two equations. (p. 196)

$$y = 2x - 6$$
$$y = -2x$$

table The tables used in this course represent numerical information by organizing it into columns and rows. The numbers may come from a graph, situation (pattern), or rule (equation). Many of the tables in this course are x-y tables like the one shown above right. (p. 124)

IN (x)	–2	4	1	6	–5
OUT (y)	–6	–2	–3	2	–9

term A term is a single number, variable, or the product of numbers and variables, such as -45, $1.2x$, and $3xy^2$. (p. 52)

terminating decimal A terminating decimal is a decimal that has only a finite number of non-zero digits, such as 4.067. Terminating decimals are a particular kind of repeating decimal for which the repeating portion is zeros, so the example could be written 4.0670000000… but it is not necessary to write the zeros at the end. (p. 5)

third quartile (Q3) The median of the upper half of an ordered set of data.

three-dimensional An object that has height, width, and depth.

tick mark A symbol that shows that a number line has been divided into intervals of equal length. See *number line*.

transformation This course studies four transformations: reflection, rotation, translation, and dilation. All of them preserve shape, and the first three preserve size. *See each term for its own definition.* (p. 233)

translation A transformation that preserves the size, shape, and orientation of a figure while sliding (moving) it to a new location. The result is called the "image" of the original figure. Note that a translation is sometimes referred to as a "slide." (p. 233)

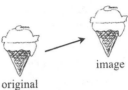

original   image

transversal A line that intersects two or more other lines on a flat surface (plane). In this course, you often work with a transversal that intersects two parallel lines. (p. 391)

triangle A polygon with three sides.

Triangle Inequality In a triangle with side lengths a, b, and c, c must be less than the sum of a and b and greater than the difference of a and b. In the example at right, a is greater than b (that is, $a > b$), so the possible values for c are all numbers such that $c > a - b$ and $c < a + b$. (p. 420)

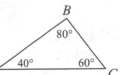

Triangle Angle Sum Theorem The sum of the measures of the interior angles in any triangle is $180°$. For example, in $\triangle ABC$ at right, $m\angle A + m\angle B + m\angle C = 180°$. (p. 405)

two-dimensional An object having length and width.

turn *See* rotation.

undefined slope The slope of a vertical line is undefined. (p. 310)

undoing In this course, "undoing" refers to a method of solving one-variable equations. In "undoing," you undo the last operation that was applied to an expression by applying its inverse operation. You then solve the resulting equation using various solution methods, including perhaps undoing again. For example, in the equation $4(x + 2) = 36$, the last operation that was applied to the left-hand side was a *multiplication* by 4. So to use "undoing," you *divide* both sides of the equation by 4, giving us $x + 2 = 9$. You then solve the equation $x + 2 = 9$ (perhaps by "undoing" again and subtracting 2 from both sides) to find that $x = 7$. (p. 35)

unit rate   A rate with a denominator of one when simplified. (p. 315)

variable   A symbol used to represent one or more numbers. In this course, letters of the English alphabet are used as variables. For example, in the expression $3x - (8.6xy + z)$, the variables are x, y, and z. (p. 52)

variable expression   See *expression*.

vertex (plural: vertices)   (1) For a two-dimensional geometric shape, a vertex is a point where two or more line segments or rays meet to form a "corner," such as in a polygon or angle. (2) For a three-dimensional polyhedron, a vertex is a point where the edges of the solid meet. (3) For a parabola it is the highest or lowest point on the parabola (depending on the parabola's orientation). (p. 109, 396)

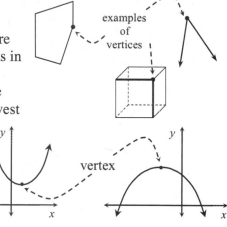

vertical   At right angles to the horizon. On a coordinate graph, the y-axis runs vertically. (p. 310)

vertical angles   The two opposite (that is, non-adjacent) angles formed by two intersecting lines. "Vertical" is a relationship between pairs of angles, so one angle cannot be called vertical. Angles that form a vertical pair are always congruent. (p. 396)

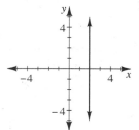

vertical lines   Vertical lines run up and down in the same direction as the y-axis and are parallel to it. All vertical lines have equations of the form $x = a$, where a can be any number. For example, the graph at right shows the vertical line $x = 2$. The y-axis has the equation $x = 0$ because $x = 0$ everywhere on the y-axis. Vertical lines have undefined slope. (p. 310)

volume   A measurement of the size of the three-dimensional region enclosed within an object. Volume is expressed as the number of $1 \times 1 \times 1$ unit cubes (or parts of cubes) that fit inside a solid.

***x*-axis**   The horizontal number line on a coordinate graph. See *axis*. (p. 11)

***x*-coordinate**   In an ordered pair, (x, y), that represents a point in the coordinate plane, x is the value of the x-coordinate. That is, the distance from the y-axis that is needed to plot the point.

Core Connections, Course 3

x-intercept(s) The point(s) where a graph intersects the x-axis. A graph may have several x-intercepts, no x-intercepts, or just one. You sometimes report the x-intercepts of a graph with coordinate pairs, but since the y-coordinate is always zero, you often just give the x-coordinates of x-intercepts. For example, you might say that the x-intercepts of the graph at right are $(0, 0)$ and $(2, 0)$, or you might just say that the x-intercepts are 0 and 2. (p. 124)

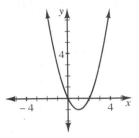

x → y table An x → y table, like the one at right, represents pairs of values of two related quantities. The input value (x) appears first, and the output value (y) appears second. For example, the x → y table at right tells us that the input value 10 is paired with the output value 18 for some rule. (p. 102)

IN (x)	OUT (y)
0	-2
-4	-10
10	18

y = mx + b When two quantities x and y have a linear relationship, that relationship can be represented with an equation in $y = mx + b$ form. The constant m is the slope, and b is the y-intercept of the graph. For example, the graph at right shows the line represented by the equation $y = 2x + 3$, which has a slope of 2 and a y-intercept of 3. This form of a linear equation is also called the slope-intercept form. (p. 162)

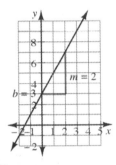

y-axis The vertical number line on a coordinate graph. See *axis*. (p. 11)

y-coordinate In an ordered pair, (x, y), that represents a point in the coordinate plane, y is the value of the y-coordinate. That is, the distance from the x-axis that is needed to plot the point.

y-intercept The point where a graph intersects the y-axis. A function has at most one y-intercept; a relation may have several. The y-intercept of a graph is important because it often represents the starting value of a quantity in a real-world situation. For example, on the graph of a tile pattern the y-intercept represents the number of tiles in Figure 0. You sometimes report the y-intercept of a graph with a coordinate pair, but since the x-coordinate is always zero, you often just give the y-coordinate of the y-intercept.

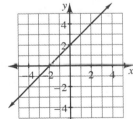

For example, you might say that the y-intercept of the graph at right is $(0, 2)$, or you might just say that the y-intercept is 2. When a linear equation is written in $y = mx + b$ form, b tells us the y-intercept of the graph. For example, the equation of the graph at right is $y = x + 2$ and its y-intercept is 2. (p. 124)

zero A number often used to represent "having none of a quantity." Zero is neither negative nor positive. Zero is the additive identity. (p. 59)

Many of the pages referenced here contain a definition or an example of the topic listed, often within the body of a Math Notes box. Others contain problems that develop or demonstrate the topic. It may be necessary to read the text on several pages to fully understand the topic. Also, some problems listed here are good examples of the topic and may not offer any explanation. The page numbers below reflect the pages in the Student Version. References to Math Notes boxes are bolded.

Checkpoint 2, 83, 499
Checkpoint 3, 141, 501
Checkpoint 4, 177, 504
Checkpoint 5, 211, 508
Checkpoint 6, 264, 511
Checkpoint 7, 327, 516
Checkpoint 8, 382, 519
Checkpoint 9, 410, 522
Chord, **128**
Chubby Bunny, 203
Circle
   area, **128**
   chord, **128**
   circumference, **128**
   diameter, **128**
   pi, **128**
   radius, **128**
   sector, 474
Circle graph, 273, **276**
   comparing data, 274
Circle the terms, **61**
Circumference, **128**
   Checkpoint 4, 177, 504
Cluster, 288, **290**
Coefficient, **52**, 208
Coinciding lines
   system of equations, **210**
Collaborative Learning Expectations, 9
Combining like terms, 50, 51, **56**
Commutative Property of Addition, **66**
Commutative Property of Multiplication, **66**, 354
Comparing the Gym Bags, 460
Complementary angles, **396**
Complete graph, 115, **124**
Compound interest, 343, 344, 345, 349, **351**
Cone, 465
   volume, 465, 472
Congruent, **245**, 249, **262**
Conjecture, 240, 393
Constant of proportionality, **315**
Constant term, **52**, 208
Continuous, 103, **105**
Converse, 443
Converse of the Pythagorean Theorem, **424**
Coordinate
   axes, **11**
   grid, 226
   system, 14
Coordinates, **124**

Corresponding, 243, **245**
   angles, 393, **401**
   sides, 255
Counterexample, 194
Critique the reasoning of others, 484
Cross multiplication, 34, **35**
Cube, 457
Cube root, 457, 458
Customer Service, 530
Cylinder, **468**
   surface area, 460, **468**
   volume, 460, **463**

D
Data
   analyzing, 19, 490
   collecting, 19
   comparing
     with circle graphs, 274
   modeling, 280
   organizing, 19
     scatterplot, 279
Decimal
   as a fraction, **5**, 429
   as a percent, **5**
   operations with
     Checkpoint 1, 37, 496
   repeating, as a fraction, 431
   terminating, as a fraction, **5**
Dependent variable, **113**, **378**
Diameter, **128**
Diamond Problems, 6
Dilation, 239, 240
   similar figures, 242
Direction, of an association, 287
Discrete, 103, **105**
Distributive Property, 138, **139**

E
Enlarge, **262**
Equal Values Method, 204, **205**, 207, 208, **210**

548

Core Connections, Course 3

Slope, 296, 297, 302, 307, **310**
  horizontal line, **310**
  in different representations, 301
  negative, 307, **310**
  positive, 307, **310**
  ratio, 307, **310**
  undefined, **310**
  vertical line, **310**
Slope-intercept form, **189**
Solution
  all numbers, **136**
  checking, 122
  infinite, **136**
  no solution, **136**
  number of, 126
  of a linear equation, 123
  system of equations, **210**
Solve
  by inspection
    systems of equations, 208
  equation, 122, 131, 135
    Checkpoint 5, 211, 508
    linear, **133**
  equations with decimals
    Checkpoint 7, 327, 516
  equations with fractions, 191, **198**
    Checkpoint 7, 327, 516
  persevere in, 488
  proportion, 31, **35**
  systems of equations, 203, 204, **205**, 207
    Checkpoint 7, 327, 516
  using algebra tiles, 76, 78, 80
  using an Equation Mat, 78
Sphere, 470
  volume, 470, 471, **475**
Square, perfect, 422
Square root, 421, **437**
  estimating, 422
Squaring a number, **437**
Stoplight Icon, explained, 104
Straight angle, **396**
Standard form of a linear equation, 189
Structure, look for and make use of, 488
Substituion, **61**
Supplementary angles, **396**
Surface area
  cylinder, 460, **468**
System of equations, 196, 197
  infinite solutions, **210**
  no solution, **210**

solution, **210**
Systems of equations, **201**
  solving, 203, 204, **205**
    by inspection, 208
    strategies, 207

T
Table, **124**, 175
  frequency, 324
  from a graph, 161
  from a pattern, 102, 161
  from a rule, 108, 159
  from a situation, 111
  relative frequency, 325
  to make a prediction, 98
Task Manager, 4
Team roles, 4
  Facilitator, 4
  Recorder/Reporter, 4
  Resource Manager, 4
  Task Manager, 4
Technology tool
  Key-Lock Transformations, **223**
Term, 50, **52**, **56**
  constant, **52**, 208
  like, 50, **56**
Terminating decimal
  as a fraction, **5**
Three Views (PI-5), 528
Tile pattern, 10, 93, 151, 152, 155, 174, 175
  finding a rule, 102
  team challenge, 151
Tiles, algebra, 47
Tools, using appropriate, 484, 485
Transformations
  Checkpoint 8, 382, 519
  rigid, 223, **233**, 236, 239
Translation, 226, **233**
Transversal, 391
Trend line. *See* line of best fit
Triangle
  Angle Sum Theorem, **405**
  angle-angle similarity, **413**
  exterior angle, 403
  finding angles in, 399
  possible side lengths, 411
  remote interior angle, 403
  side length patterns, **419**
  Sierpinski, 531
  similar, 407, 408

Triangle Inequality, **419**
Turn
    rigid transformation, 223
    rotation, 226

U
Undoing
    division, 32, **35**
Unit rate, **315**
    Checkpoint 3, 141, 501
    of change, **310**

V
Variable, 47, **52**
    categorical, 324
    dependent, **113**, **378**
    independent, **113**, **378**
Vertex, 109
    angle, **396**
Vertical angles, **396**
Vertical line
    slope, **310**
Volume
    application, 474
    cone, 465, 472
    cylinder, 460, **463**
    pyramid, 465, **472**
    sphere, 470, 471, **475**

W
Web, multiple representations, 157, 168, 173
Weighing Pumpkins (PI-9), 531
What's My Number? (PI-11), 533
Which is the Fake? (PI-1), 525
Word problem
    writing rule, 200

X
$x \rightarrow y$ table
    from a pattern, 102
x-axis, **11**
x-intercept, 116, **124**
x-value, 14
xy-coordinate system, 14

Y
$y = mx + b$, 162, 293
y-axis, **11**
y-intercept, 116, **124**, 171, **189**
y-value, 14

Z
Zero, 59

Common Core State Standards for Mathematics

Mathematics | Grade 8

In Grade 8, instructional time should focus on three critical areas: (1) formulating and reasoning about expressions and equations, including modeling an association in bivariate data with a linear equation, and solving linear equations and systems of linear equations; (2) grasping the concept of a function and using functions to describe quantitative relationships; (3) analyzing two- and three-dimensional space and figures using distance, angle, similarity, and congruence, and understanding and applying the Pythagorean Theorem.

(1) Students use linear equations and systems of linear equations to represent, analyze, and solve a variety of problems. Students recognize equations for proportions ($y/x = m$ or $y = mx$) as special linear equations ($y = mx + b$), understanding that the constant of proportionality (m) is the slope, and the graphs are lines through the origin. They understand that the slope (m) of a line is a constant rate of change, so that if the input or x-coordinate changes by an amount A, the output or y-coordinate changes by the amount $m \cdot A$. Students also use a linear equation to describe the association between two quantities in bivariate data (such as arm span vs. height for students in a classroom). At this grade, fitting the model, and assessing its fit to the data are done informally. Interpreting the model in the context of the data requires students to express a relationship between the two quantities in question and to interpret components of the relationship (such as slope and y-intercept) in terms of the situation.

Students strategically choose and efficiently implement procedures to solve linear equations in one variable, understanding that when they use the properties of equality and the concept of logical equivalence, they maintain the solutions of the original equation. Students solve systems of two linear equations in two variables and relate the systems to pairs of lines in the plane; these intersect, are parallel, or are the same line. Students use linear equations, systems of linear equations, linear functions, and their understanding of slope of a line to analyze situations and solve problems.

(2) Students grasp the concept of a function as a rule that assigns to each input exactly one output. They understand that functions describe situations where one quantity determines another. They can translate among representations and partial representations of functions (noting that tabular and graphical representations may be partial representations), and they describe how aspects of the function are reflected in the different representations.

(3) Students use ideas about distance and angles, how they behave under translations, rotations, reflections, and dilations, and ideas about congruence and similarity to describe and analyze two-dimensional figures and to solve problems. Students show that the sum of the angles in a triangle is the angle formed by a straight line, and that various

configurations of lines give rise to similar triangles because of the angles created when a transversal cuts parallel lines. Students understand the statement of the Pythagorean Theorem and its converse, and can explain why the Pythagorean Theorem holds, for example, by decomposing a square in two different ways. They apply the Pythagorean Theorem to find distances between points on the coordinate plane, to find lengths, and to analyze polygons. Students complete their work on volume by solving problems involving cones, cylinders, and spheres.

8 Grade 8 Overview

The Number System

- Know that there are numbers that are not rational, and approximate them by rational numbers.

Expressions and Equations

- Work with radicals and integer exponents.
- Understand the connection between proportional relationships, lines, and linear equations.
- Analyze and solve linear equations and pairs of simultaneous linear equations.

Functions

- Define, evaluate, and compare functions.
- Use functions to model relationships between quantities.

Geometry

- Understand congruence and similarity using physical models, transparencies, or geometry software.
- Understand and apply the Pythagorean Theorem.
- Solve real-world and mathematical problems involving volume of cylinders, cones, and spheres.

Statistics and Probability

- Investigate patterns of association in bivariate data.

Mathematical Practices

1. Make sense of problems and persevere in solving them.
2. Reason abstractly and quantitatively.
3. Construct viable arguments and critique the reasoning of others.
4. Model with mathematics.
5. Use appropriate tools strategically.
6. Attend to precision.
7. Look for and make use of structure.
8. Look for and express regularity in repeated reasoning.

The Number System   8.NS

Know that there are numbers that are not rational, and approximate them by rational numbers.

1. Know that numbers that are not rational are called irrational. Understand informally that every number has a decimal expansion; for rational numbers show that the decimal expansion repeats eventually, and convert a decimal expansion which repeats eventually into a rational number.

2. Use rational approximations of irrational numbers to compare the size of irrational numbers, locate them approximately on a number line diagram, and estimate the value of expressions (e.g., π2). *For example, by truncating the decimal expansion of √2, show that √2 is between 1 and 2, then between 1.4 and 1.5, and explain how to continue on to get better approximations.*

Expressions and Equations   8.EE

Work with radicals and integer exponents.

1. Know and apply the properties of integer exponents to generate equivalent numerical expressions. *For example, $3^2 \times 3^{-5} = 3^{-3} = 1/3^3 = 1/27$.*

2. Use square root and cube root symbols to represent solutions to equations of the form $x^2 = p$ and $x^3 = p$, where p is a positive rational number. Evaluate square roots of small perfect squares and cube roots of small perfect cubes. Know that √2 is irrational.

3. Use numbers expressed in the form of a single digit times an integer power of 10 to estimate very large or very small quantities, and to express how many times as much one is than the other. *For example, estimate the population of the United States as 3×10^8 and the population of the world as 7×10^9, and determine that the world population is more than 20 times larger.*

4. Perform operations with numbers expressed in scientific notation, including problems where both decimal and scientific notation are used. Use scientific notation and choose units of appropriate size for measurements of very large or very small quantities (e.g., use millimeters per year for seafloor spreading). Interpret scientific notation that has been generated by technology.

Understand the connections between proportional relationships, lines, and linear equations.

5. Graph proportional relationships, interpreting the unit rate as the slope of the graph. Compare two different proportional relationships represented in different ways. *For example, compare a distance-time graph to a distance-time equation to determine which of two moving objects has greater speed.*

6. Use similar triangles to explain why the slope m is the same between any two distinct points on a non-vertical line in the coordinate plane; derive the equation $y = mx$ for a line through the origin and the equation $y = mx + b$ for a line intercepting the vertical axis at b.

Analyze and solve linear equations and pairs of simultaneous linear equations.

7. Solve linear equations in one variable.
   a. Give examples of linear equations in one variable with one solution, infinitely many solutions, or no solutions. Show which of these possibilities is the case by successively transforming the given equation into simpler forms, until an equivalent equation of the form $x = a$, $a = a$, or $a = b$ results (where a and b are different numbers).
   b. Solve linear equations with rational number coefficients, including equations whose solutions require expanding expressions using the distributive property and collecting like terms.

8. Analyze and solve pairs of simultaneous linear equations.

     a.   Understand that solutions to a system of two linear equations in two variables correspond to points of intersection of their graphs, because points of intersection satisfy both equations simultaneously.

     b.   Solve systems of two linear equations in two variables algebraically, and estimate solutions by graphing the equations. Solve simple cases by inspection. *For example, 3x + 2y = 5 and 3x + 2y = 6 have no solution because 3x + 2y cannot simultaneously be 5 and 6.*

     c.   Solve real-world and mathematical problems leading to two linear equations in two variables. *For example, given coordinates for two pairs of points, determine whether the line through the first pair of points intersects the line through the second pair.*

Functions   8.F

Define, evaluate, and compare functions.

1.   Understand that a function is a rule that assigns to each input exactly one output. The graph of a function is the set of ordered pairs consisting of an input and the corresponding output.[1]

2.   Compare properties of two functions each represented in a different way (algebraically, graphically, numerically in tables, or by verbal descriptions). *For example, given a linear function represented by a table of values and a linear function represented by an algebraic expression, determine which function has the greater rate of change.*

3.   Interpret the equation $y = mx + b$ as defining a linear function, whose graph is a straight line; give examples of functions that are not linear. *For example, the function $A = s^2$ giving the area of a square as a function of its side length is not linear because its graph contains the points (1,1), (2,4) and (3,9), which are not on a straight line.*

Use functions to model relationships between quantities.

4.   Construct a function to model a linear relationship between two quantities. Determine the rate of change and initial value of the function from a description of a relationship or from two (x, y) values, including reading these from a table or from a graph. Interpret the rate of change and initial value of a linear function in terms of the situation it models, and in terms of its graph or a table of values.

5.   Describe qualitatively the functional relationship between two quantities by analyzing a graph (e.g., where the function is increasing or decreasing, linear or nonlinear). Sketch a graph that exhibits the qualitative features of a function that has been described verbally.

Geometry   8.G

Understand congruence and similarity using physical models, transparencies, or geometry software.

1.   Verify experimentally the properties of rotations, reflections, and translations:

     a.   Lines are taken to lines, and line segments to line segments of the same length.

     b.   Angles are taken to angles of the same measure.

     c.   Parallel lines are taken to parallel lines.

2.   Understand that a two-dimensional figure is congruent to another if the second can be obtained from the first by a sequence of rotations, reflections, and translations; given two congruent figures, describe a sequence that exhibits the congruence between them.

3.   Describe the effect of dilations, translations, rotations, and reflections on two-dimensional figures using coordinates.

---

[1] Function notation is not required in Grade 8.

Grade 8

4. Understand that a two-dimensional figure is similar to another if the second can be obtained from the first by a sequence of rotations, reflections, translations, and dilations; given two similar two-dimensional figures, describe a sequence that exhibits the similarity between them.

5. Use informal arguments to establish facts about the angle sum and exterior angle of triangles, about the angles created when parallel lines are cut by a transversal, and the angle-angle criterion for similarity of triangles. *For example, arrange three copies of the same triangle so that the sum of the three angles appears to form a line, and give an argument in terms of transversals why this is so.*

Understand and apply the Pythagorean Theorem.

6. Explain a proof of the Pythagorean Theorem and its converse.

7. Apply the Pythagorean Theorem to determine unknown side lengths in right triangles in real-world and mathematical problems in two and three dimensions.

8. Apply the Pythagorean Theorem to find the distance between two points in a coordinate system.

Solve real-world and mathematical problems involving volume of cylinders, cones, and spheres.

9. Know the formulas for the volumes of cones, cylinders, and spheres and use them to solve real-world and mathematical problems.

Statistics and Probability   8.SP

Investigate patterns of association in bivariate data.

1. Construct and interpret scatter plots for bivariate measurement data to investigate patterns of association between two quantities. Describe patterns such as clustering, outliers, positive or negative association, linear association, and nonlinear association.

2. Know that straight lines are widely used to model relationships between two quantitative variables. For scatter plots that suggest a linear association, informally fit a straight line, and informally assess the model fit by judging the closeness of the data points to the line.

3. Use the equation of a linear model to solve problems in the context of bivariate measurement data, interpreting the slope and intercept. *For example, in a linear model for a biology experiment, interpret a slope of 1.5 cm/hr as meaning that an additional hour of sunlight each day is associated with an additional 1.5 cm in mature plant height.*

4. Understand that patterns of association can also be seen in bivariate categorical data by displaying frequencies and relative frequencies in a two-way table. Construct and interpret a two-way table summarizing data on two categorical variables collected from the same subjects. Use relative frequencies calculated for rows or columns to describe possible association between the two variables. *For example, collect data from students in your class on whether or not they have a curfew on school nights and whether or not they have assigned chores at home. Is there evidence that those who have a curfew also tend to have chores?*

THIS BOOK IS THE
PROPERTY OF:

Book No._____

ISSUED TO	Year Used	CONDITION	
		ISSUED	RETURNED
_____	_____		
_____	_____		
_____	_____		
_____	_____		
_____	_____		
_____	_____		
_____	_____		
_____	_____		

PUPILS to whom this texbook is issued must not write on any part of it in any way, unless otherwise instructed by the teacher.